IMAGES
of America

Tacoma's Theater District

On the Cover: On May 20, 1934, hundreds of children line up outside the Rialto Theater to take advantage of a special offer of free admission for Tacoma's youth, sponsored by the *Tacoma Times* and Rialto Theater. The children were treated to the double feature of *Parachute Jumper*, starring Bette Davis and Douglas Fairbanks, and *Dr. Bull*, with Will Rogers and Marian Nixon. (Courtesy of the Tacoma Public Library.)

IMAGES
of America

TACOMA'S THEATER DISTRICT

Kimberly M. Davenport

ARCADIA
PUBLISHING

ISBN 978-1-4671-3402-6

Published by Arcadia Publishing
Charleston, South Carolina

Printed in the United States of America

Library of Congress Control Number: 2015935344

For all general information, please contact Arcadia Publishing:
Telephone 843-853-2070
Fax 843-853-0044
E-mail sales@arcadiapublishing.com
For customer service and orders:
Toll-Free 1-888-313-2665

Visit us on the Internet at www.arcadiapublishing.com

To my father, whose stories of the Tacoma of his youth have nurtured my love of the city and my desire to explore its history

Contents

ACKNOWLEDGMENTS

This project could not have been completed without the personal and professional support and encouragement of many people. First, I thank my parents for their love, support, and guidance. My interest in history and telling stories stems directly from my father. I have always emulated his ability to share important ideas or paint a picture of another time and place through words. My mother provides patience, which I do not possess, offering a willingness to listen to me talk at great length about a topic that excites me and then quietly suggest a brilliant idea that brings it all together.

A sincere thank-you to Jody Gripp of the Northwest Room at the Tacoma Public Library for her support and guidance; Peter Serko and Chip van Gilder for sharing their phenomenal photographs; and Tom Blackwell and the Puget Sound Theater Organ Society for their website, which was of great help in my research, and for sharing some of the photographs featured there. I would also like to thank Max Grinnell for his Arcadia book on Hyde Park, Illinois; not only did it serve as the catalyst to reunite old friends, but it also planted the thought in my mind to pursue an Arcadia project someday. Additional thanks goes to Joe Chynoweth for encouraging me to write, Nicole Blair for her boundless enthusiasm, Dawn Lucien for welcoming me into her home to discuss memories of the efforts to renovate the Pantages Theater, and Michael Sullivan for sharing his ideas and his willingness to serve as a sounding board on issues of local history. Last but certainly not least, a thank-you to my Arcadia editor, Matt Todd, for his prompt responses to my many questions.

INTRODUCTION

Although small in size, Tacoma's theater district is rich in history. To share that history is to tell stories of people, individually and collectively; buildings that have stood the test of time and those that live only in memory; and the ever-changing social, urban, and entertainment landscape of the City of Destiny. To share that history through photographs is particularly satisfying, as it helps illustrate both what we have left behind and what remains vibrant in today's Tacoma.

The theater district, for the purposes of this book, is defined as just a few blocks, primarily on Broadway, and centered on the intersection of Broadway with Ninth Street. It was here, where the Tacoma Theater opened in 1890, that a district would coalesce around first the Tacoma and then the Pantages and Rialto Theaters in 1918. Because the latter two venues are still in operation, the history of the theater district spans most of the history of Tacoma itself. And because the area was home to not only theaters, but also a vibrant shopping district and community gathering space, this small area offers us a broad range of stories over many decades.

The first chapter explores the beginnings of the district. Even before downtown streets were paved, the population of Tacoma, which began to boom in the 1880s, was eager for theater entertainment. Many early facilities fit the bill, even if just for a short time, and fortunately, a photographic record exists of several of these. The year 1890 saw the opening of the first truly grand theater in the city, the Tacoma Theater; with its "largest stage on the west coast," it was designed to be a theater fit for the prominent city Tacoma's boosters were sure it would become. Around it, other grand buildings—from hotels to churches, office buildings, and other theaters—would gradually rise, solidifying the district as an important entertainment and shopping destination in the city center.

Chapter 2, "Golden Age of the Stage," speaks to the era before film became a dominant means of entertainment, when much of the activity in the theaters still involved live performance. From the 1890s through the 1920s and beyond, stages in the theater district were home to vaudeville shows, operas, stage plays, musical acts of all genres, magicians, comedians, and more, as well as early silent films. Even as movies became the primary focus for the theaters, live performances continued.

Chapter 3, "The Silver Screen," shares a range of film-related stories. In the mid-1920s, Tacoma had its very own film studio, H.C. Weaver Productions, which released three silent films before succumbing to the success of the new sound era that it was not prepared for. Several local musicians started their performing careers as organists for theaters during the silent era; actors and actresses who were born or raised in Tacoma and went on to success in Hollywood were celebrated each time one of their films appeared at a hometown venue. Theater district businesses took advantage of the appearance of popular films to sell everything from cars to jewelry. Finally, citizens of all ages enjoyed first-run Hollywood films as well as newsreels at venues of varying styles and sizes.

Chapter 4 provides a glimpse into the wide range of public gatherings that took place on the streets surrounding the theater venues themselves. From parades to speeches, presidential visits to holiday gatherings, the intersection of Ninth Street and Broadway has long been a vital gathering spot for the people of Tacoma. For more than 50 years, the theater district was home to a vibrant shopping district, with several major department stores and specialty shops. In the early 20th century, it was possible to shop for a car, piano, jewelry, the latest appliances, and clothes for the entire family, all within two blocks of the Pantages Theater.

Chapter 5 shares a dramatic story of decline followed by rejuvenation. Beginning in the 1960s, the theater district entered a challenging period. The Tacoma Theater (then the Music Box) was lost to fire in 1963, at the same time that many businesses were leaving downtown in favor of new malls outside of the city center. The next decade would see the demolition of many historic structures, as well as failed attempts to bring people back downtown with new parking garages and pedestrian plazas. Fortunately, the people and government of Tacoma worked together to pull through this difficult era. Remaining historic theaters were restored and reestablished as active venues, once again making the theater district a destination for cultural events. As the Pantages and Rialto Theaters approach their centennial, Tacoma's theater district is once again poised to serve as an anchor for a vibrant downtown core.

One

Theater District Beginnings

The earliest theaters in downtown Tacoma were located on Pacific Avenue, specifically between Seventh and Eleventh Streets. The first on record was Smith's Place, which opened on the east side of Pacific Avenue between Seventh and Ninth Streets in 1877. Cogswell's Hall, on Eighth Street just off Pacific Avenue, opened in 1881. Both venues were quite small and without many amenities, such as heat or comfortable seating, for either performers or audience. Upon its opening in 1882, the Alpha Opera House, located at Tenth Street and Pacific Avenue, was a dramatic improvement over these first attempts; much larger than previous venues, it could seat about 700, which was approximately a quarter of the population of Tacoma at this date. The Germania Hall opened to great fanfare in February 1889 at the corner of Thirteenth Street and Fawcett Avenue and was successful for a time; it eventually failed, however, as it was a bit too far from the core of downtown, occupied an unpaved street, and proved difficult to heat.

With the opening of the Tacoma Theater at Ninth Street and Broadway in 1890, citizens of the City of Destiny at last had a significant theater venue to call their own. It was grand in size, boasting the largest stage on the West Coast and seating for 1,200. Renowned theater architect J.M. Wood of Chicago brought his national reputation to the project, designing a stunning Modern Romanesque structure of blue-gray stone and vibrant red brick. Thomas Moses, also of Chicago, designed and hand painted dozens of stage sets to accommodate the needs of any first-class touring company.

Over the next few decades, several more theaters opened around downtown Tacoma and, indeed, throughout the city as various neighborhood districts developed. Pacific Avenue remained a busy downtown thoroughfare with multiple theater venues. And yet, it was the Tacoma Theater, larger and grander than the other early Tacoma theaters, that would prove to become the anchor for downtown Tacoma's theater district. By the time the Pantages and Rialto Theaters opened in 1918, the intersection of Ninth Street and Broadway was solidified as the heart of this new district.

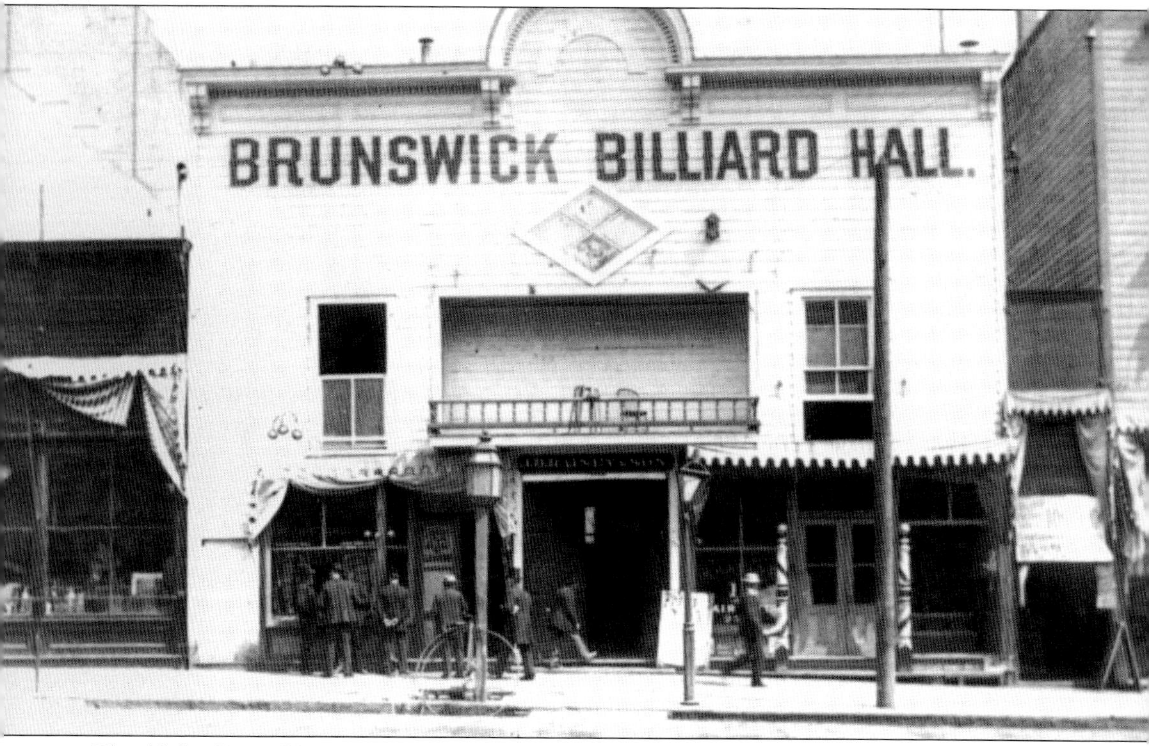

The Alpha Opera House, Tacoma's first true theater building, opened in this structure at Tenth Street and Pacific Avenue in 1882. By the time this photograph was taken in 1891, the building was home to Brunswick Billiard Hall; the property was torn down the following year. The theater was managed by Charles Sprague and Steve Baker, the sons of railroad and bank executives, respectively. In its heyday, the Alpha Opera House hosted plays, operas, vaudeville, and town meetings, including Tacoma's celebration of Washington's statehood in 1889. Double doors entered directly into a hall that could seat about 700 people, which was roughly a quarter of the population of Tacoma at its opening in 1882. The Alpha's reign as the preeminent downtown theater came to an end in 1890 with the opening of the Tacoma Theater at Ninth Street and Broadway. (Courtesy of the Tacoma Public Library.)

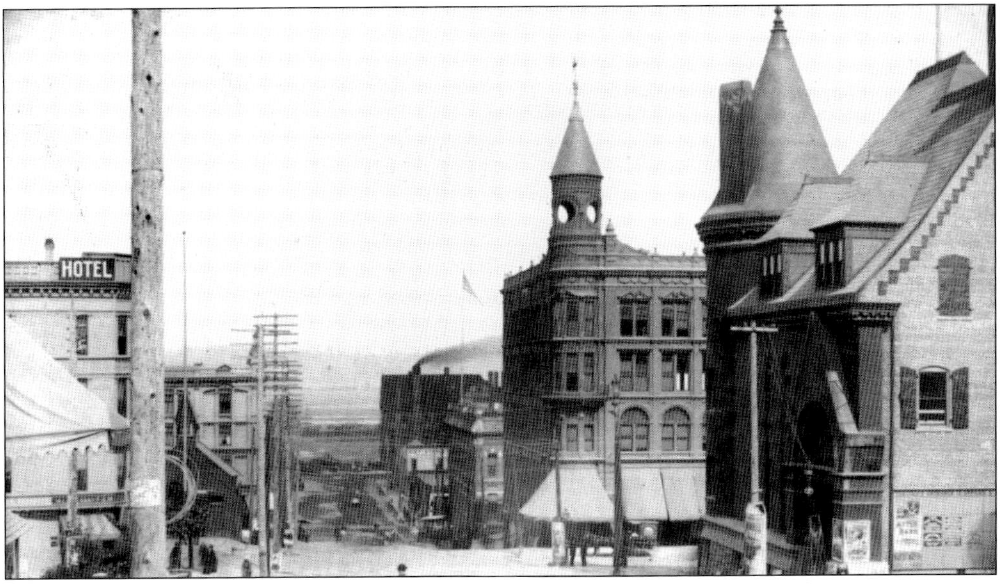

In 1890, this was the view looking down the hill from the intersection of Ninth and C Streets. In the foreground are the Tacoma Theater (right) and Bostwick Building (left). The small building at left with the steeple is a fire station. The farthest building visible at right, perched over Commencement Bay, is the Tacoma Hotel. (Courtesy of the Tacoma Public Library.)

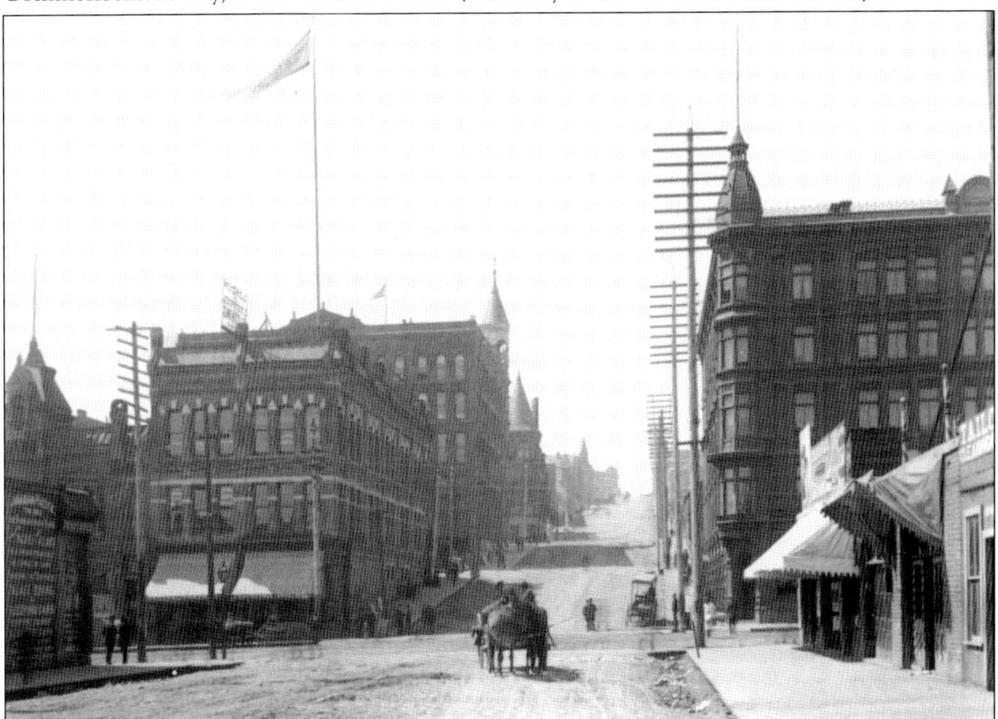

F. Jay Haynes took this photograph, looking west up Ninth Street from A Street, about 1890 for a collection titled *Northern Pacific Railroad Scenery*. Although there were wood sidewalks, the streets are still not paved. The rooftop dome of the newly opened Tacoma Theater can be seen in the distance at left. (Courtesy of the Tacoma Public Library.)

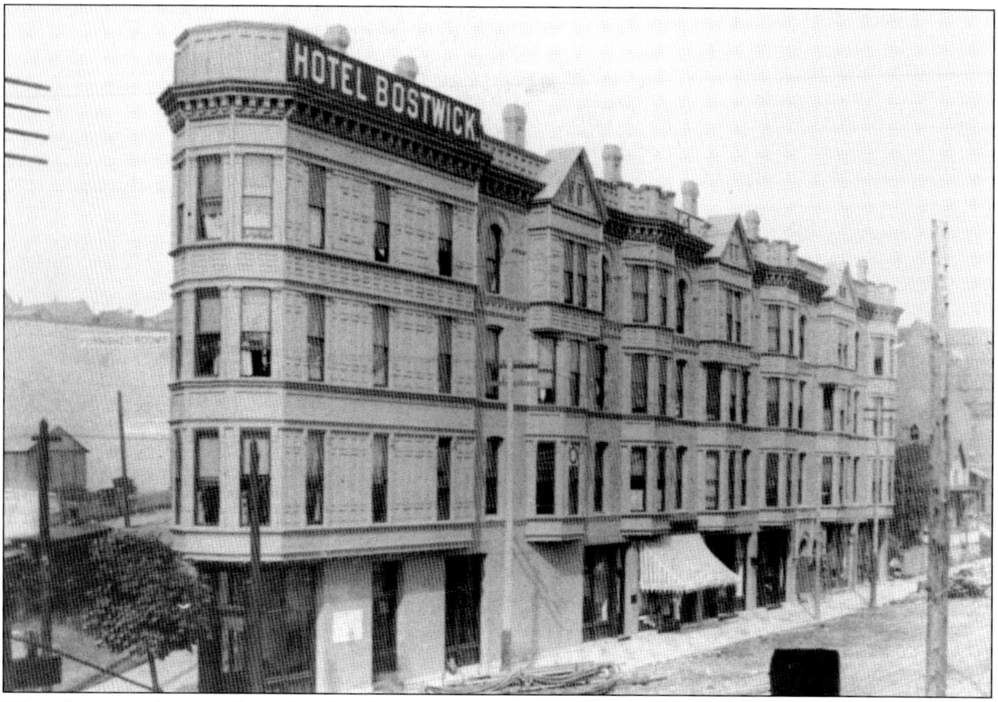

This photograph was taken shortly after the Bostwick Building was completed in 1889. Designed by early Tacoma architect O.P. Dennis, the Bostwick was remodeled in 1924, facing the original wood-clad exterior with stucco. The unique triangular building has been home to hotels, apartments, and a wide range of businesses—from jewelers to malt shops—in its prominent street-level storefronts. (Courtesy of the Tacoma Public Library.)

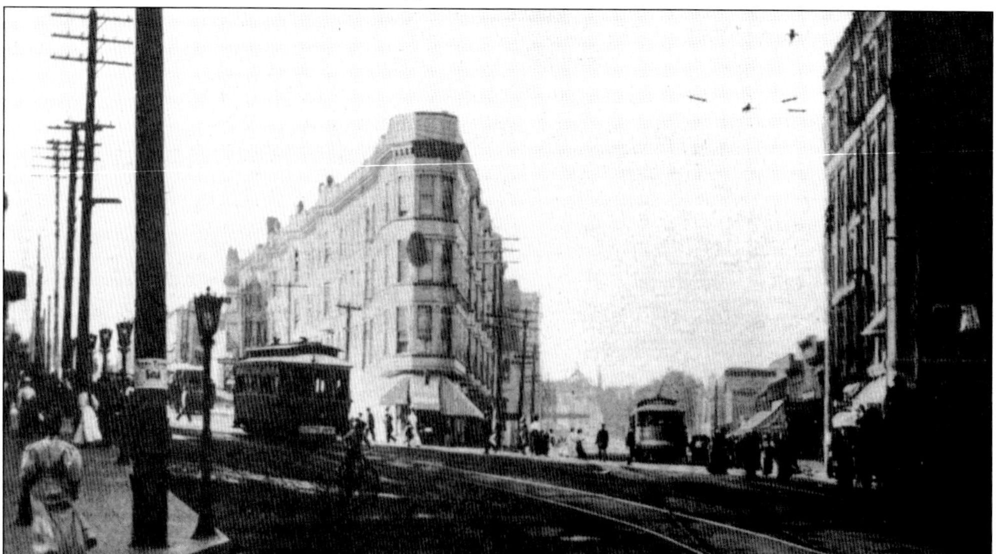

The exact date of this photograph, depicting a late 1890s scene at the intersection of Ninth Street and Broadway, is unknown. The recently opened Bostwick Hotel is at the center, while multiple streetcars occupy the streets and the newly paved sidewalks are full of pedestrian traffic. (Courtesy of the Tacoma Public Library.)

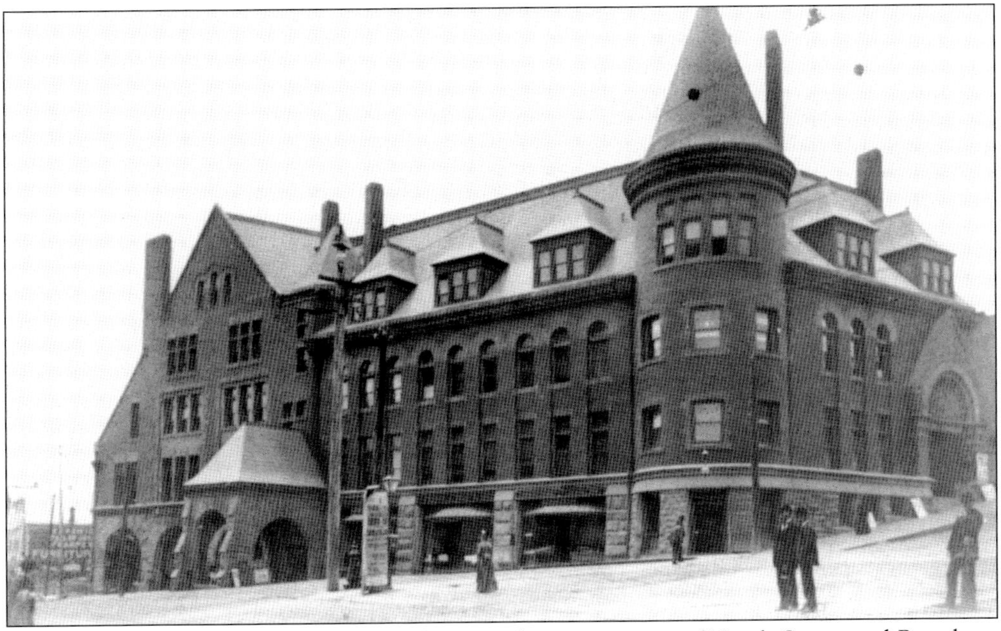

The impressive Tacoma Theater looms large at the intersection of Ninth Street and Broadway soon after its opening in 1890. While the interior boasted the largest stage on the West Coast, the exterior was also unique, featuring among other architectural details a porte cochere, or covered carriage entrance, facing Broadway at left. (Courtesy of the Tacoma Public Library.)

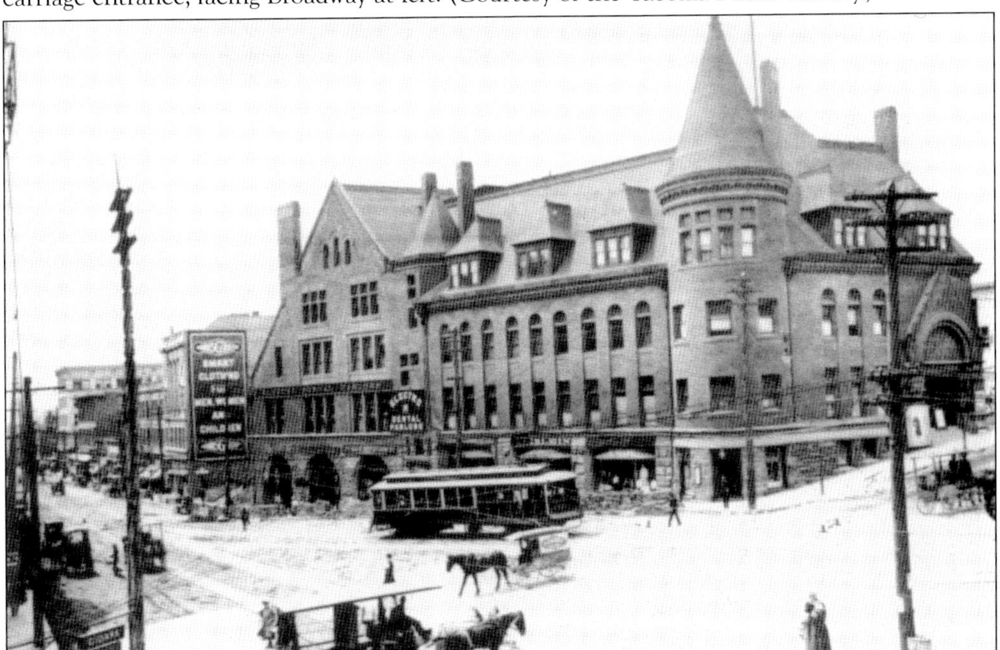

The W.D. Harney Photogravure Company of Racine, Wisconsin, visited Tacoma in 1907, capturing this dramatic view looking south from the intersection of Ninth Street and Broadway. The Tacoma Theater fills most of the photograph. The Pythian temple, with a large wall advertisement, can be seen to the south. A few automobiles are visible, but horse-drawn carriages and streetcars are still the more popular means of transportation. (Courtesy of the Tacoma Public Library.)

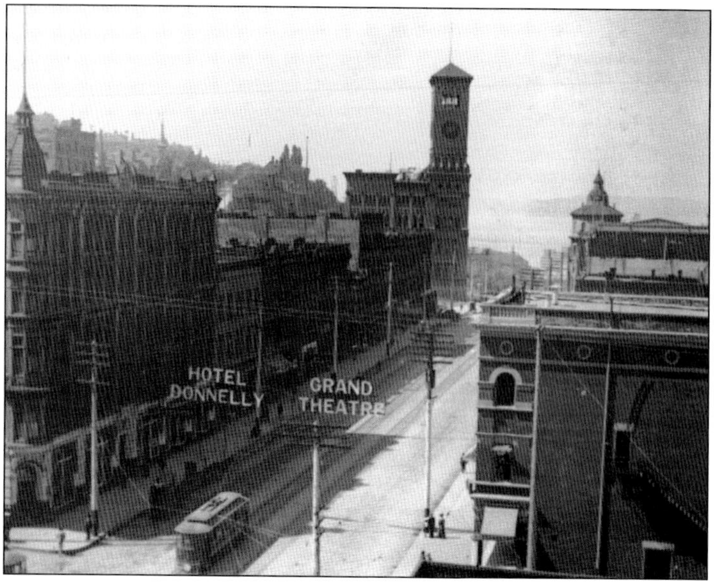

Looking north down Pacific Avenue from its intersection with Ninth Street, the old city hall (built in 1893) is featured prominently in the background. Signage for the Hotel Donnelly, one of the earliest hotels in Tacoma, and the Grand Theater, which opened in 1905, stretches across Pacific Avenue as a streetcar passes below. (Courtesy of the Tacoma Public Library.)

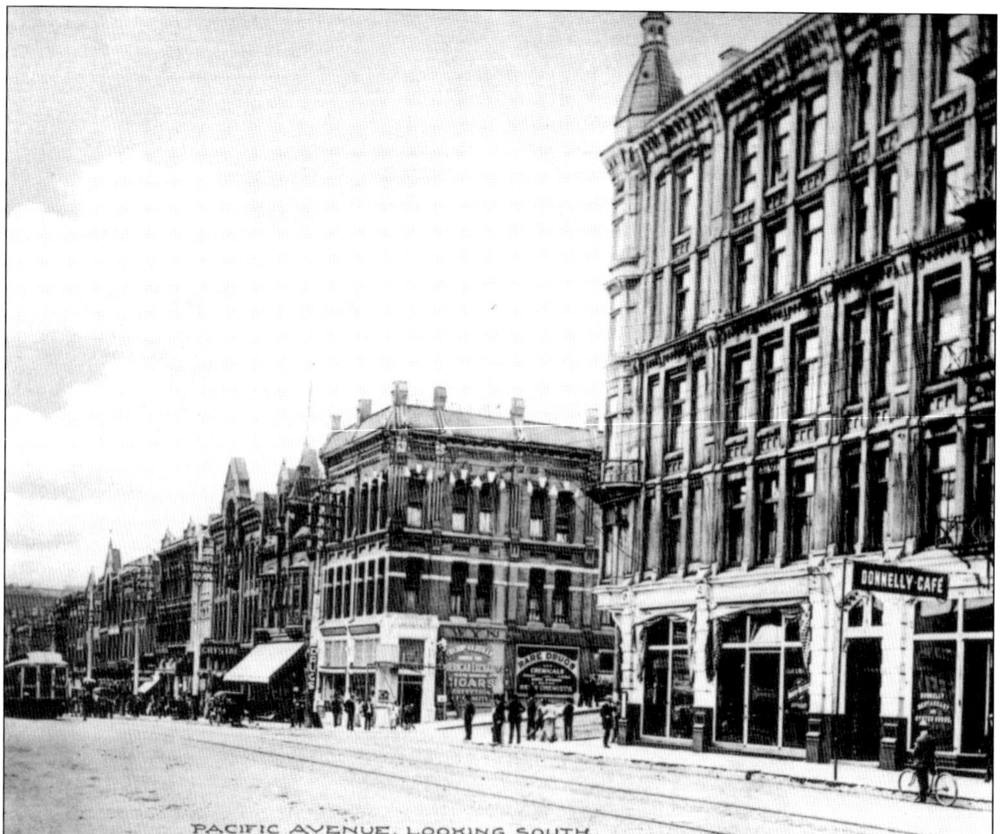

This image of Pacific Avenue is from about 1907. The Hotel Donnelly occupies the northwest corner of Ninth Street and Pacific Avenue, and across Ninth Street is the Wynkoop-Vaughn Drug Co. A few doors south is the Crystal Theater, which would soon be remodeled to become the first Pantages Theater in Tacoma. (Courtesy of the Tacoma Public Library.)

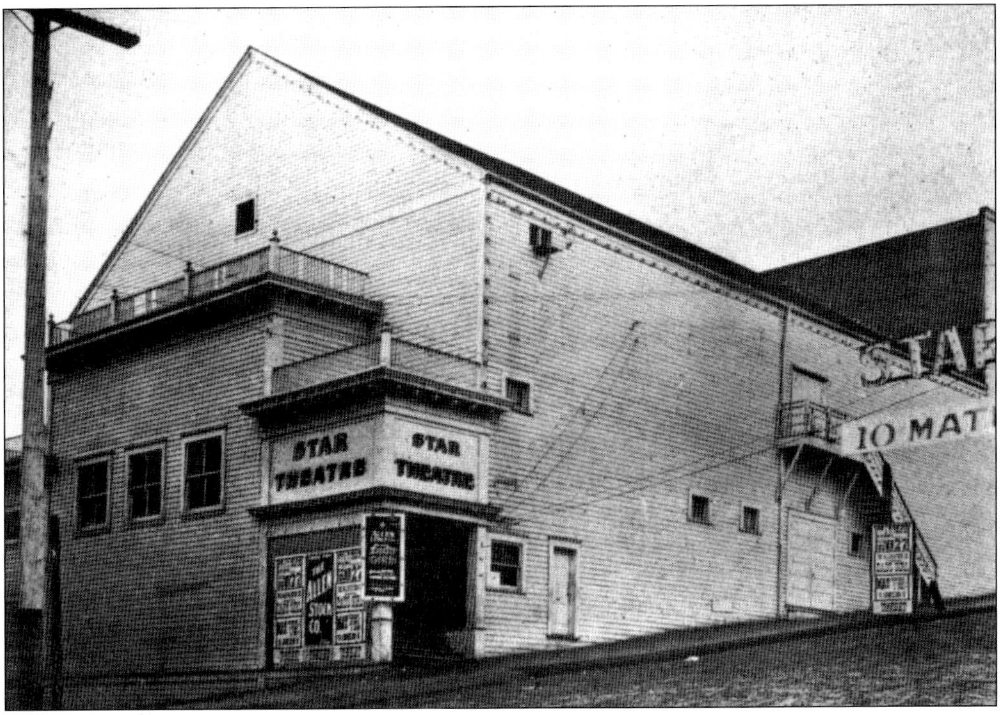

This theater was built in 1892 and operated as the Olympic (1892–1895), the Ninth Street (1895–1898), the Lyceum (1899–1904), and finally, the Star, as seen here, beginning in 1905 until the wood-frame building was lost to fire in 1909. The Rialto Theater was later built on this same site, facing Ninth Street and next door to the Tacoma Theater. (Courtesy of the Tacoma Public Library.)

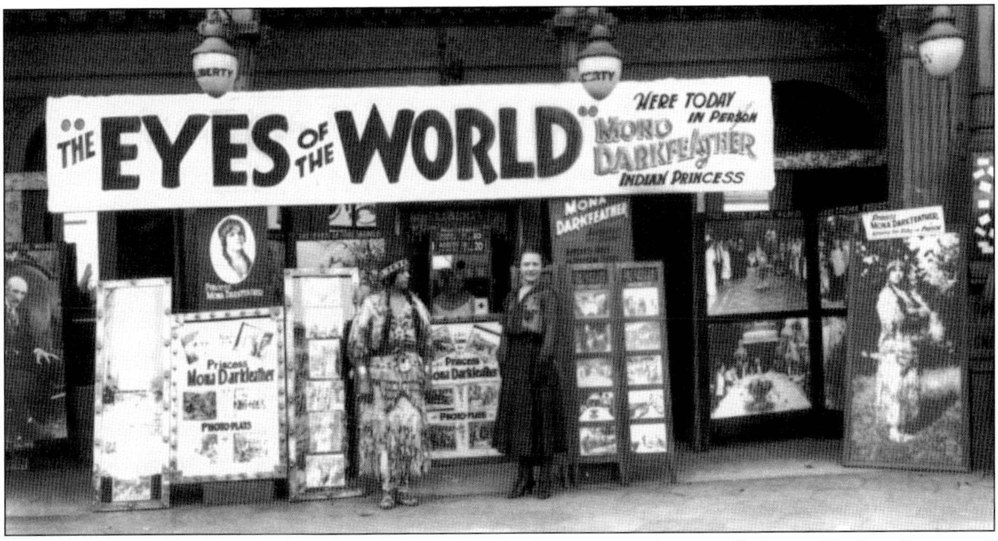

Appearing at the Liberty Theater, 906–908 Pacific Avenue, in August 1918 was "Indian Princess" Mona Darkfeather. Born Josephine Workman, she became a screen actress after answering an advertisement calling for young women to play Indian maidens in feature films. She spent several days in Tacoma during the run of her film *The Eyes of the World*, appearing on stage after each showing. (Courtesy of the Tacoma Public Library.)

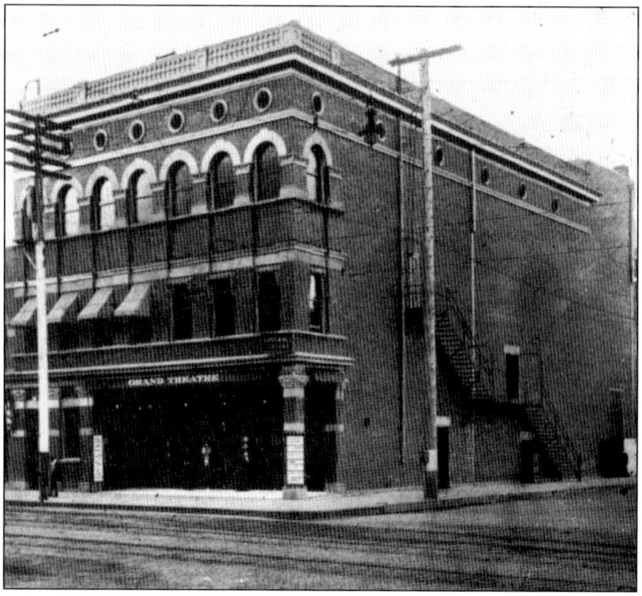

Described as the "costliest home of vaudeville in the country" when it was built in 1905 at the corner of Ninth Street and Pacific Avenue, this theater operated under several different names in the following years. In this c. 1905–1910 photograph, it was the Grand Theater. Subsequent names included Majestic, Empress, Regent, and Hippodrome. (Courtesy of the Tacoma Public Library.)

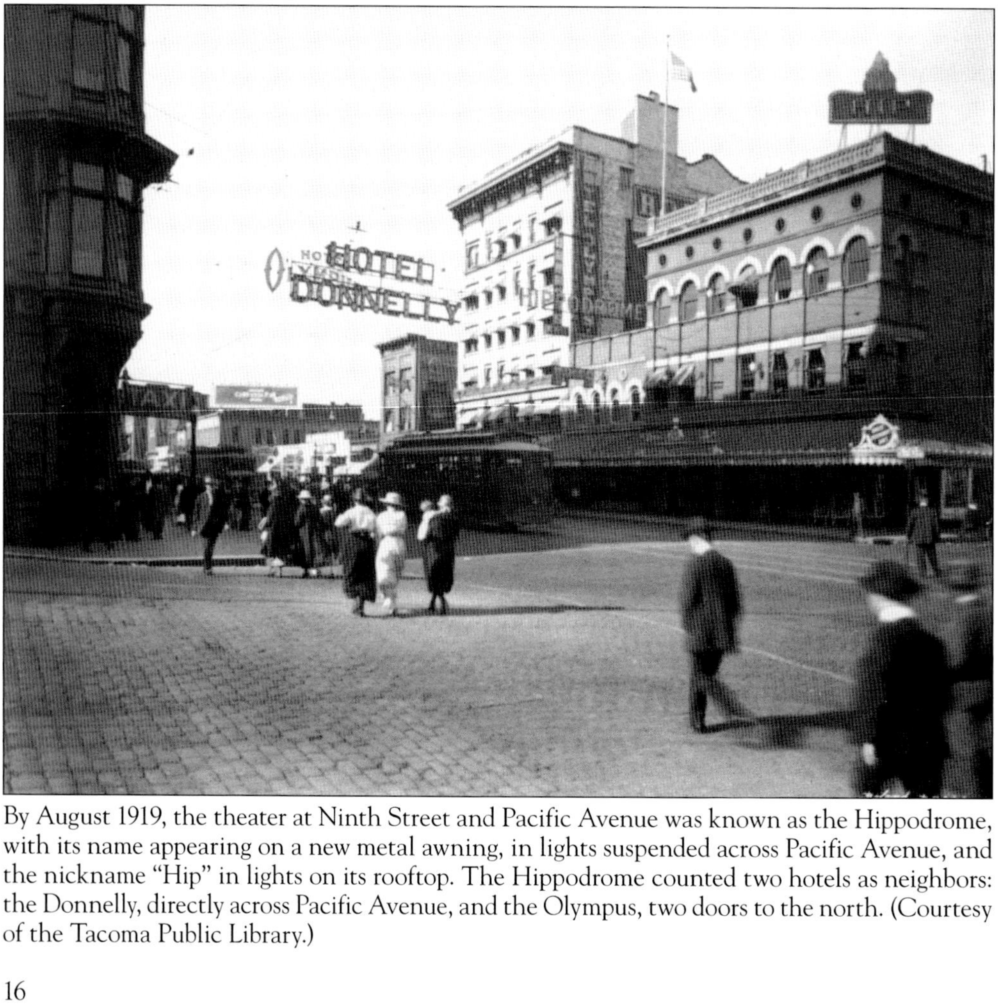

By August 1919, the theater at Ninth Street and Pacific Avenue was known as the Hippodrome, with its name appearing on a new metal awning, in lights suspended across Pacific Avenue, and the nickname "Hip" in lights on its rooftop. The Hippodrome counted two hotels as neighbors: the Donnelly, directly across Pacific Avenue, and the Olympus, two doors to the north. (Courtesy of the Tacoma Public Library.)

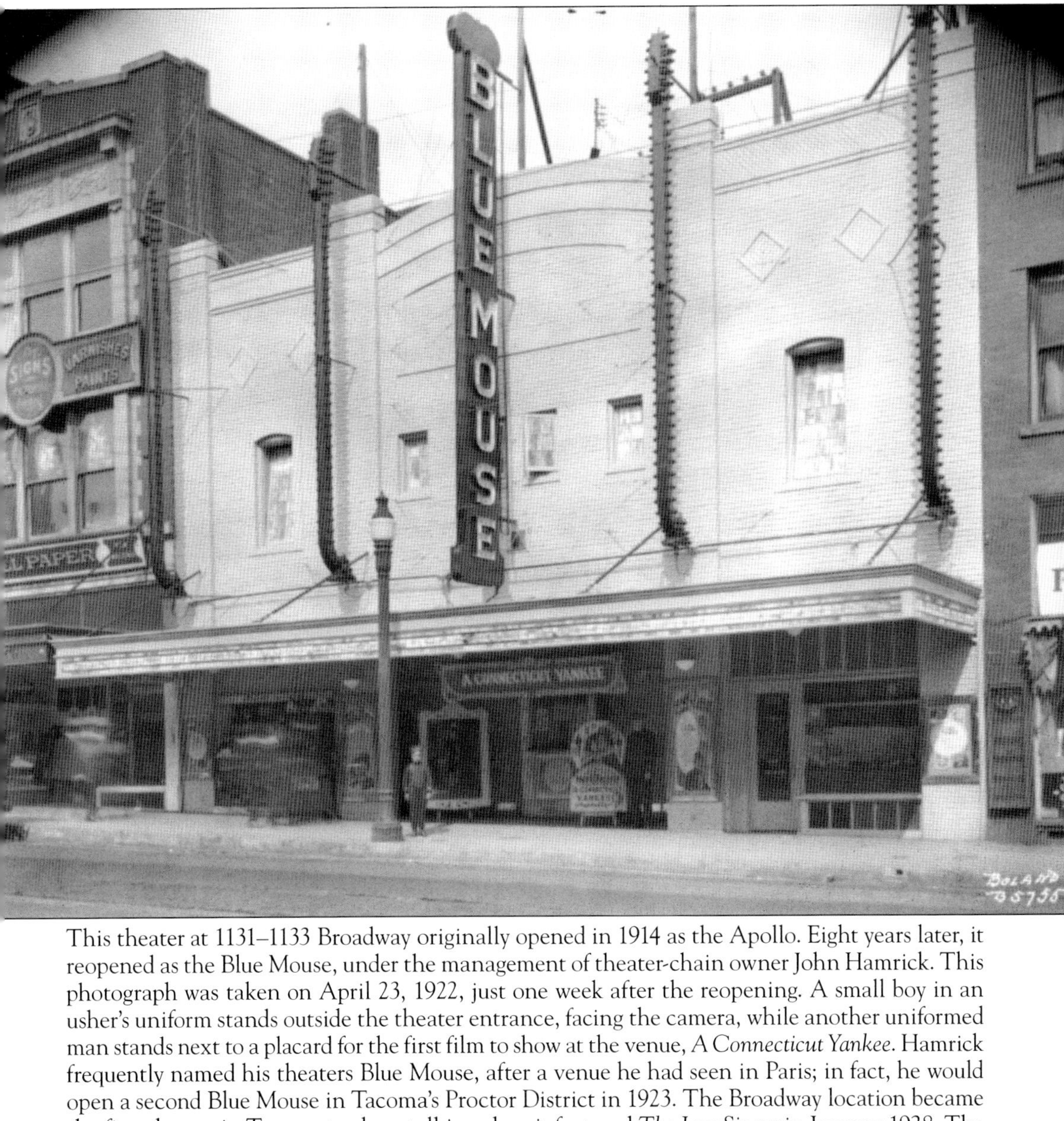

This theater at 1131–1133 Broadway originally opened in 1914 as the Apollo. Eight years later, it reopened as the Blue Mouse, under the management of theater-chain owner John Hamrick. This photograph was taken on April 23, 1922, just one week after the reopening. A small boy in an usher's uniform stands outside the theater entrance, facing the camera, while another uniformed man stands next to a placard for the first film to show at the venue, *A Connecticut Yankee*. Hamrick frequently named his theaters Blue Mouse, after a venue he had seen in Paris; in fact, he would open a second Blue Mouse in Tacoma's Proctor District in 1923. The Broadway location became the first theater in Tacoma to show talkies when it featured *The Jazz Singer* in January 1928. The theater was a favorite among Tacoma moviegoers until its demolition in 1960 to make way for a moving sidewalk. (Courtesy of the Tacoma Public Library.)

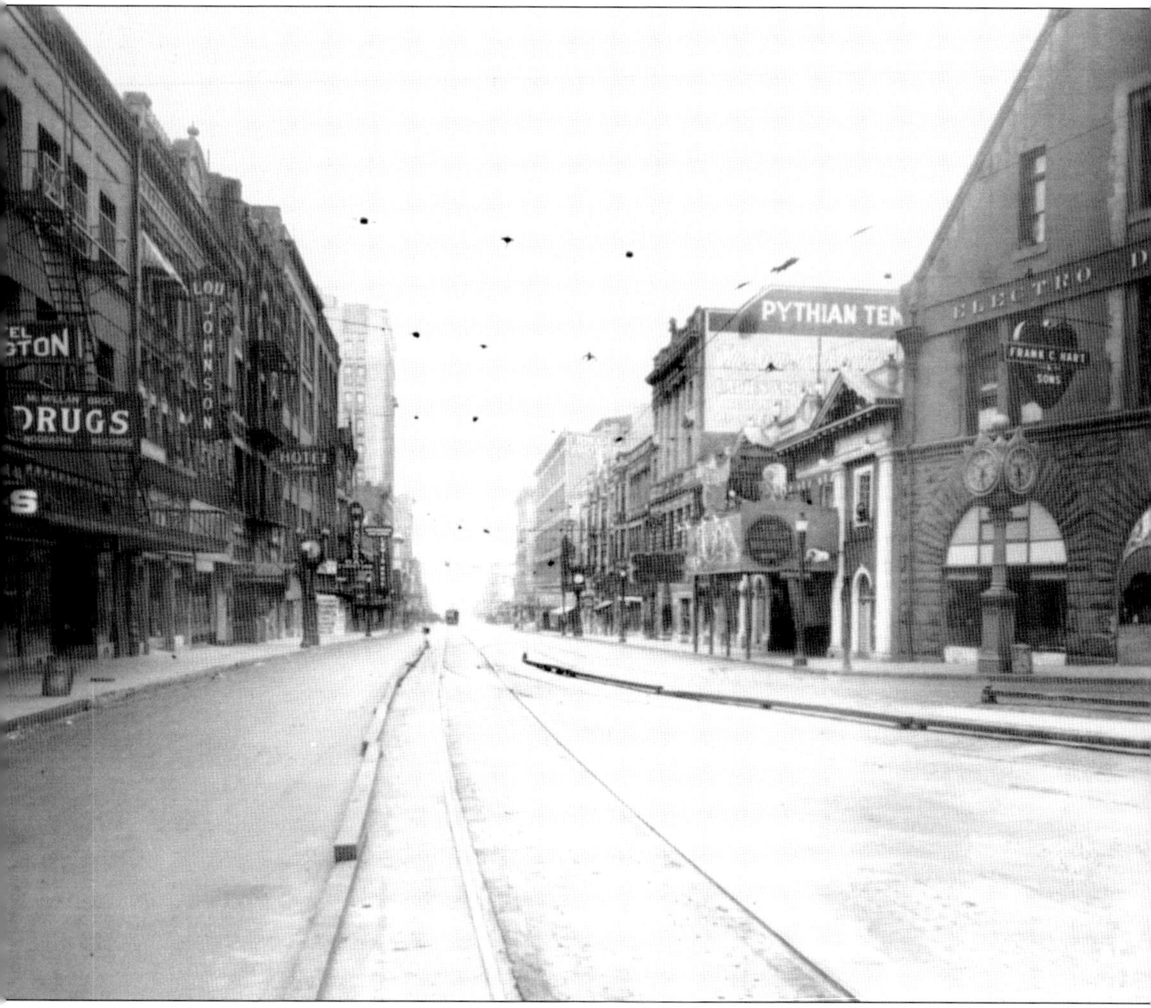

In this view of the 900 block of Broadway in August 1924, a wide range of business establishments can be seen coexisting with the many theaters in the district. The Pantages Theater, just out of view, would be directly to the left of the photographer. Visible on the left side of the street are the Hotel Illington, McMillan Bros. Drugs, Lou Johnson (women's clothing), the Hotel Pierce, and Lewis Brothers (clothing). Rhodes Brothers department store occupies the far end of the street at right, while the Pythian temple and Colonial Theater are closer in the foreground. A portion of the Tacoma Theater building is visible at far right, with two of its commercial occupants, Frank C. Hart & Sons (jewelers) and the Electro Dental Parlors. A streetcar is visible in the distance along the tracks. (Courtesy of the Tacoma Public Library.)

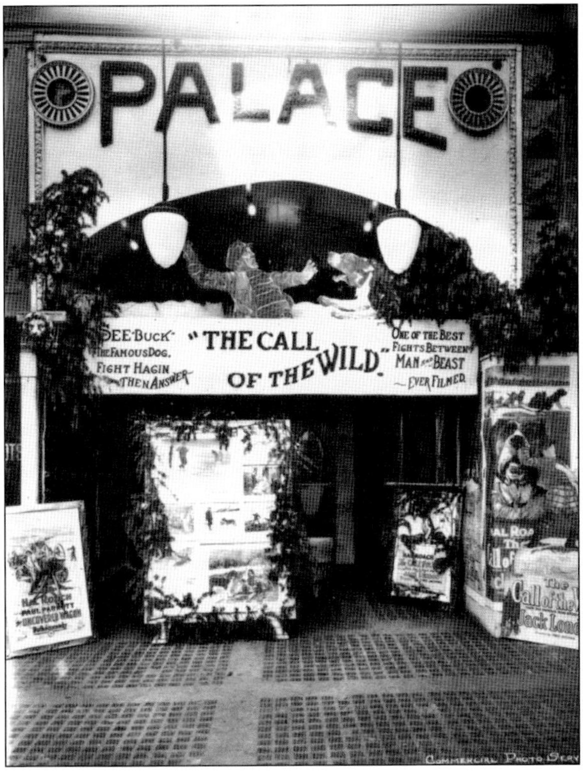

The Palace Theater was in operation at 1128 Pacific Avenue from 1911 until 1928. It would later reopen as the Cameo Theater in 1941, remaining in business until the building was demolished in 1960. These two photographs from the mid-1920s provide both a close-up view of the theater's entrance and a sense of its context amidst other businesses. At this date, it appears that the Palace was the only entertainment venue on the 1100 block of Pacific Avenue, sharing the block with two hotels (the Regal and the Bristol) and two dental clinics (Dr. J.T. Wilson and the Chicago Dentists), as well as the Club Cigar Store and Oxford Café. (Both, courtesy of the Tacoma Public Library.)

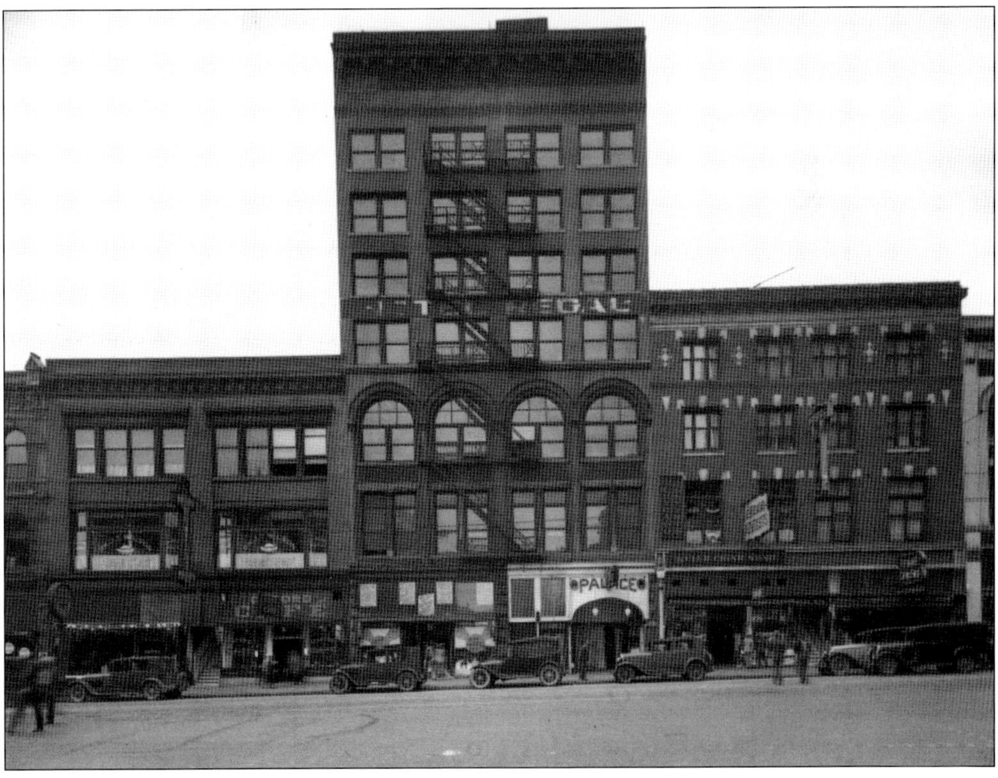

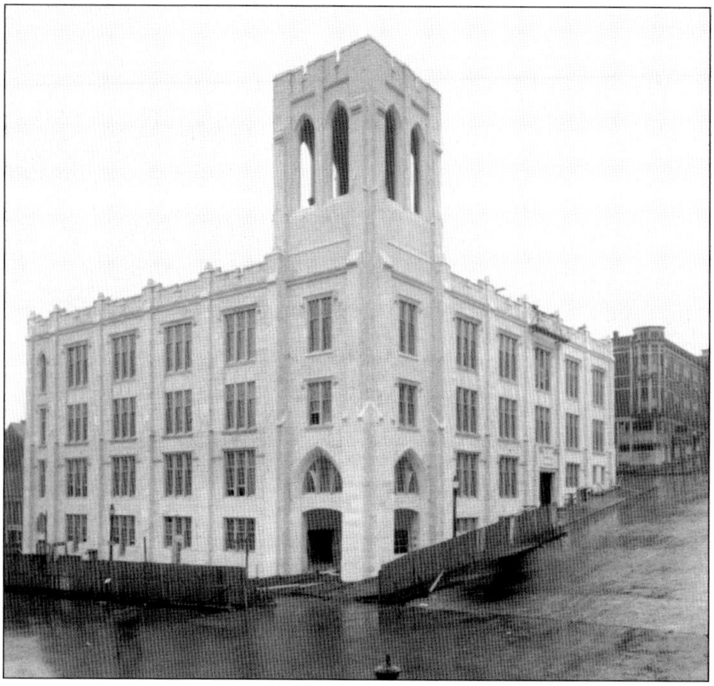

Just before its dedication in June 1925, the Wilkeson sandstone exterior of the new First Baptist Church can be seen in its original glory. First Baptist had been a downtown church since its founding in 1892. After outgrowing previous buildings on this site (Ninth and Market Streets), the congregation voted in 1921 to hold weekly services at the Tacoma Theater until their grand new facility could be completed. (Courtesy of the Tacoma Public Library.)

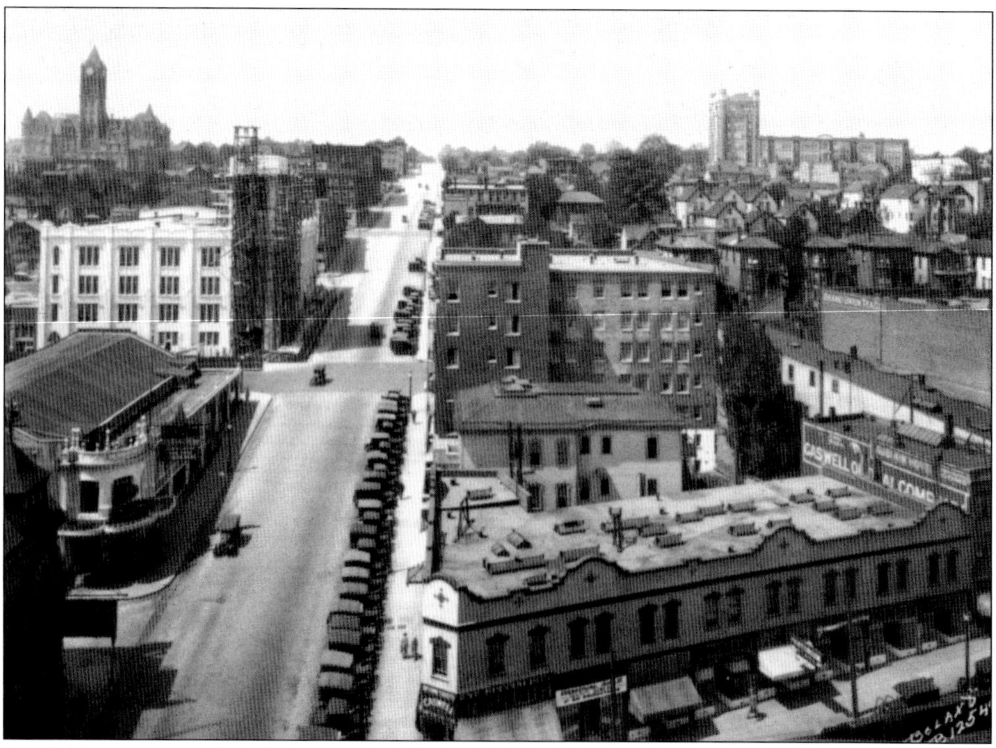

Scaffolding surrounds the bell tower of the almost-complete First Baptist Church, seen here at left up the hill from the Rialto and Tacoma Theaters in May 1925. The new First Baptist would serve not only as the home for its congregation, but also frequently as a venue for concerts. (Courtesy of the Tacoma Public Library.)

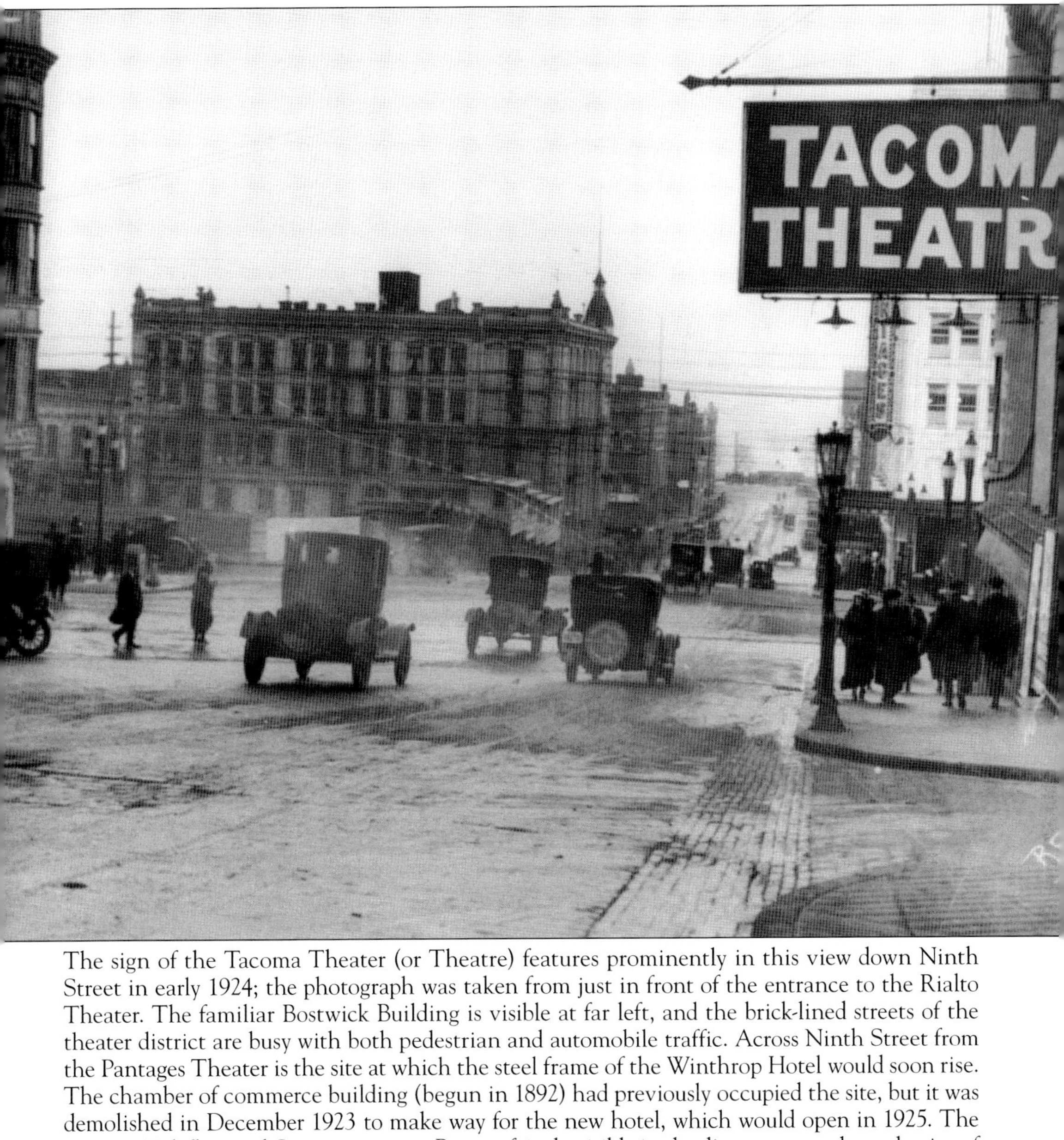

The sign of the Tacoma Theater (or Theatre) features prominently in this view down Ninth Street in early 1924; the photograph was taken from just in front of the entrance to the Rialto Theater. The familiar Bostwick Building is visible at far left, and the brick-lined streets of the theater district are busy with both pedestrian and automobile traffic. Across Ninth Street from the Pantages Theater is the site at which the steel frame of the Winthrop Hotel would soon rise. The chamber of commerce building (begun in 1892) had previously occupied the site, but it was demolished in December 1923 to make way for the new hotel, which would open in 1925. The Tacoma Tideflats and Commencement Bay are faintly visible in the distance, past the end point of Ninth Street at the bottom of the hill. (Courtesy of the Washington State Historical Society.)

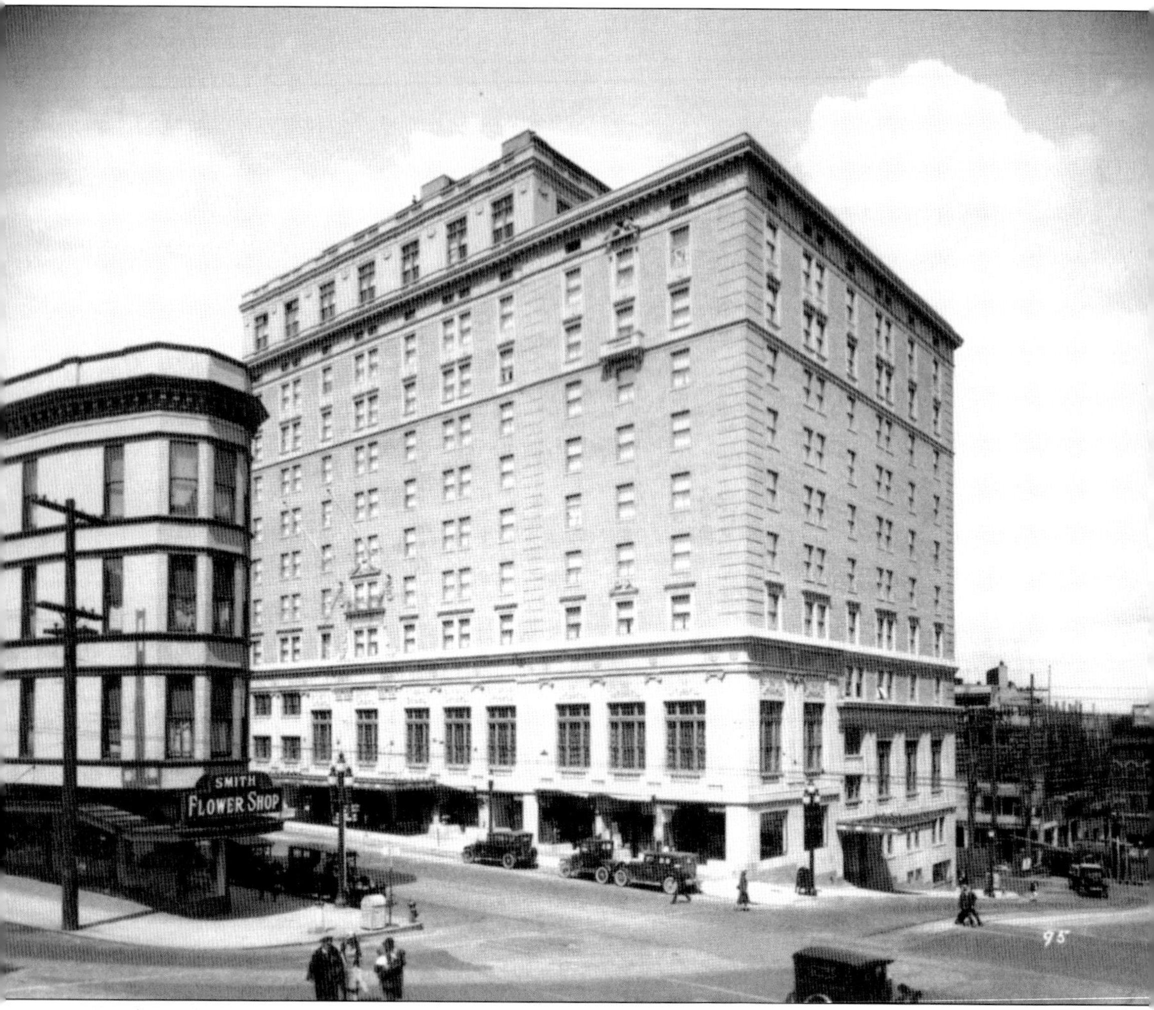

Looking from the vantage point of the Tacoma Theater, the 12-story Hotel Winthrop features prominently in this photograph taken soon after its opening in May 1925. The Bostwick Building is at left, with the Smith Flower Shop occupying its street-level storefront at this date. The new hotel was expected to provide a significant boost to the local economy, and it was built to last: the building was constructed from granite, structural steel, and terra cotta and faced with tapestry brick. The Winthrop was truly a community effort: the Citizens Hotel Corporation raised the construction cost of $2.5 million through a subscription drive. The hotel was then named for writer and Northwest explorer Theodore Winthrop, after George L. Dickson's entry in the *Tacoma Daily Ledger*'s name-the-hotel contest was selected as the winner. (Courtesy of the Tacoma Public Library.)

Two

Golden Age of the Stage

With the opening of the Tacoma Theater in 1890, city residents could boast of having the "largest stage on the Pacific coast." Newspaper accounts of the opening spoke to the vision of the Tacoma pioneers who had supported the theater project:

> It was long before the present magnificent edifice was planned that the project was first thought of. Tacoma was marked out as the City of Destiny, and there were men within its borders who foresaw the tens of thousands who would make their homes upon the shores of Commencement Bay. A beautiful theater, fashioned in most modern elegance, a fit place of amusement in the metropolis of the new northwest, was one of the things which it was known must be provided.

This new venue made possible a tremendous range of performances by both local and traveling acts, from magicians to concert violinists, stage plays to big bands, lectures to vaudeville shows. Even just a brief sampling of the more famous visitors to the Tacoma Theater during its earliest decades reads like a who's who of the entertainment world of the time: Mark Twain, Harry Houdini, John and Ethel Barrymore, John Philip Sousa, Sarah Bernhardt, Al Jolson, Sergei Rachmaninoff, and the list goes on.

In 1918, two new theaters joined the Tacoma on the Ninth Street hill. Alexander Pantages opened his stunning, state-of-the-art vaudeville house on the corner of Ninth Street and Broadway. The Rialto, the only of these three venues to be originally designed as a movie theater, was the other new neighbor to the Tacoma, its box office just across an alley from that of the grand old theater.

Through the 1920s and 1930s, despite changes in ownership and management for all three theaters, periods of economic downturn, and a gradual change in balance between stage and screen, the theater district—with the Pantages, Tacoma, and Rialto theaters as its core—continued to play host to a broad range of live performances, providing entertainment for Tacomans of all ages and tastes.

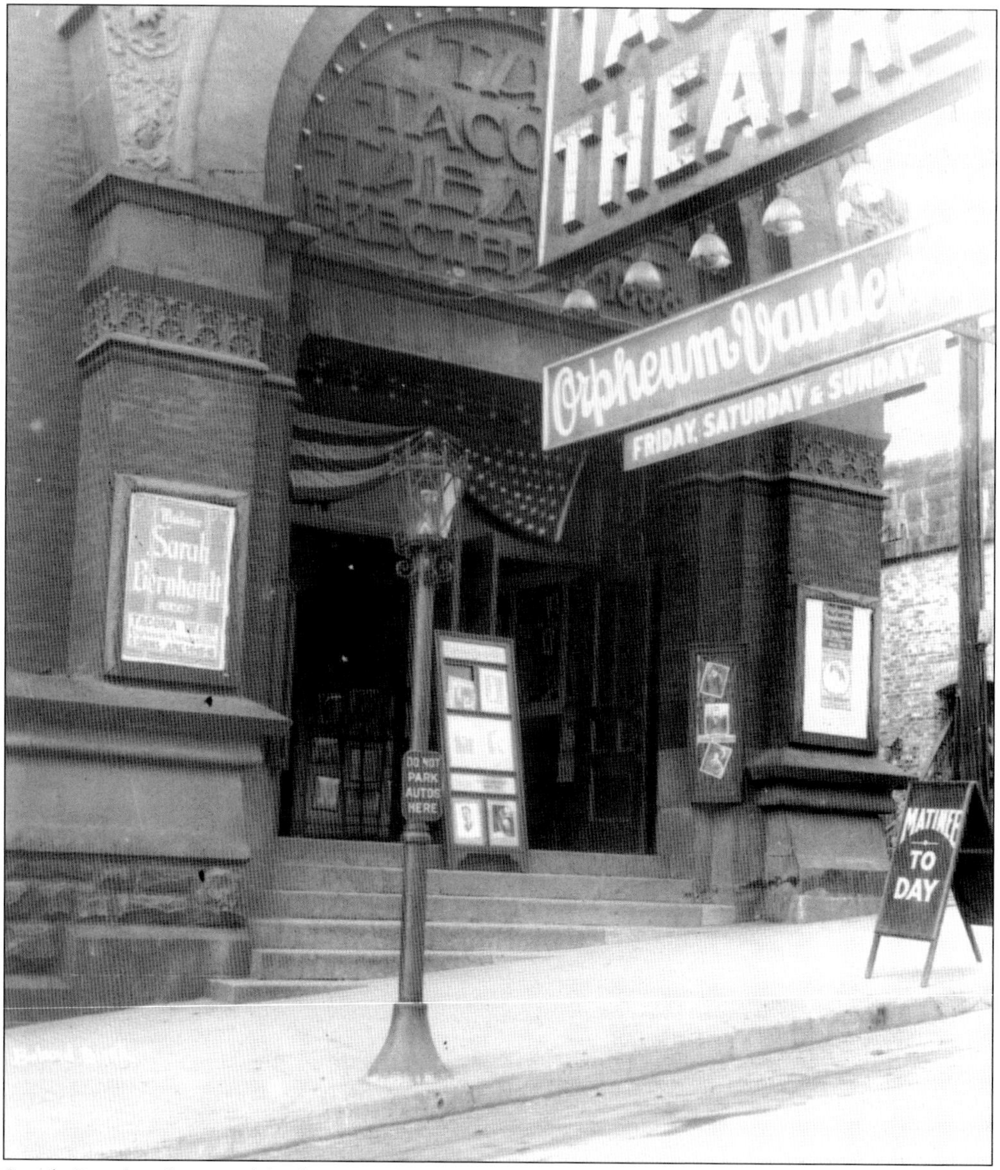

Sarah Bernhardt, arguably the most famous actress in the world at the time, appeared at the Tacoma Theater from June 14 through 16, 1918. Bernhardt and her company were sharing the closing bill of the Orpheum Vaudeville season with several other acts, including soprano Marion Weeks, Mayo and Lynn, Madden and Ford, Albert Donnelly, and Bensee and Baird. This visit was at least the second by Bernhardt to the Tacoma Theater's stage; the actress had appeared, to the great excitement of Tacoma audiences, in 1891, soon after the theater's opening. The year 1918 also marked the period in which the Tacoma Theater was joined on the Ninth Street hillside by two new venues; the Pantages had opened in January, and the Rialto's opening followed in September. In this view of the theater's front entrance on Ninth Avenue, both the original relief lettering and the more modern protruding sign can be seen. (Courtesy of the Tacoma Public Library.)

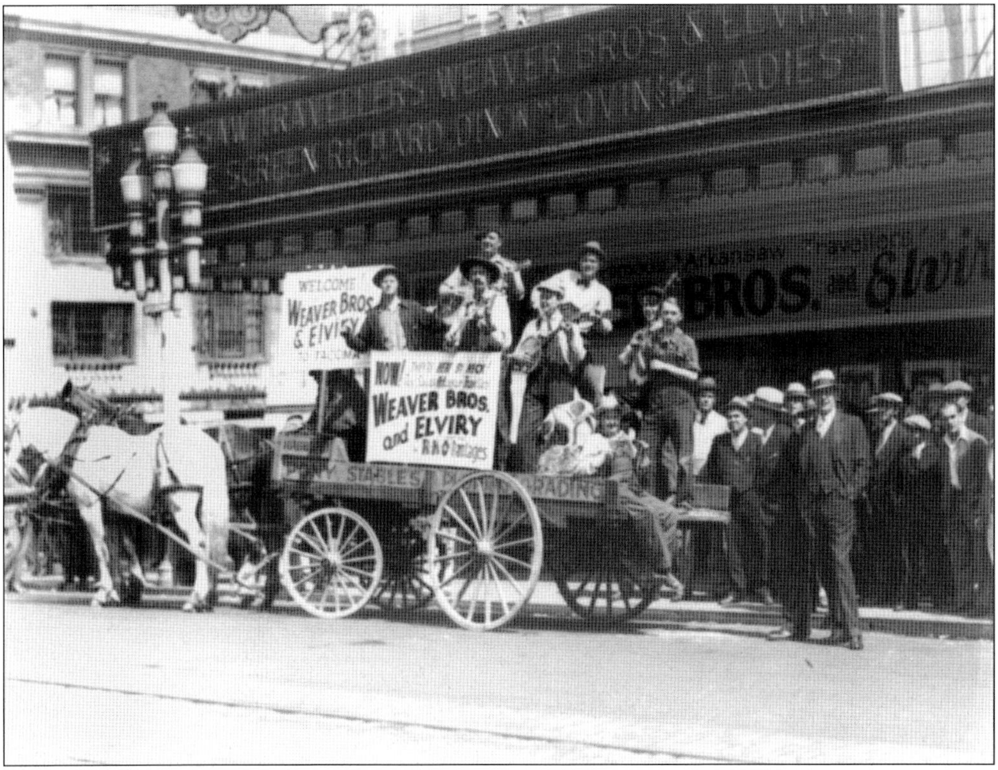

The musical-comedy team of the Weaver Brothers and Elviry, signed by Alexander Pantages to a contract in the early 1920s, is seen here outside Tacoma's Pantages Theater before a performance. The family act enjoyed a lengthy vaudeville career before venturing into film. Although their movies were hugely popular, the family missed the audience interaction of vaudeville and eventually left Hollywood to return to live performance. (Courtesy of the Tacoma Public Library.)

Members of the Tacoma Drama League are seen here in rehearsal for their December 16, 1924, performance of *The Torch Bearers* at the Tacoma Theater. In choosing *The Torch Bearers*, a 1922 play by American playwright George Kelly, the drama league was showing a willingness to laugh at itself: the play is a satire of amateur theater, with characters depicted as narcissistic and undisciplined. (Courtesy of the Tacoma Public Library.)

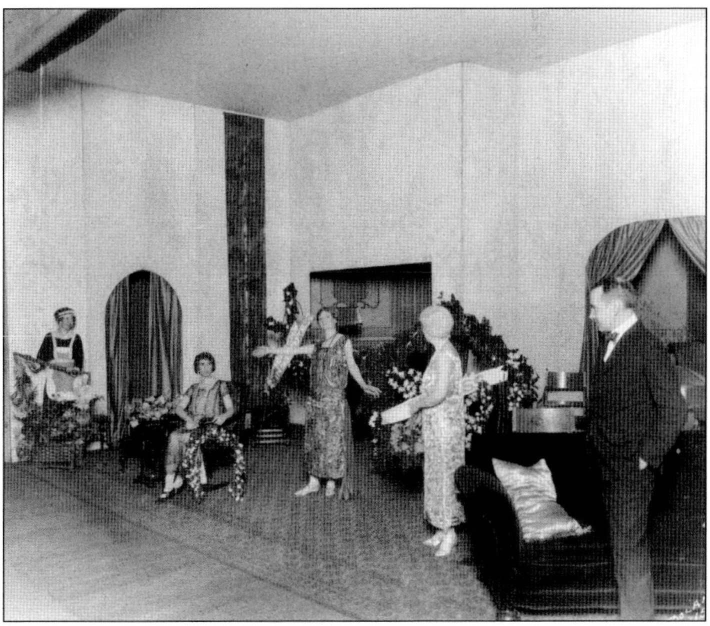

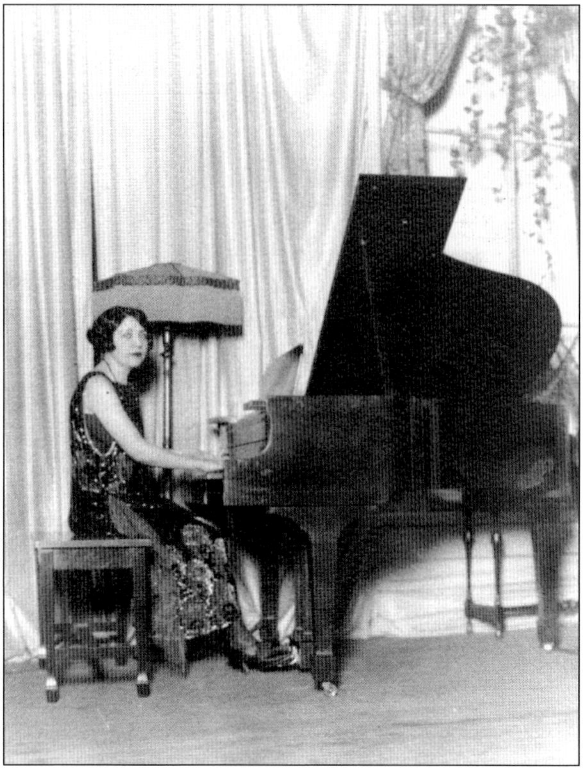

Esther Stayner, seen here playing a baby grand piano on the stage of the Rialto Theater, was named as the Rialto's organist in November 1924, succeeding Alice Piercy in the job. Stayner had spent the three previous years at the Clemmer Theater in Spokane, Washington. A framed window with accompanying foliage is also part of the stage décor. (Courtesy of the Tacoma Public Library.)

In the mid-1920s, live performers often shared the bill with films at Tacoma's theaters. In this photograph from January 1925, eight musicians, believed to be Eddie Hillabrand and his Hollywood Studio Jazz Band, appear on the stage of the Rialto behind the theater's organ. Hillabrand's band performed three times daily, at 3:00, 7:00, and 9:00 p.m. (Courtesy of the Tacoma Public Library.)

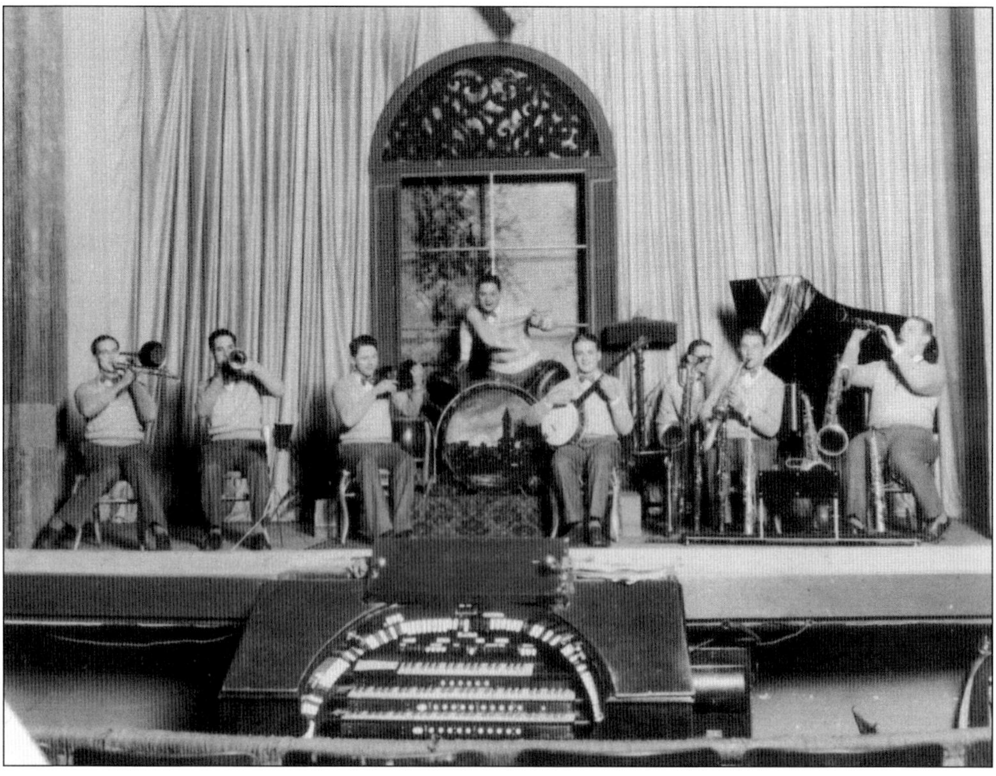

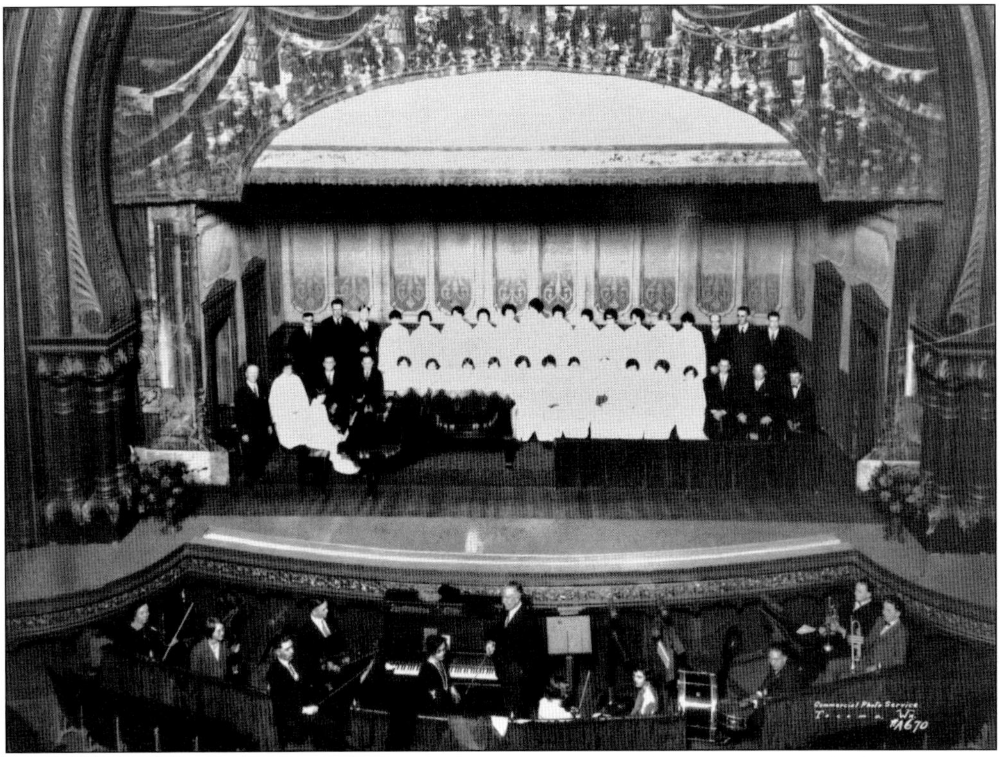

When the Tacoma Theater was built in 1889, it boasted the largest stage on the Pacific coast, measuring 67 feet in width, 42 feet in depth, and 55 feet in height from stage to loft. The sheer size and grandeur of the stage can be seen in these two photographs from the mid-1920s, taken prior to the theater's 1925–1927 remodel. The stage was well equipped to host a variety of events, whether a full choir with grand piano and accompanying pit orchestra, or a fully staged play with a cast of dozens. A variety of hand-painted curtains and sets were also available to provide background for a diverse range of performances. (Both, courtesy of the Tacoma Public Library.)

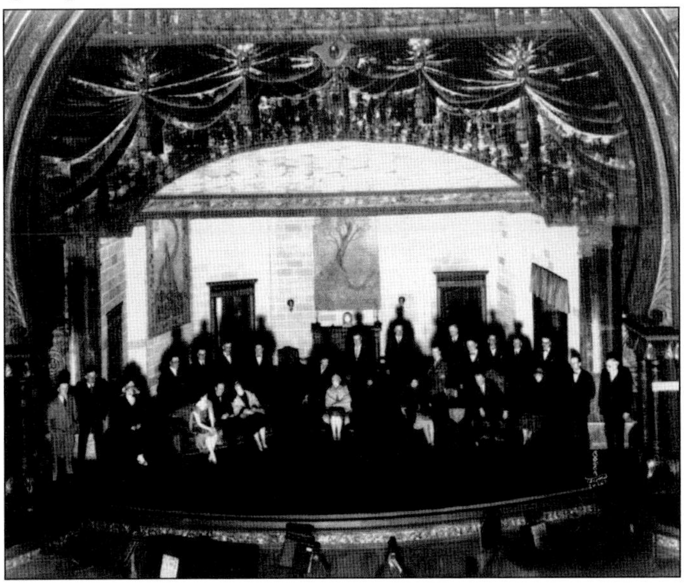

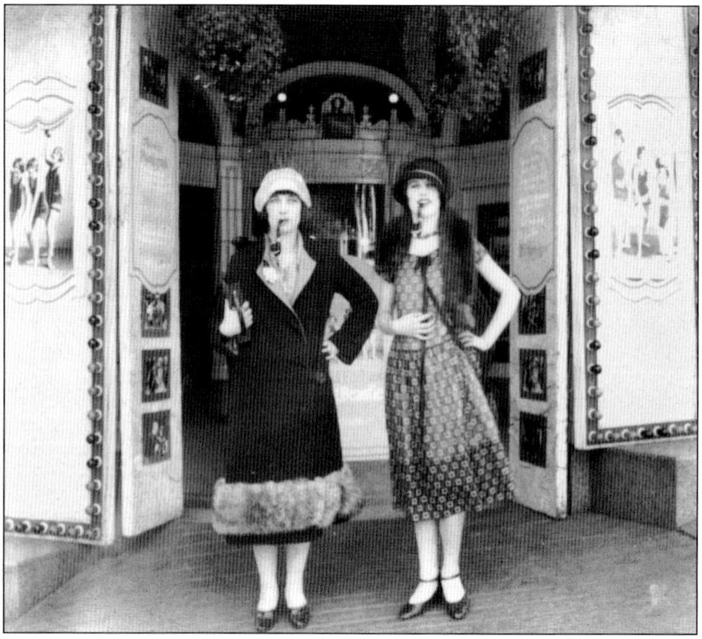

In June 1925, Arline Abel (left) and Hazel Green, performers in the Ziegfeld Follies *Phantograph*, pose in front of the Rialto Theater. The Follies act starred six beautiful bathing beauties, a comedian, and a German police dog in a live-action skit. Each audience member was given an early form of three-dimensional glasses, which seemed to bring the action even closer to their seats. (Courtesy of the Tacoma Public Library.)

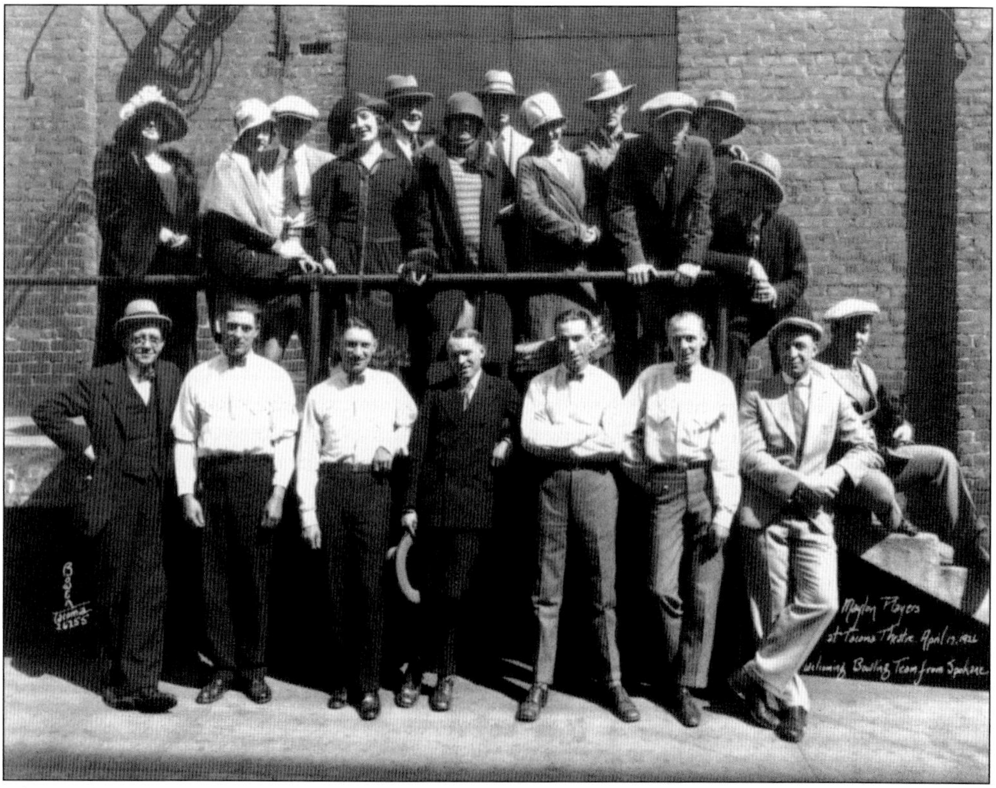

The Maylon Players, a theater troupe that performed throughout the region, is seen here on April 17, 1926, posing outside the Tacoma Theater. The troupe performed *Best People*, a 1924 play by Avery Hopwood and David Gray, at the theater the following evening. (Courtesy of the Tacoma Public Library.)

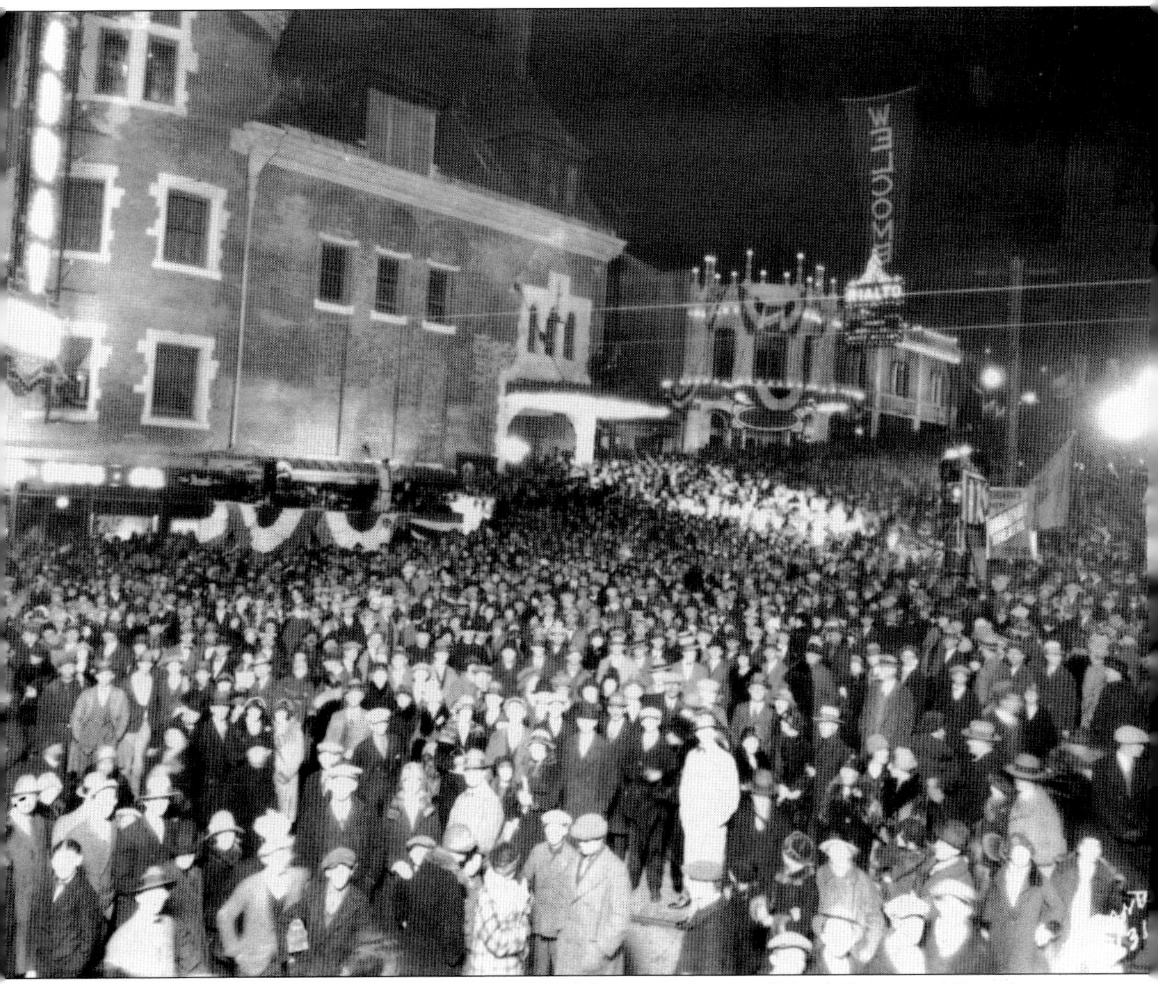

On February 4, 1927, thousands of Tacomans filled the intersection of Ninth Street and Broadway to celebrate the grand opening of the new Broadway—formerly the Tacoma—Theater. The Tacoma Theater, originally opened in 1889, had closed in 1925 for an extensive remodel, reopening two years later with new capabilities for showing films in addition to stage acts. For the grand opening, streets were closed to traffic, and crowds began gathering as early as 3:00 p.m. By later in the evening, when this photograph was taken, much of Tacoma's theatergoing public seemed to have joined the party. A street dance on Market Street near Ninth Street, public singing on Ninth Street near Broadway, and an informal ball at the Hotel Winthrop contributed to the festive atmosphere. The streets were illuminated by high lights advertised as two million candlepower. The Broadway's bill that evening promoted the first-run production of Harold Lloyd's *The Kid Brother*, Fanchon and Marco's *Pyramids* revue, and Oliver Wallace and his Broadway Revelers as musical accompaniment. (Courtesy of the Tacoma Public Library.)

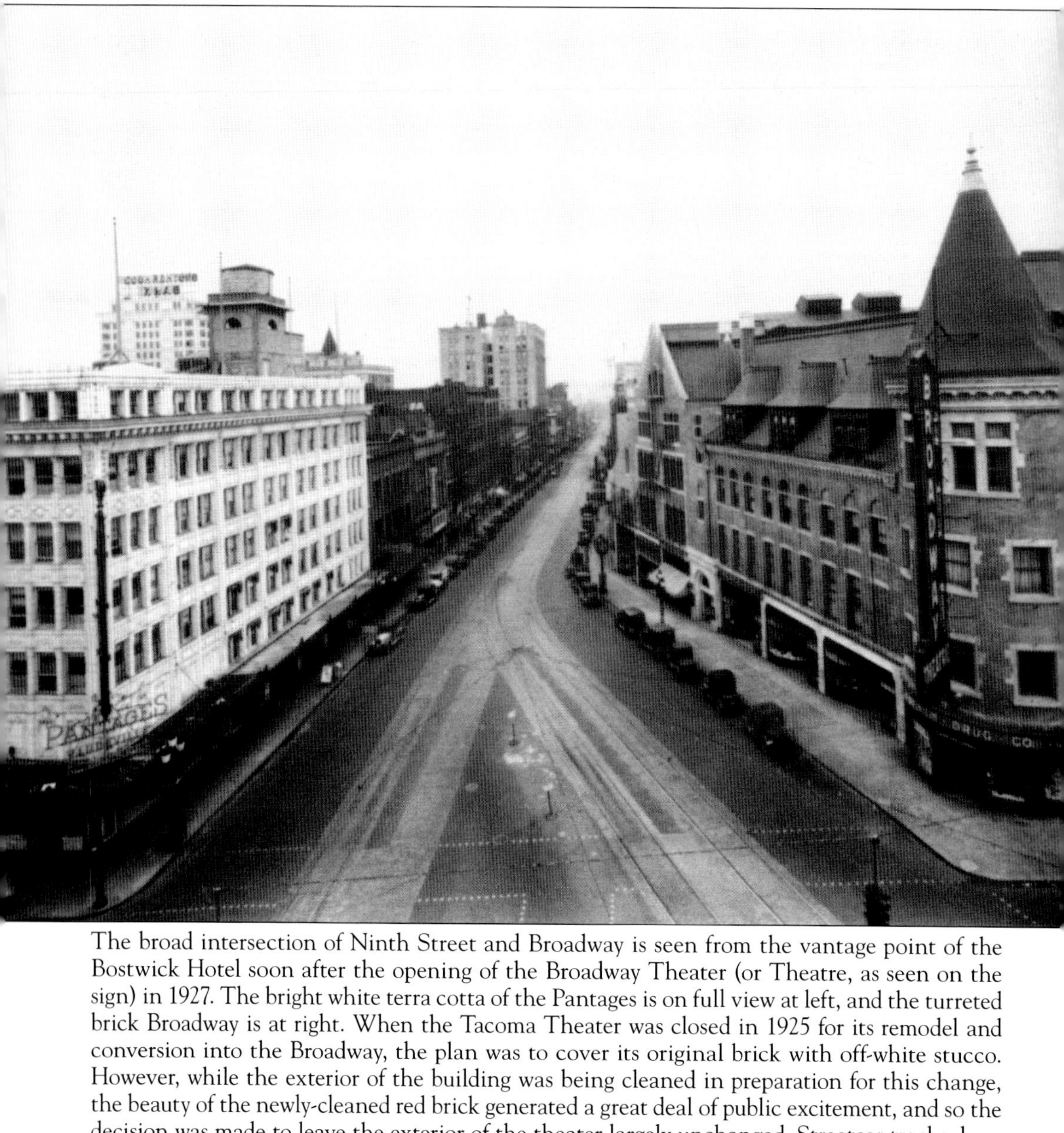

The broad intersection of Ninth Street and Broadway is seen from the vantage point of the Bostwick Hotel soon after the opening of the Broadway Theater (or Theatre, as seen on the sign) in 1927. The bright white terra cotta of the Pantages is on full view at left, and the turreted brick Broadway is at right. When the Tacoma Theater was closed in 1925 for its remodel and conversion into the Broadway, the plan was to cover its original brick with off-white stucco. However, while the exterior of the building was being cleaned in preparation for this change, the beauty of the newly-cleaned red brick generated a great deal of public excitement, and so the decision was made to leave the exterior of the theater largely unchanged. Streetcar tracks, long a presence throughout downtown Tacoma, were joined by an increasing number of cars at this time. (Courtesy of the Tacoma Public Library.)

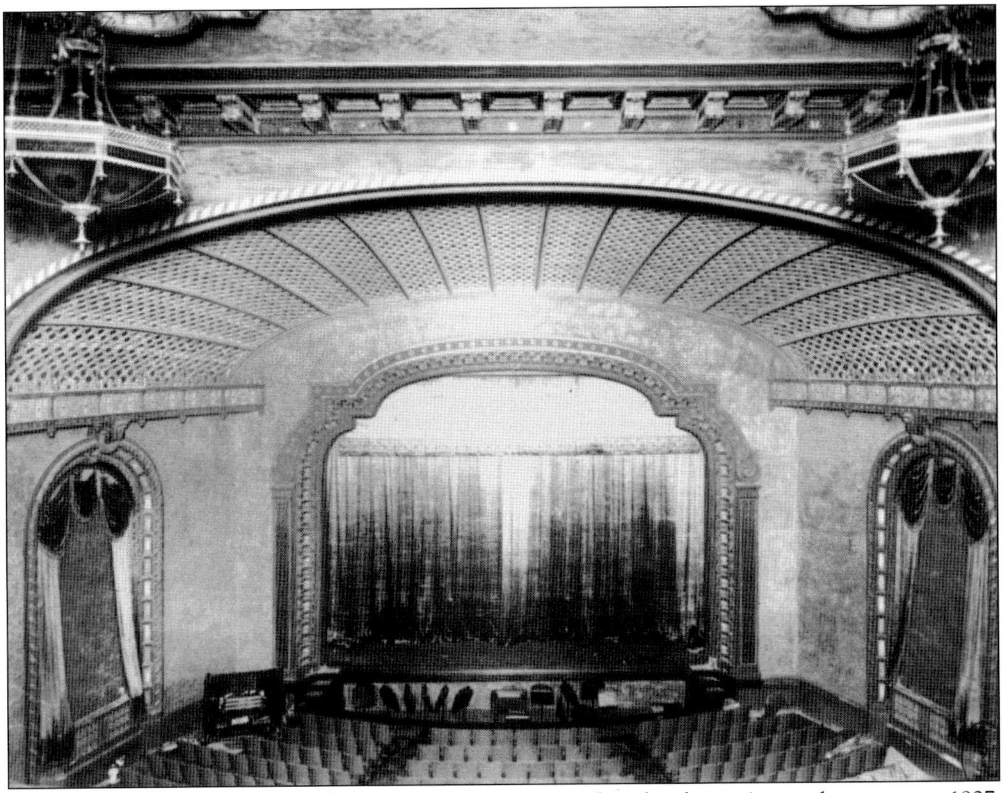

The interior of the Broadway Theater is seen here soon after the theater's grand opening in 1927. In the process of remodeling the old Tacoma Theater into the new Broadway, the interior was completely gutted, with the stage made smaller to increase the seating capacity from 1,200 to 1,600. (Courtesy of the Tacoma Public Library.)

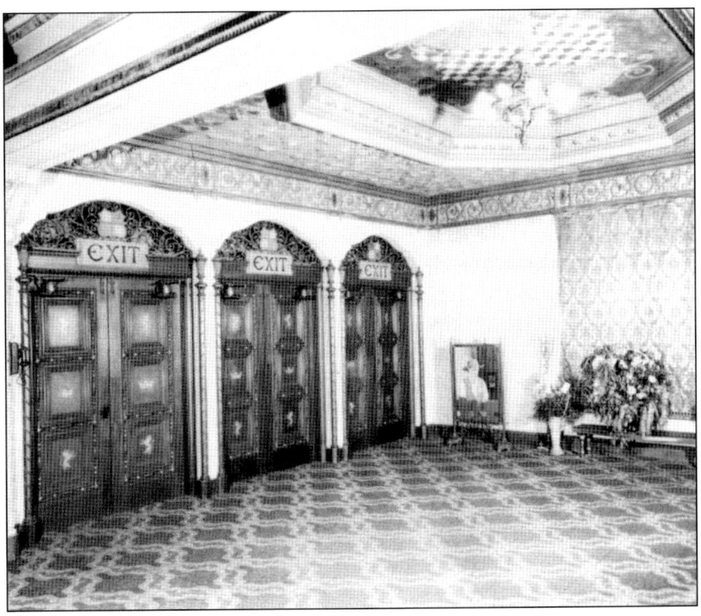

One of the lobby areas of the newly opened Broadway Theater displays the changes made to the interior of the old Tacoma Theater to reflect the style of the late 1920s. A number of practical changes also modernized the facility. The entrance was moved to accommodate a larger ticket booth. An elevator was installed, and a projection booth was added. (Courtesy of the Tacoma Public Library.)

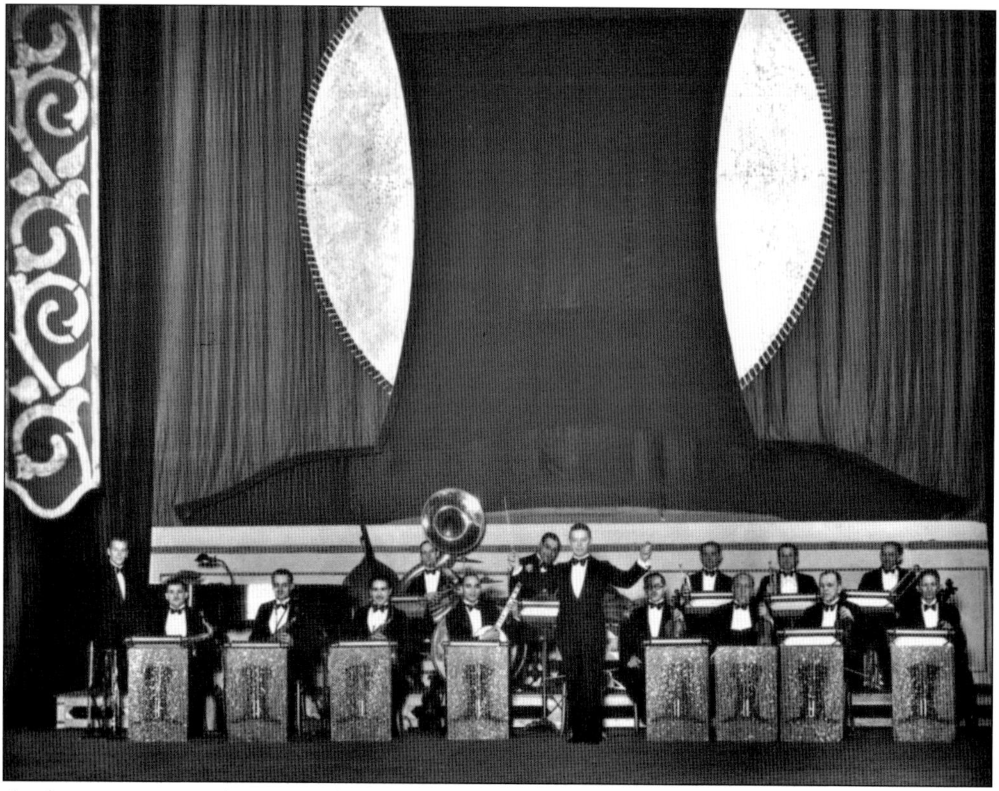

As these two images from 1928 demonstrate, even after reducing the size of the original Tacoma Theater stage, the Broadway Theater remained a venue that could support large stage acts. Well into the 1930s, stages in Tacoma's theater district supported a mix of films, vaudeville acts, and musical performances. One photograph shows a 14-piece orchestra posing in front of a "top hat and moon" backdrop. In the other, a large party fills the stage for a farewell party for musician Oliver Wallace, who—after many years as a theater organist and band leader in the region—would move to Hollywood, where he went on to compose scores for several of Walt Disney's animated classics. (Both, courtesy of the Tacoma Public Library.)

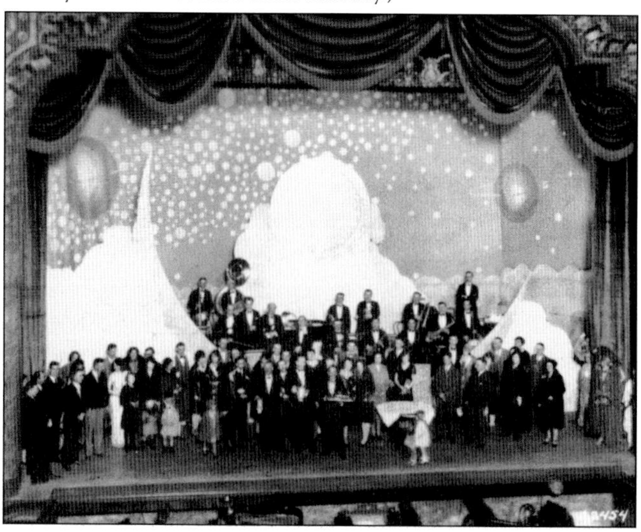

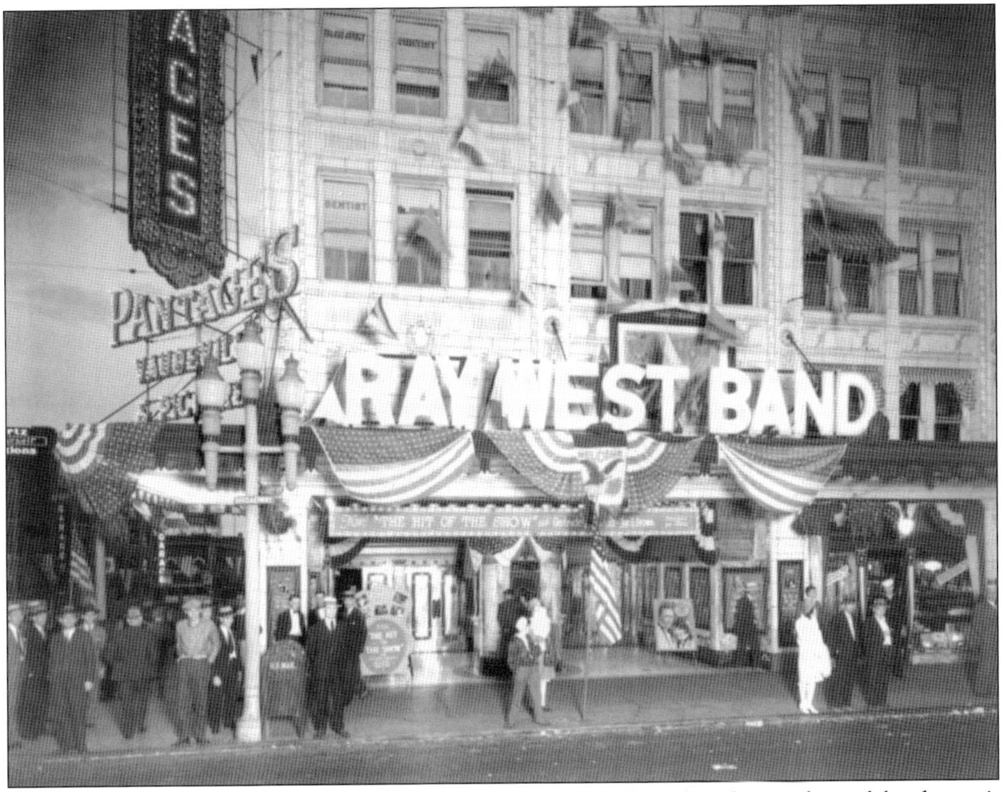

A small crowd mingles outside the Pantages in 1928. As is reflected in the wording of the theater's permanent marquee, "Pantages Vaudeville & Pictures," the traveling live acts appearing at the venue during this period often received more prominent billing than the films currently on view. Ray West Band appears in large letters atop the box office, while the 1928 film *The Hit of the Show* is advertised with smaller signs below. (Courtesy of the Tacoma Public Library.)

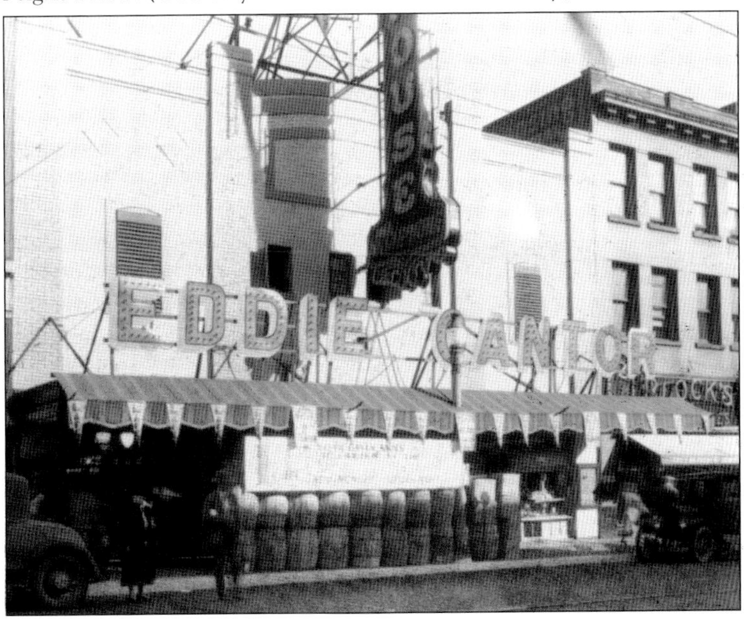

Eddie Cantor is featured at the Blue Mouse Theater (or Theatre, as seen on the sign) in the early 1930s. Cantor's lengthy show business career included work on the stage as well as in radio, film, and television. He turned down the lead role in *The Jazz Singer*, which was the first talking film to be shown in Tacoma, at the Blue Mouse. (Courtesy of the Tacoma Public Library.)

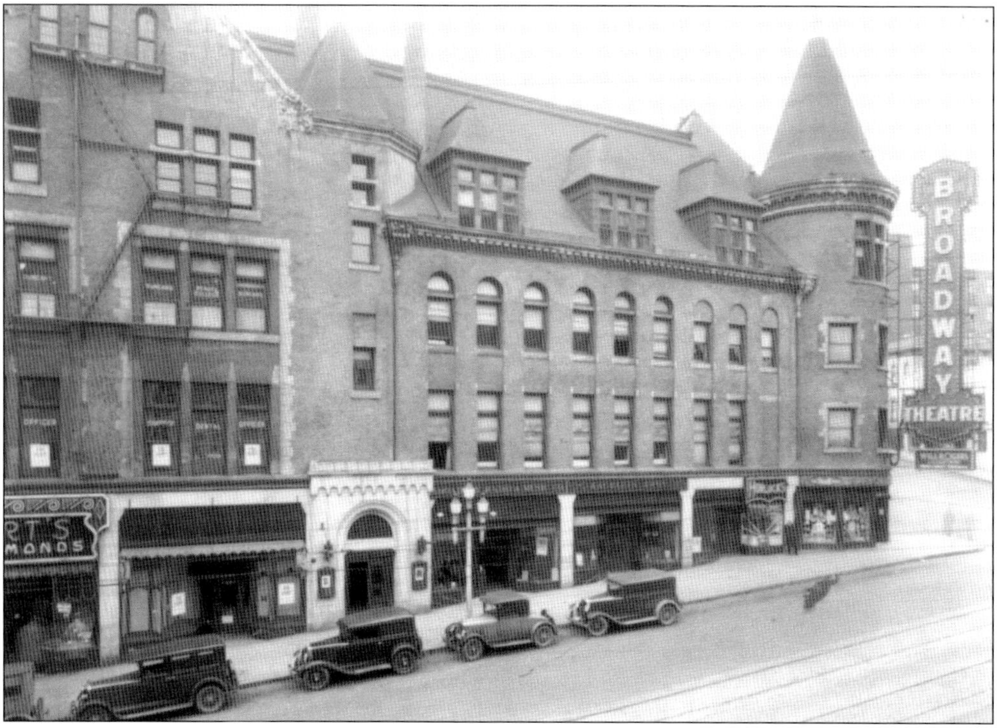

Several "for rent" signs are visible in storefronts in the Broadway Theater building in 1930, reflecting the difficult economic times. Remaining businesses include, from left to right, Robert's Diamonds, Broadway Radio & Music Co., Kachlein Bros. (opticians), Horlucks (lunch counter), and French Drugstore. The Will Rogers vehicle *Lightnin'* was the film showing at the Broadway. (Courtesy of the Tacoma Public Library.)

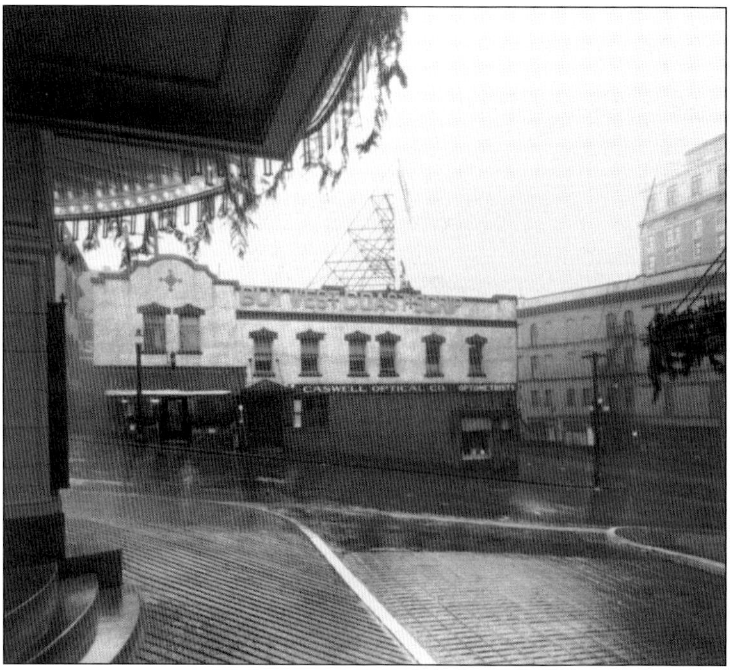

Looking north toward Ninth Street from Court C, the alley between the Broadway (right) and the Rialto (left) Theaters, Caswell Optical Co., a long-standing business in the theater district, takes center stage. Evergreen garlands adorn the marquees of both theaters, and rain has soaked the brick streets in this wintry view from the late 1920s. (Courtesy of the Tacoma Public Library.)

Noted local harpist Noreen Newbegin poses with her instrument in 1927. Newbegin performed as a soloist with the Tacoma Symphony in a concert that took place on March 7, 1927, at the First Baptist Church at Ninth and Market Streets. Even with the many other theaters within a few blocks of the church, First Baptist was frequently used as a concert venue. (Courtesy of the Tacoma Public Library.)

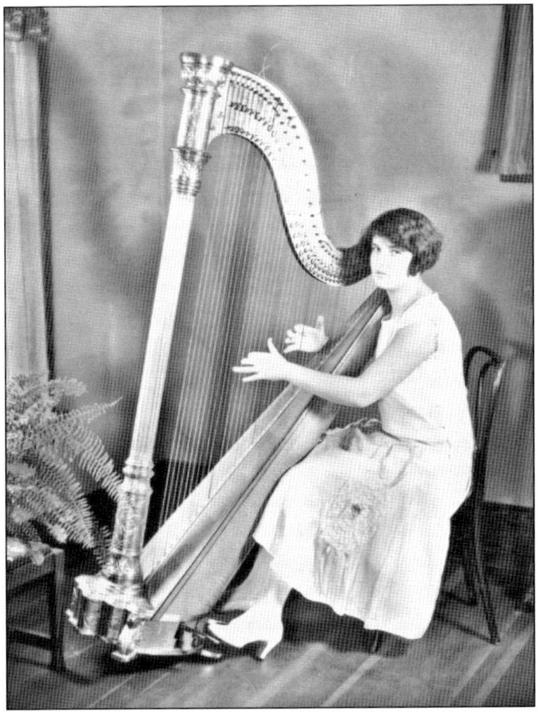

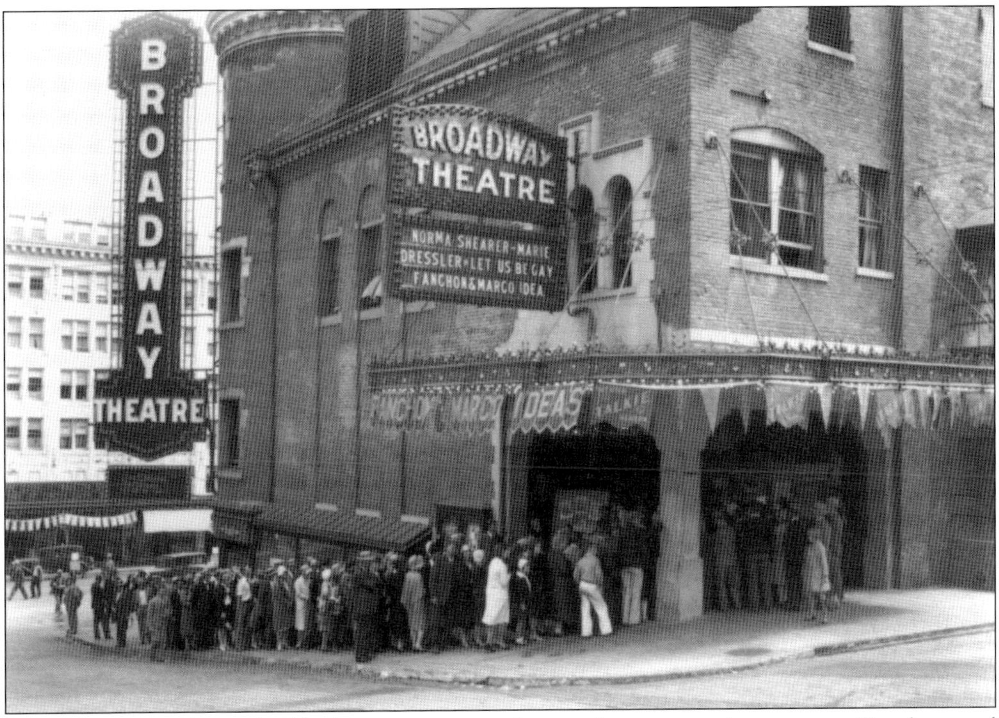

A line stretches down the block as patrons purchase tickets to see the stage act Fanchon and Marco and the 1930 film *Let Us Be Gay* at the Broadway Theater. The sister and brother team of Fanchon Simon and Marco Wolff produced full stage shows that shared billing with films at theaters around the country. (Courtesy of the Tacoma Public Library.)

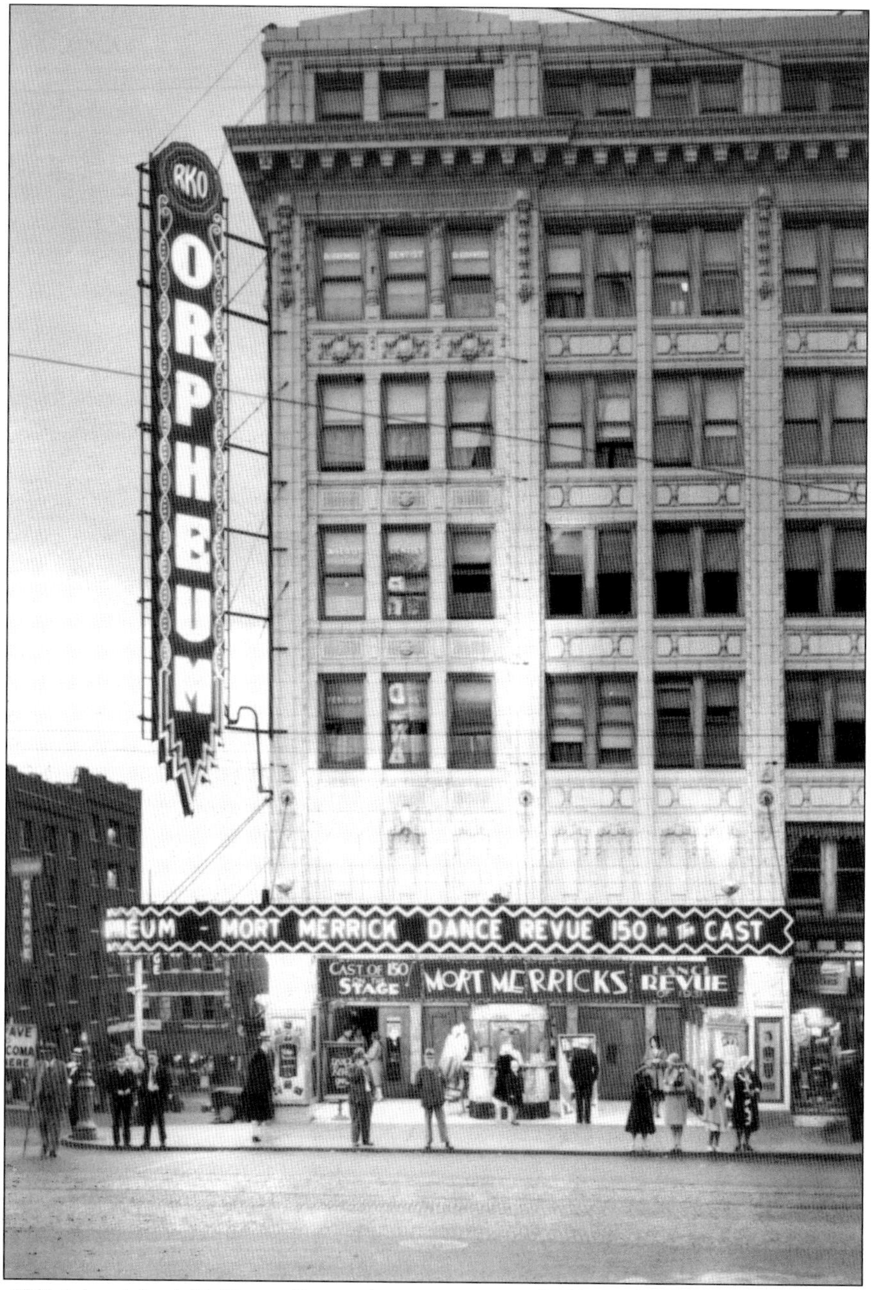

In July 1931, Mort Merrick's Dance Revue, boasting a cast of 150 on the stage, was the featured act at the RKO Orpheum on the corner of Ninth Street and Broadway. Mortimer Merrick managed a dance studio in Seattle and brought his dance revue to RKO Orpheum theaters in both Seattle and Tacoma. This theater spent only a few years of its life under RKO Orpheum ownership. It opened in 1918 as the Pantages and was sold to RKO in 1929, but by 1932, it was doing business as the Roxy. In this evening view, it appears that in addition to patrons purchasing tickets and entering the theater, there are also several men and women waiting for the streetcar. The reflection of the Broadway Theater's marquee from across the street can be seen in the windows of the Orpheum. (Courtesy of the Tacoma Public Library.)

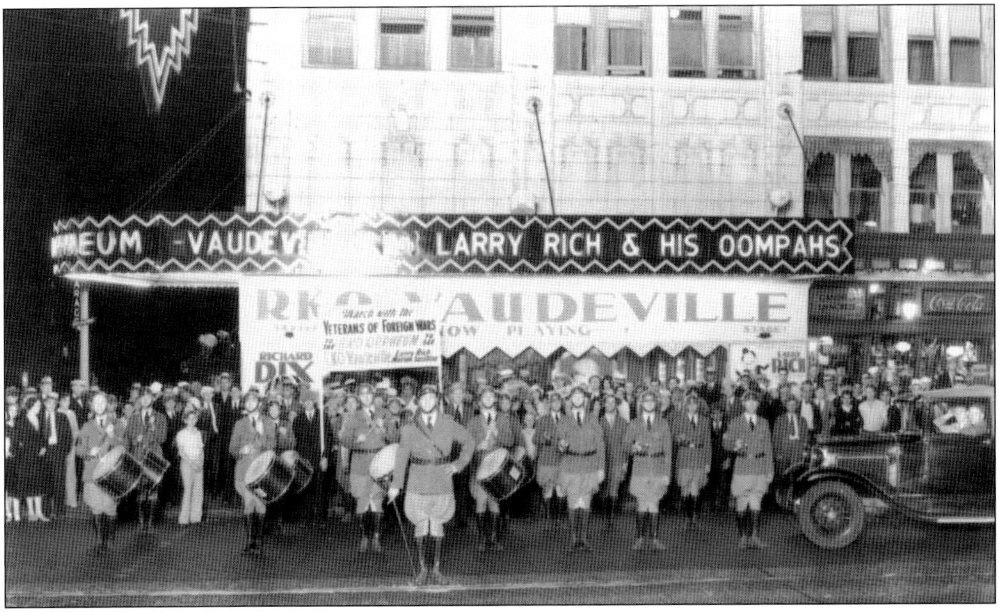

In July 1931, the Veterans of Foreign Wars drum and bugle corps poses in front of the RKO Orpheum Theater with a sign that reads, "March with the Veterans of Foreign Wars to the RKO Orpheum to see RKO Vaudeville Larry Rich and Marion Sunshine." Larry Rich was a comic bandleader who toured the vaudeville circuit with his band, the 14 Oompahs, and singer Marion Sunshine. (Courtesy of the Tacoma Public Library.)

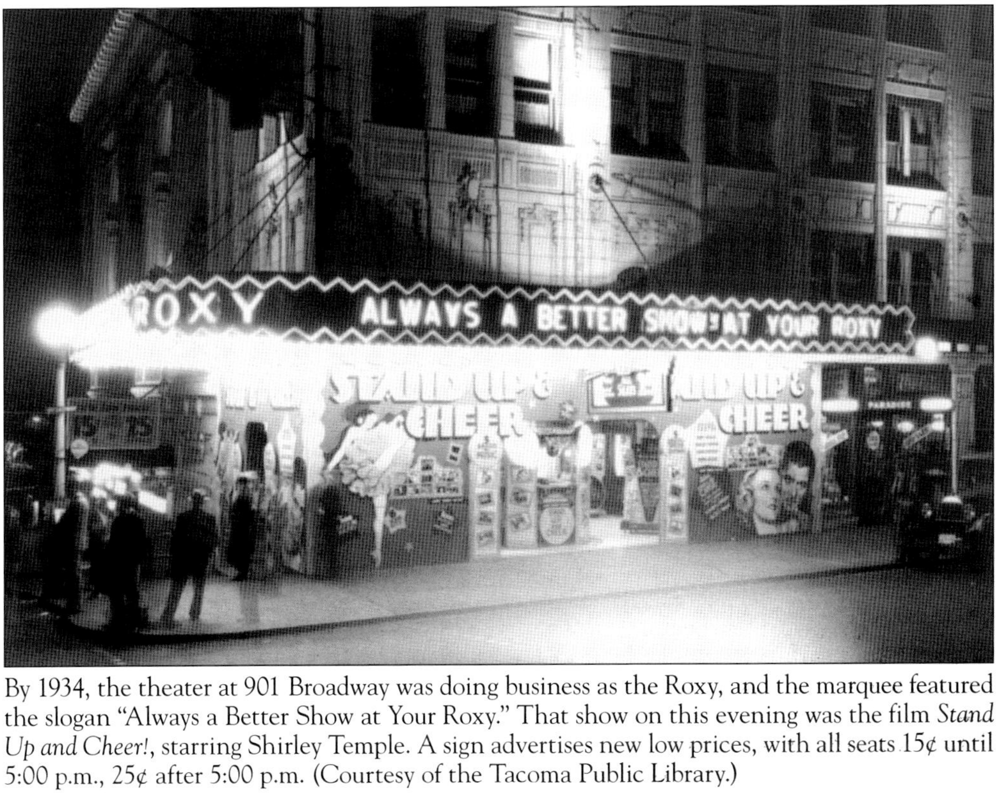

By 1934, the theater at 901 Broadway was doing business as the Roxy, and the marquee featured the slogan "Always a Better Show at Your Roxy." That show on this evening was the film *Stand Up and Cheer!*, starring Shirley Temple. A sign advertises new low prices, with all seats 15¢ until 5:00 p.m., 25¢ after 5:00 p.m. (Courtesy of the Tacoma Public Library.)

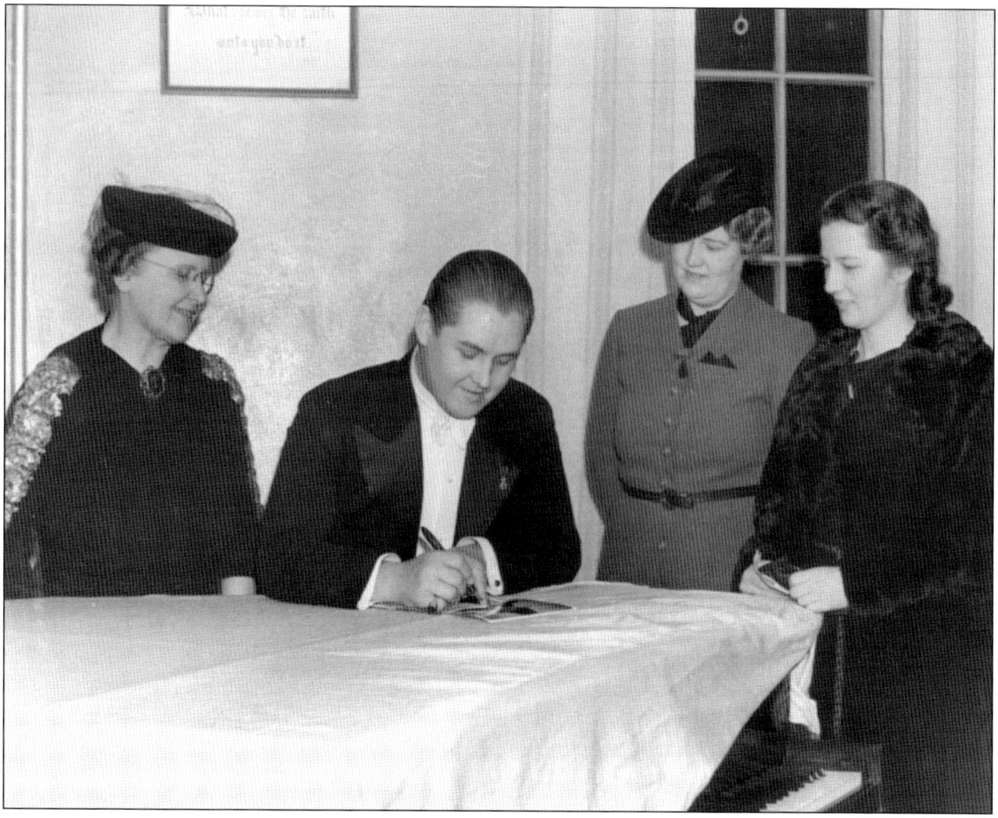

On January 5, 1939, Swedish tenor Jussi Björling of the Metropolitan Opera was featured in concert at the First Baptist Church by the Ladies' Musical Club of Tacoma. Following the performance, he is seen here autographing a portrait as Hilma Lynn (left), Ethel McFarland Siefert (center), and Margrete Anderson look on. (Courtesy of the Tacoma Public Library.)

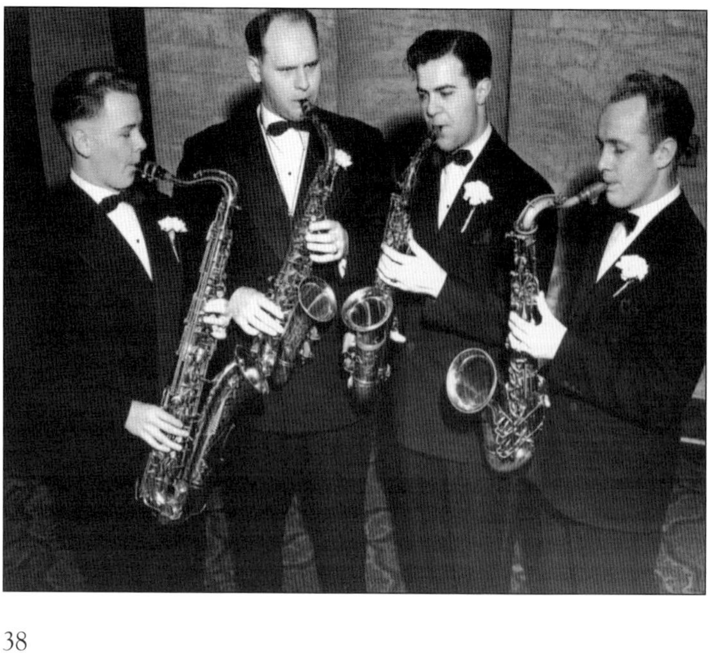

A saxophone quartet plays at the Music Box (formerly the Broadway) Theater in 1940. The musicians, from left to right, Bob Newman, Bob Earle, Art Doll, and Hal Gullett, were members of the Brad Bannon Orchestra, a popular 11-piece dance band that performed frequently at venues around the region. Art Doll wrote and arranged much of the group's music. (Courtesy of the Tacoma Public Library.)

Three

THE SILVER SCREEN

In a time before television, going to the movies was a vital piece of the entertainment pie for Tacomans of all ages. It was also a community activity, centering around Tacoma's many neighborhood movie houses as well as the larger venues in the downtown theater district. It was not only as moviegoers, however, that citizens of the growing City of Destiny participated in the booming success of the film industry in the first half of the 20th century.

In the mid-1920s, Tacoma had its very own film studio, H.C. Weaver Productions, which released three silent films before succumbing to the success of the new sound era, for which it was not prepared. The theater district played several roles in Weaver's brief success—whether as the location for a premiere, providing filming locations, or through shops in the district promoting the Weaver films.

Several local musicians started their performing careers as organists for theaters during the silent era; some of these musicians remained local, while others used their start as a stepping stone to a brighter opportunity elsewhere. Actors and actresses who were born or raised in Tacoma and went on to success in Hollywood were celebrated each time one of their films appeared at a hometown venue.

Events in Tacoma occasionally appeared in newsreels viewed across the nation, and of course, many in Tacoma kept up with world events, especially during times of war, by viewing newsreels at their local theater. Finally, especially in the downtown theater district, businesses took advantage of the appearance of popular films to sell everything from cars to jewelry.

Then, of course, there were the films themselves. For nearly 50 years, the downtown theater district was home to multiple theaters showing first-run Hollywood films. From silent films to the dawn of the sound era and from black and white to color, generations grew up around regular visits to their favorite downtown theater venue.

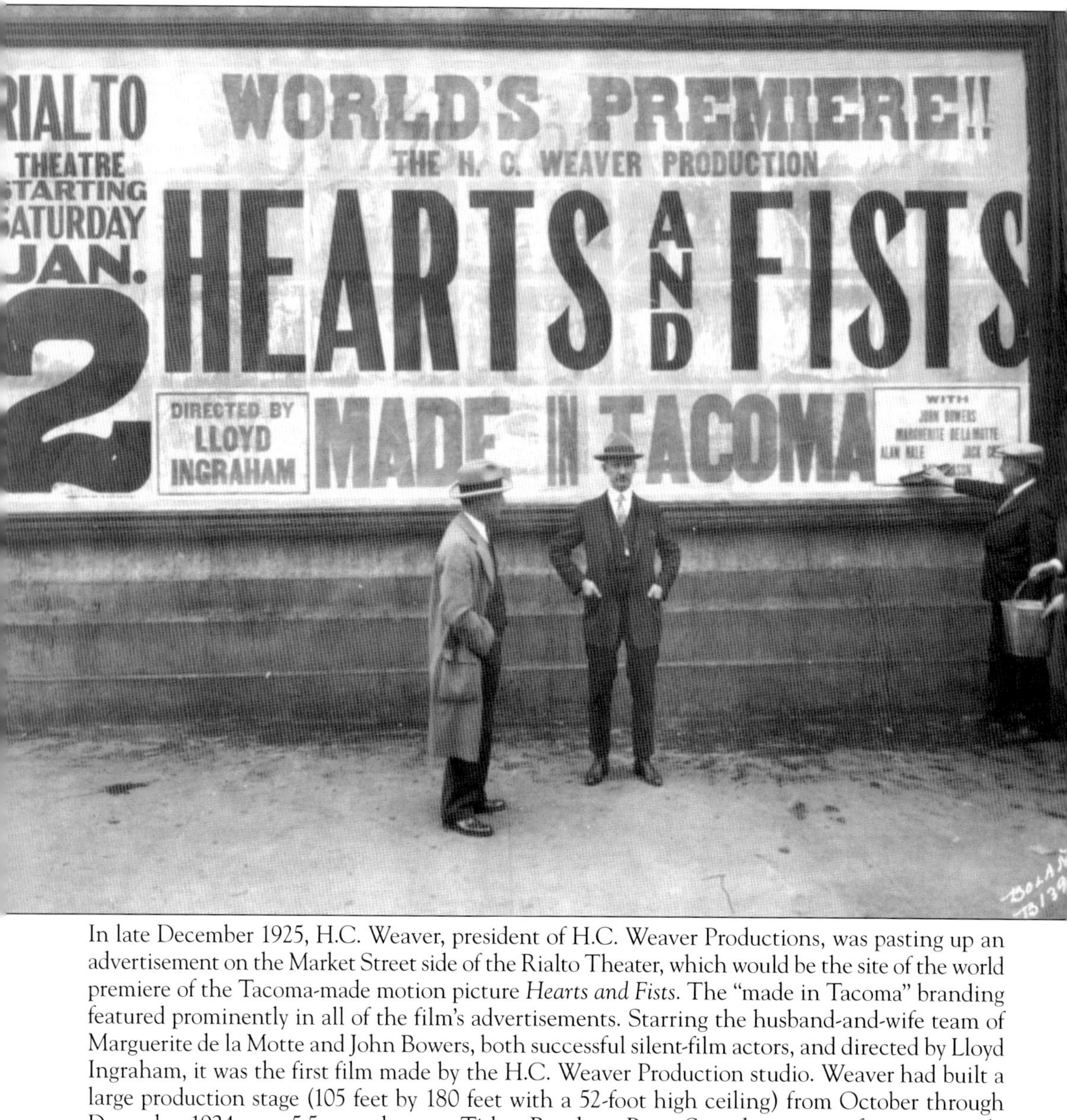

In late December 1925, H.C. Weaver, president of H.C. Weaver Productions, was pasting up an advertisement on the Market Street side of the Rialto Theater, which would be the site of the world premiere of the Tacoma-made motion picture *Hearts and Fists*. The "made in Tacoma" branding featured prominently in all of the film's advertisements. Starring the husband-and-wife team of Marguerite de la Motte and John Bowers, both successful silent-film actors, and directed by Lloyd Ingraham, it was the first film made by the H.C. Weaver Production studio. Weaver had built a large production stage (105 feet by 180 feet with a 52-foot high ceiling) from October through December 1924, on a 5.5-acre plot near Titlow Beach on Puget Sound, at a cost of approximately $50,000. At the time, it was the third-largest freestanding film production space in America, with the two larger facilities being located in Hollywood. The studio was publicly dedicated on December 14, 1924. (Courtesy of the Tacoma Public Library.)

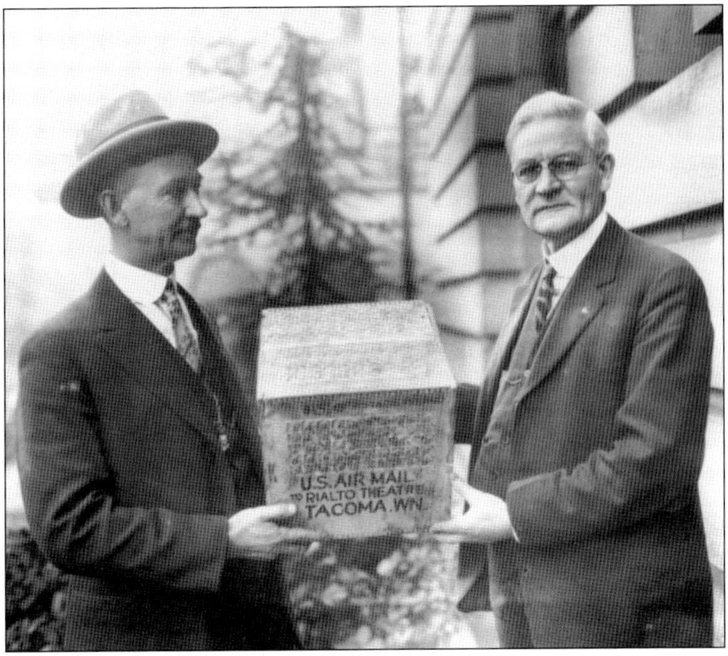

Henry T. Moore (left), manager of the Rialto Theater, and postmaster Clyde J. Backus are shown holding a wooden box, sent airmail from New York, that contained the reels for *Hearts and Fists*, the first film of Tacoma-based H.C. Weaver Productions. It took 72 hours and $151.68 in postage, but the reels arrived just in time, minutes before the premiere on January 2, 1926. (Courtesy of the Tacoma Public Library.)

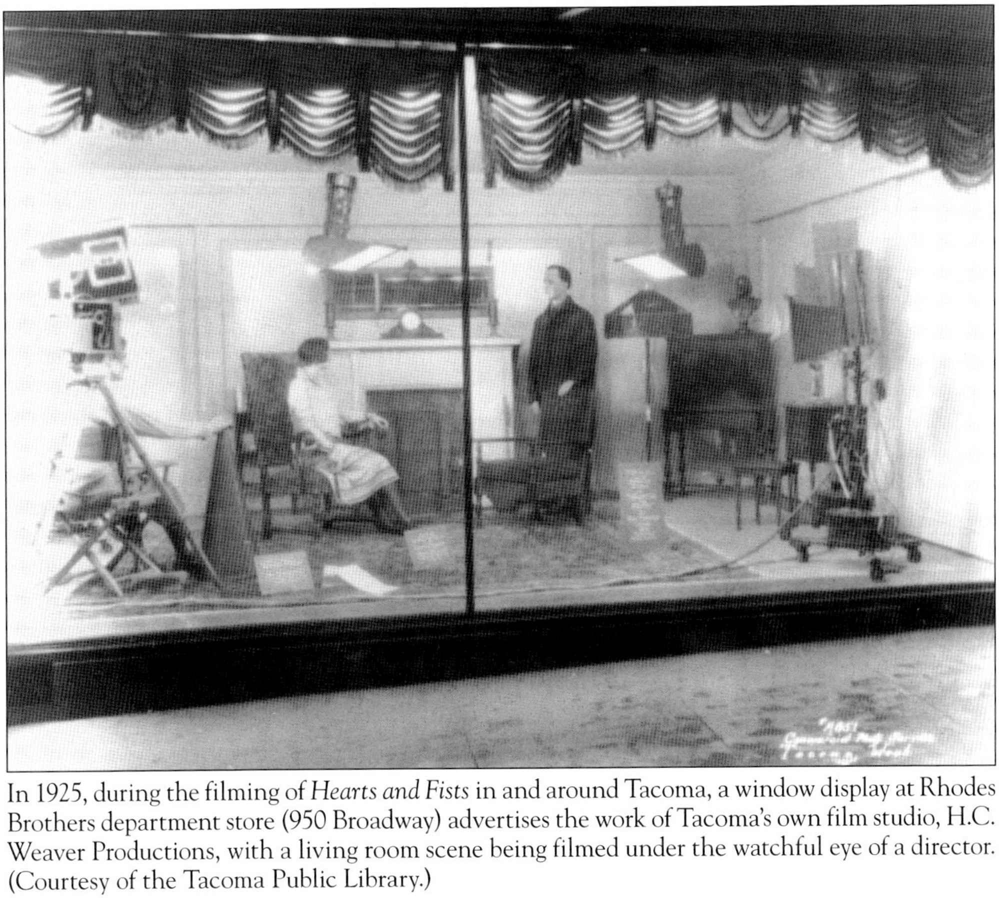

In 1925, during the filming of *Hearts and Fists* in and around Tacoma, a window display at Rhodes Brothers department store (950 Broadway) advertises the work of Tacoma's own film studio, H.C. Weaver Productions, with a living room scene being filmed under the watchful eye of a director. (Courtesy of the Tacoma Public Library.)

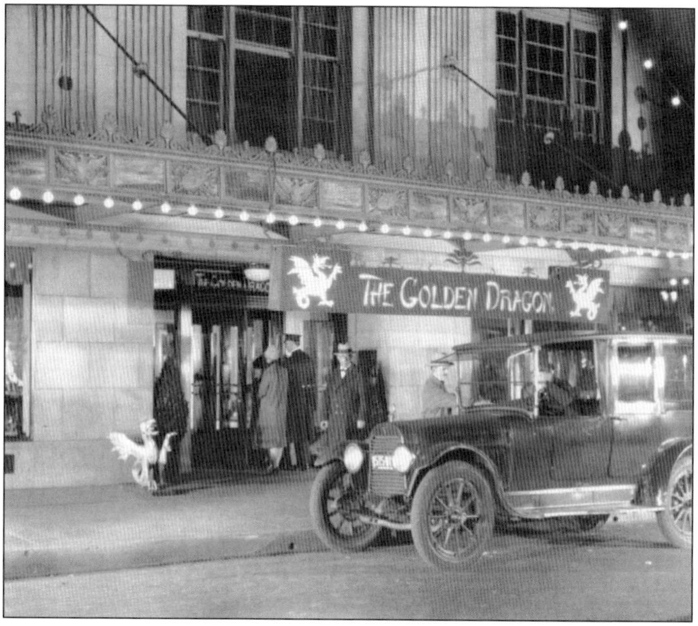

For one evening in March 1926, the Hotel Winthrop (773 Broadway) was transformed into the infamous Chinese cabaret "The Golden Dragon" during the filming of *Eyes of the Totem*, the second full-length silent film project of Tacoma's own company, H.C. Weaver Productions. In the film's script, the cabaret is the location where innocent young girls are lured into a licentious lifestyle. (Courtesy of the Tacoma Public Library.)

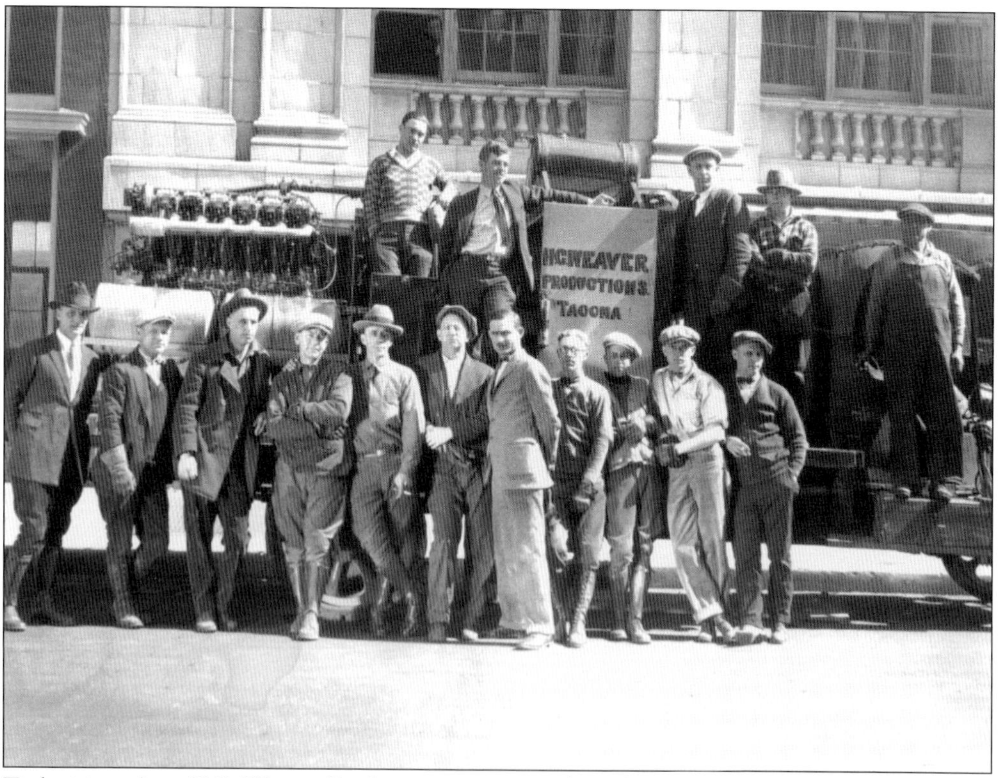

Technicians from H.C. Weaver Productions pose outside of the Winthrop Hotel (773 Broadway) with their new chief electrician (W.A. Seward, first row, fifth from right) and state-of-the-art portable generator in May 1926. The generator was used at Weaver's Titlow Beach Studio and when mounted on a truck, as shown here, could be used on location, making it possible to film in a variety of lighting conditions. (Courtesy of the Tacoma Public Library.)

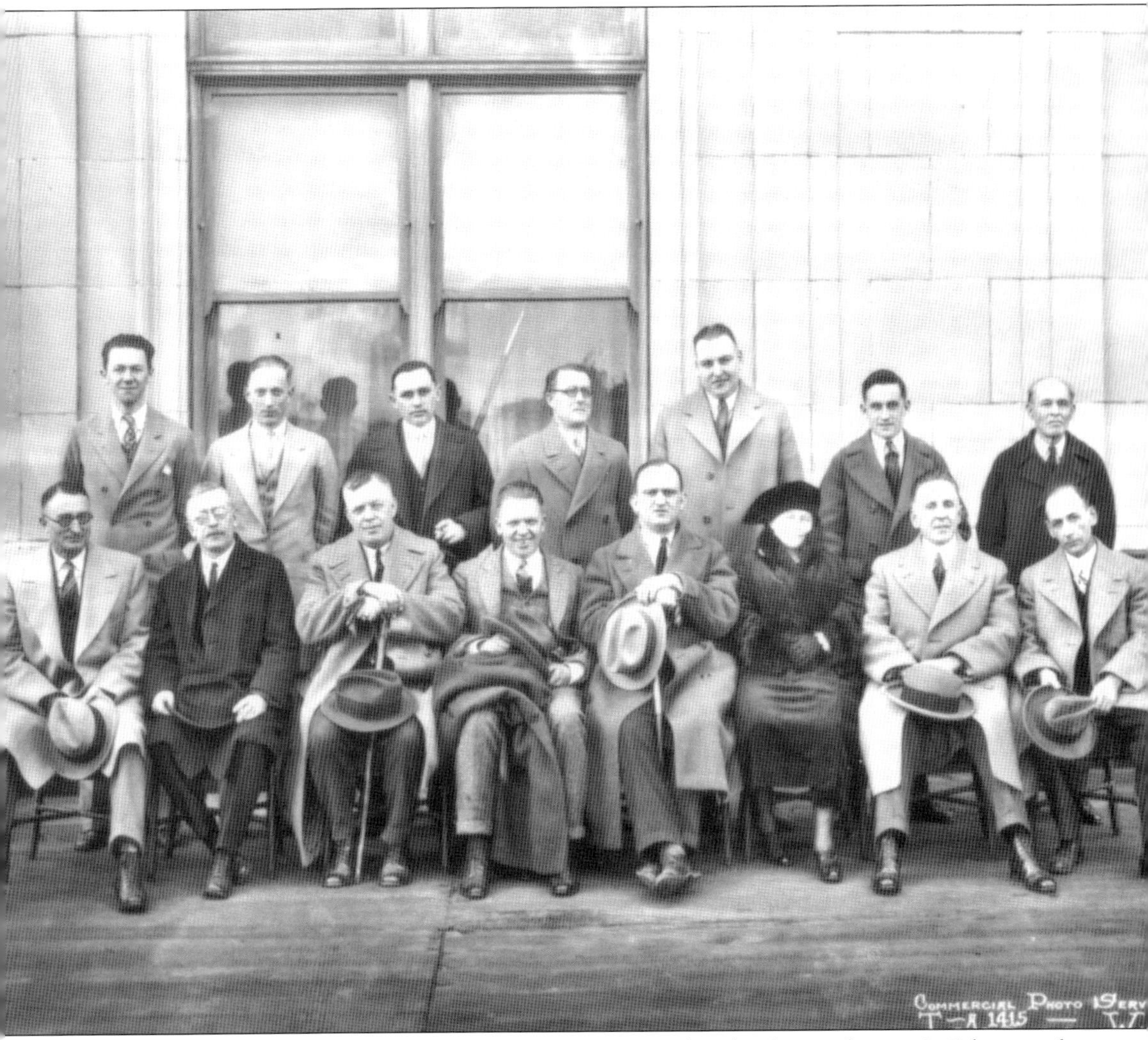

In 1926, Tacoma had over 25 movie theaters, including several in the theater district. In February of that year, members of the Picture Theater Managers' Association of Tacoma pose for a photograph after one of their meetings at the Hotel Winthrop. (Courtesy of the Tacoma Public Library.)

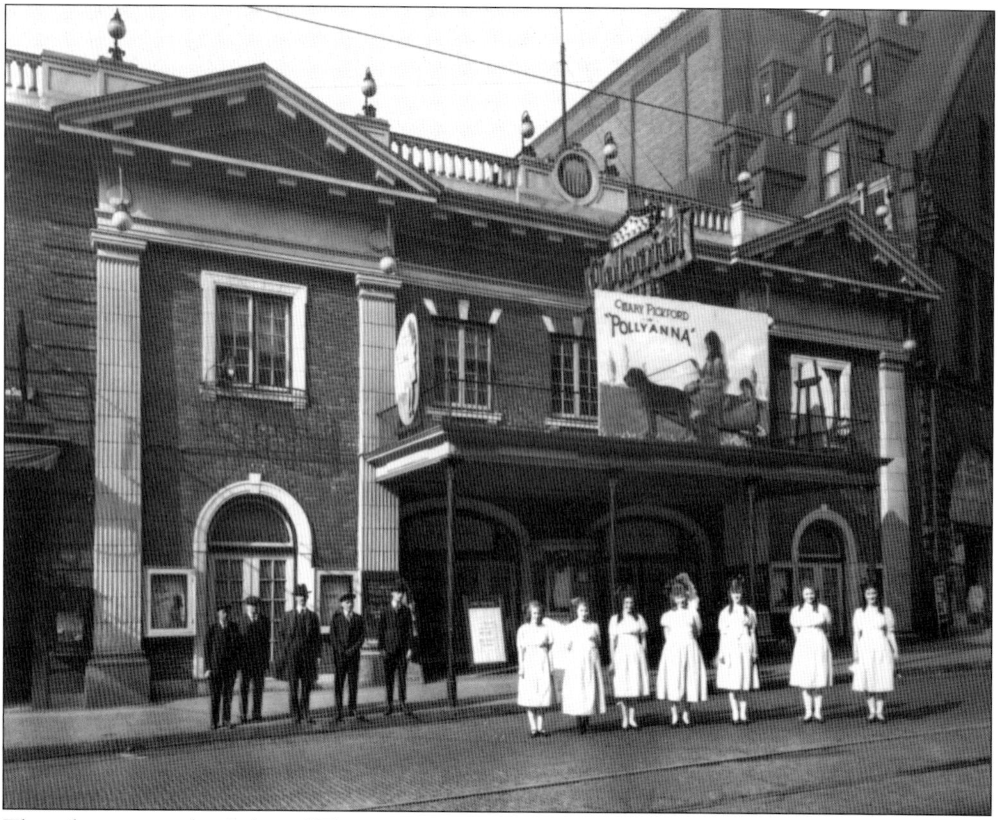

The usherettes at the Colonial Theater, 916–918 Broadway, wore gingham dresses for the opening of the silent film *Pollyanna* in February 1920. Mary Pickford, the film's star, was 27 when she played the role of the 12-year-old title character. In 1919, Pickford was a cofounder of United Artists; this film grossed $1 million for the new studio. (Courtesy of the Tacoma Public Library.)

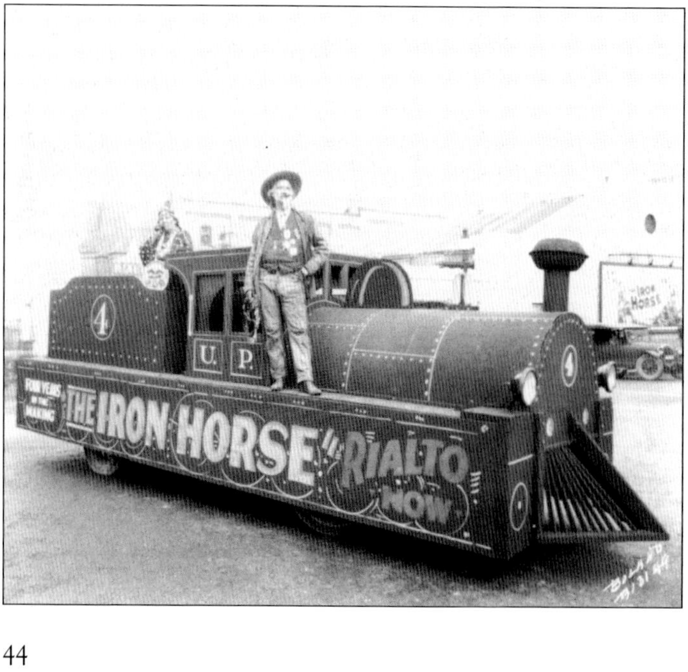

In August 1925, to promote the John Ford Western *The Iron Horse*, then showing at the Rialto Theater, this locomotive appeared in Tacoma with 84-year-old scout and interpreter Col. Alfred L. Chapman. Chapman was instrumental in securing the services of 800 Native Americans for the film, which dealt with the challenges of construction of the Union Pacific and Central Pacific Railways to the West. (Courtesy of the Tacoma Public Library.)

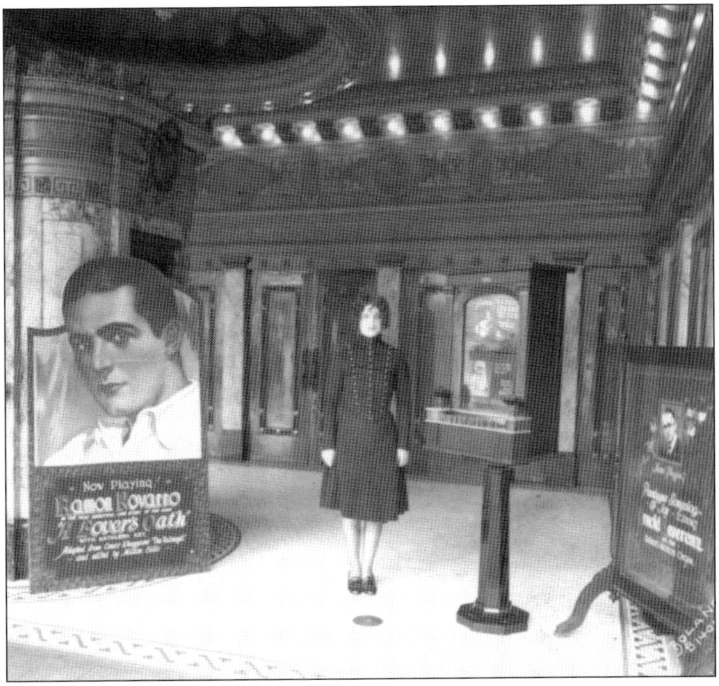

An unidentified usherette stands at attention outside the Pantages Theater in January 1926. Two shows are being promoted: the silent film *A Lovers Oath*, starring Ramon Navarro and Kathleen Key, and the *Pantages Songolog of Joy*, featuring Arnold Leverenz at the organ. The organ would also have been played as musical accompaniment to the silent film. (Courtesy of the Tacoma Public Library.)

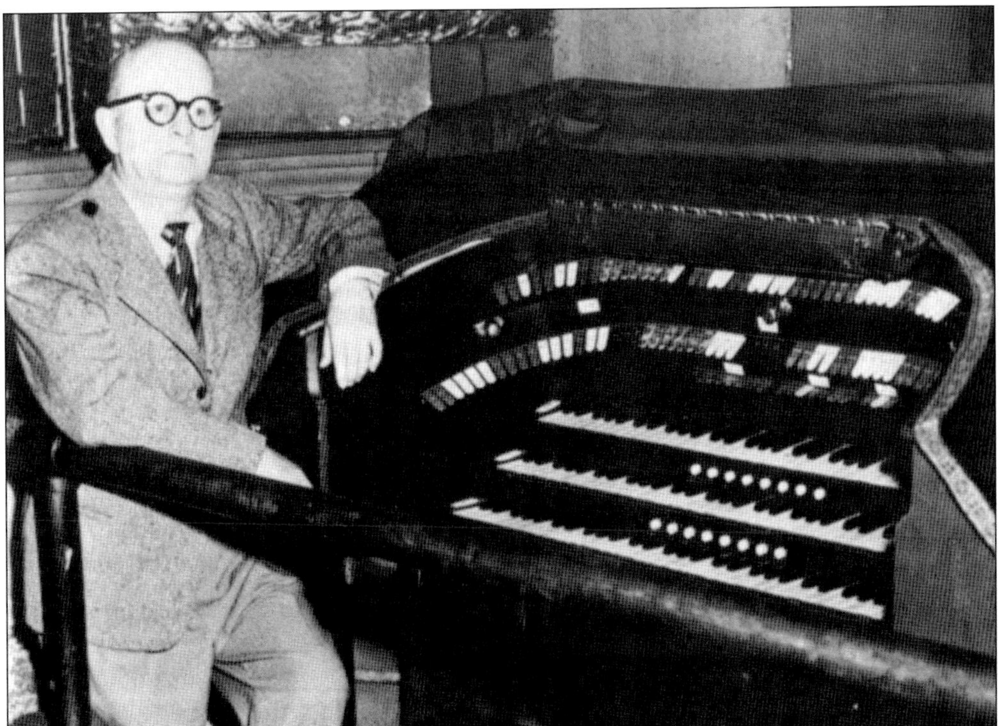

Noted Northwest musician Arnold Leverenz is seen here with the organ at the Pantages Theater. Leverenz accompanied silent films at many Northwest theaters, including the Colonial and Rialto in Tacoma's theater district. He was most well known for his silent film accompaniments and sing-alongs at the Pantages. (Courtesy of the Puget Sound Theater Organ Society.)

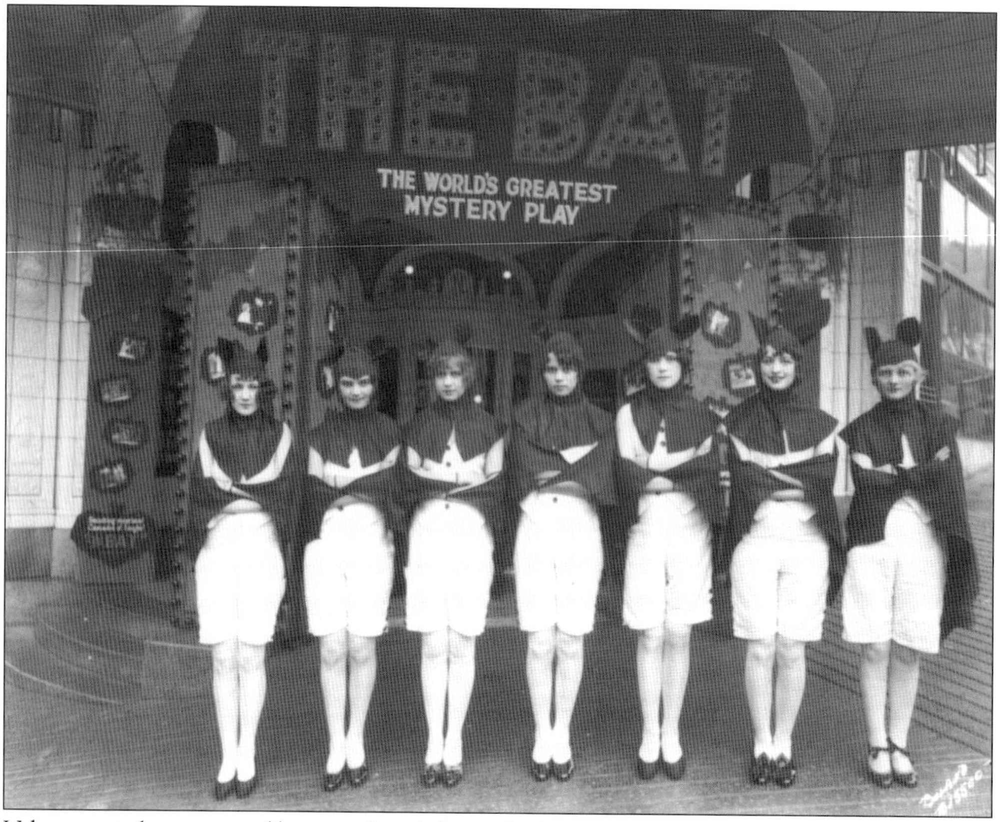

Usherettes in bat capes and bat ears, from left to right, Rose Travaglio, Mary Marko, Lillian Hansen, Ann Brower, Irene Carnahan, Helen Morley, and Florence Lloyd are lined up outside the Rialto Theater where the silent film *The Bat* was showing in 1926. Both the film and the costumes were a hit with Tacoma audiences, who could choose from a 35¢ matinee or a 50¢ evening showing. (Courtesy of the Tacoma Public Library.)

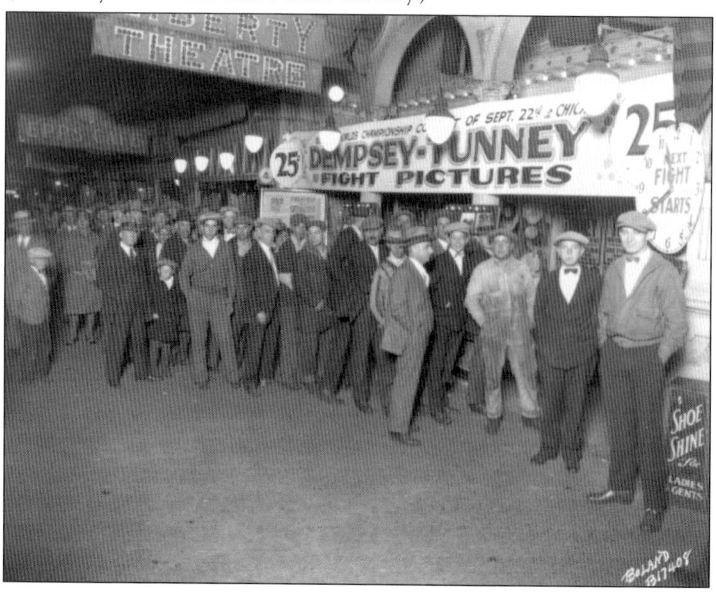

A large crowd gathers at the Liberty Theater, 906–908 Pacific Avenue, to watch the "fight pictures" from the recent championship match between boxers Jack Dempsey and Gene Tunney that occurred on September 22, 1927, at Soldier Field in Chicago. For 25¢, Tacoma fans could feel as though they were part of the roaring crowd from the original event. (Courtesy of the Tacoma Public Library.)

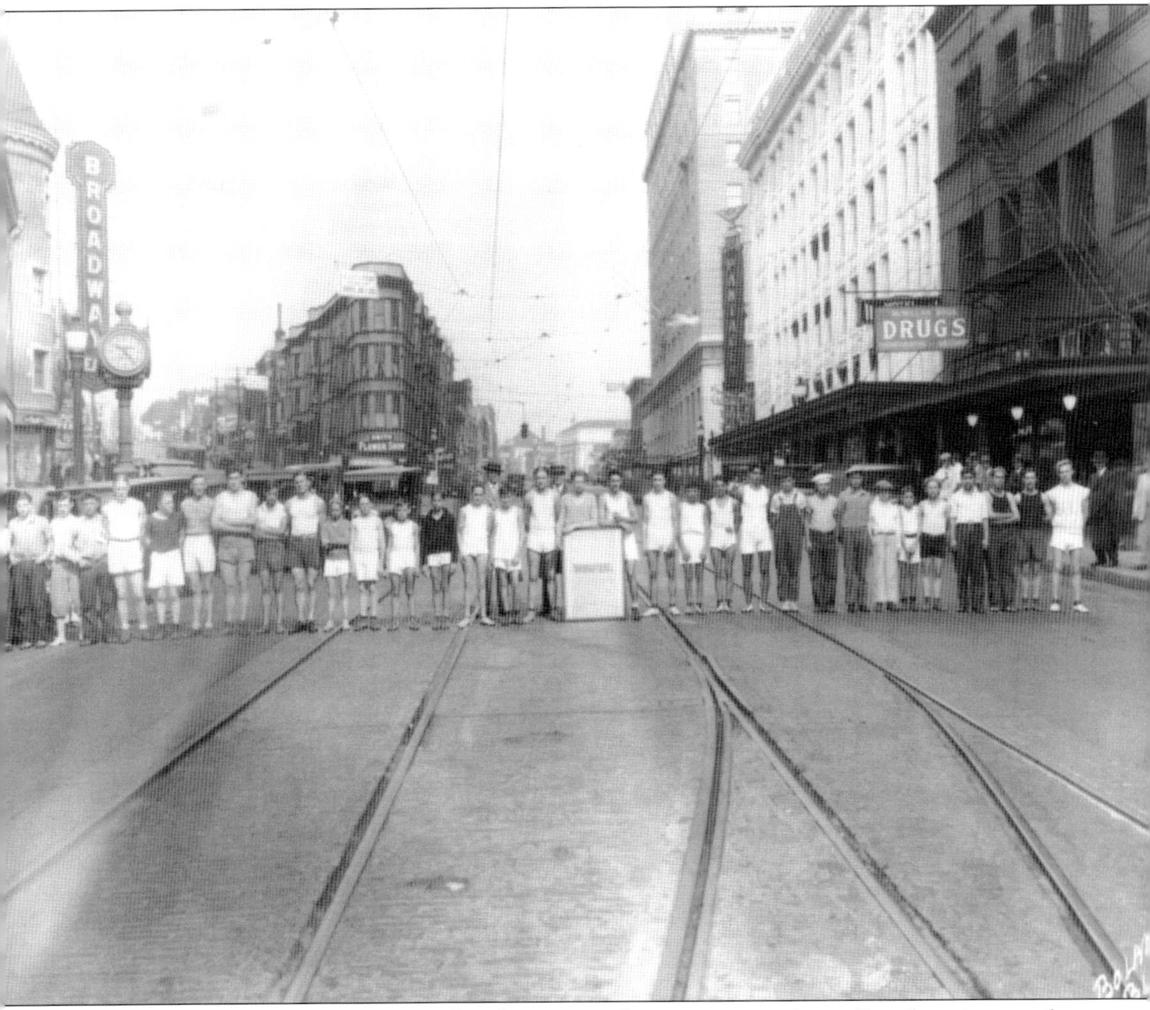

On September 17, 1927, contestants lined up across the streetcar tracks on Broadway just south of Ninth Street for the *Running Wild* marathon, an event cosponsored by the Colonial Theater and the *Tacoma Times*. The winner of the race would claim a prize of $25 in gold. Nine other prizes were offered, as well as guest passes for all participants to see W.C. Fields in *Running Wild* at the Colonial. The race was open to all, including professionals. The route, as it was described in newspaper accounts, was likely just over three miles in length, beginning and ending on Broadway in front of the Colonial, with a loop through the south end of downtown. The Colonial Theater is just out of view to the left, the Broadway Theater is on the far left, and the Pantages is on the right. The uniquely shaped Bostwick Building is just left of center, and the Winthrop Hotel is to the north, across the street from the Pantages. (Courtesy of the Tacoma Public Library.)

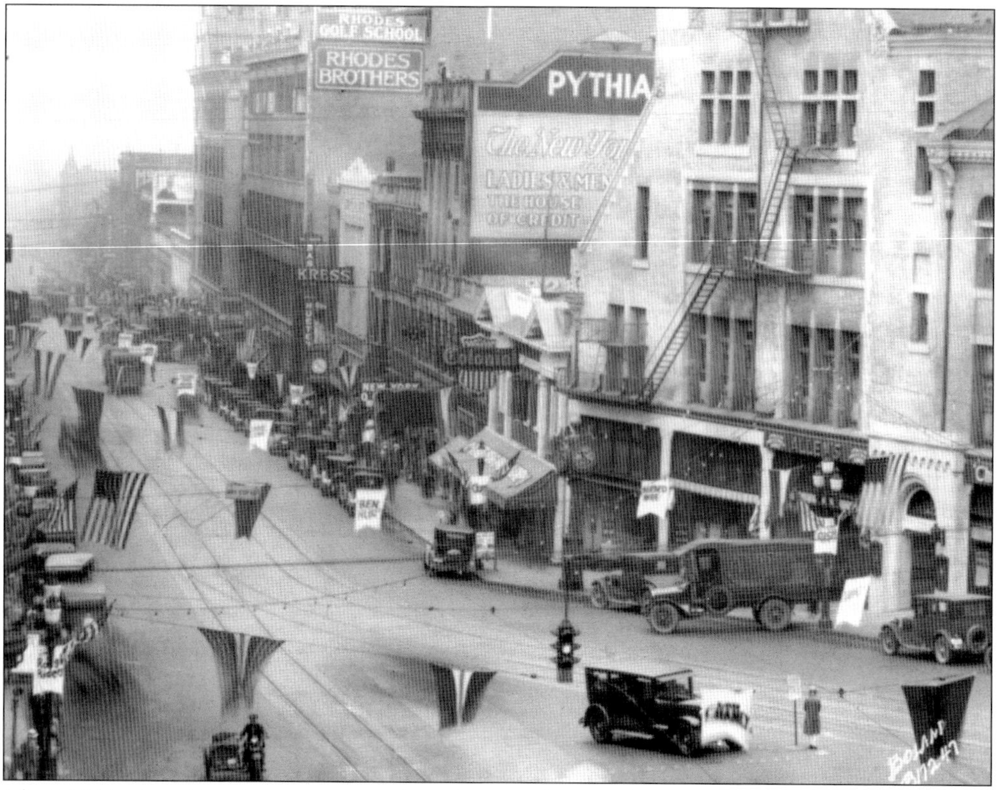

The 900 block of Broadway is seen in this photograph from the summer of 1927, when Tacoma's theater district was a bustling mix of theaters, small shops, and large department stores. Traffic lights were a fairly recent addition, sharing space above the streets with the many banners advertising the films currently appearing at the nearby Colonial (visible center right), Broadway, Pantages, and Rialto Theaters. (Courtesy of the Tacoma Public Library.)

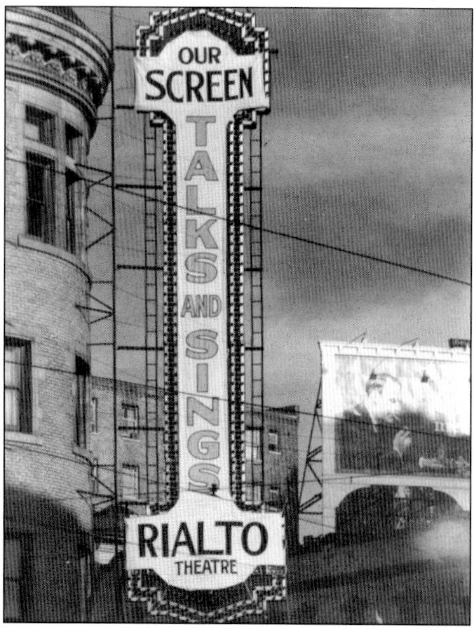

In the late 1920s, the new talkies were beginning to take over theater screens previously dominated by silent films. This banner advertisement, appearing on and obscuring the marquee of the Broadway Theater, brags that the Rialto's screen "talks and sings." The first talkie to be shown in Tacoma was *The Jazz Singer*, which appeared first at the Blue Mouse (1131 Broadway) in late 1927. (Courtesy of the Tacoma Public Library.)

Nine young women pose with a new Durant-Star coupe outside the Central Motors building at 605 St. Helens Avenue in September 1928. The car was one of the prizes in a promotional contest sponsored by the Colonial and Rialto Theaters in conjunction with the release of *Hot News*, a film starring Bebe Daniels. Prizes in the contest totaled $2,600 in value, a substantial sum in 1928. (Courtesy of the Tacoma Public Library.)

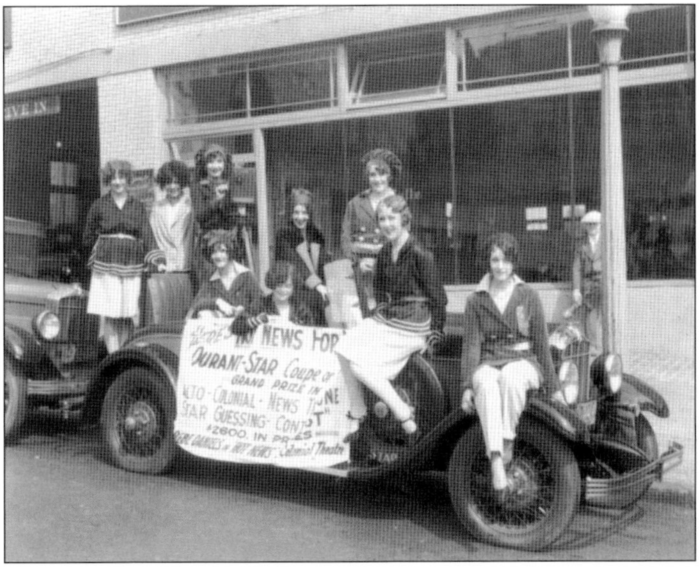

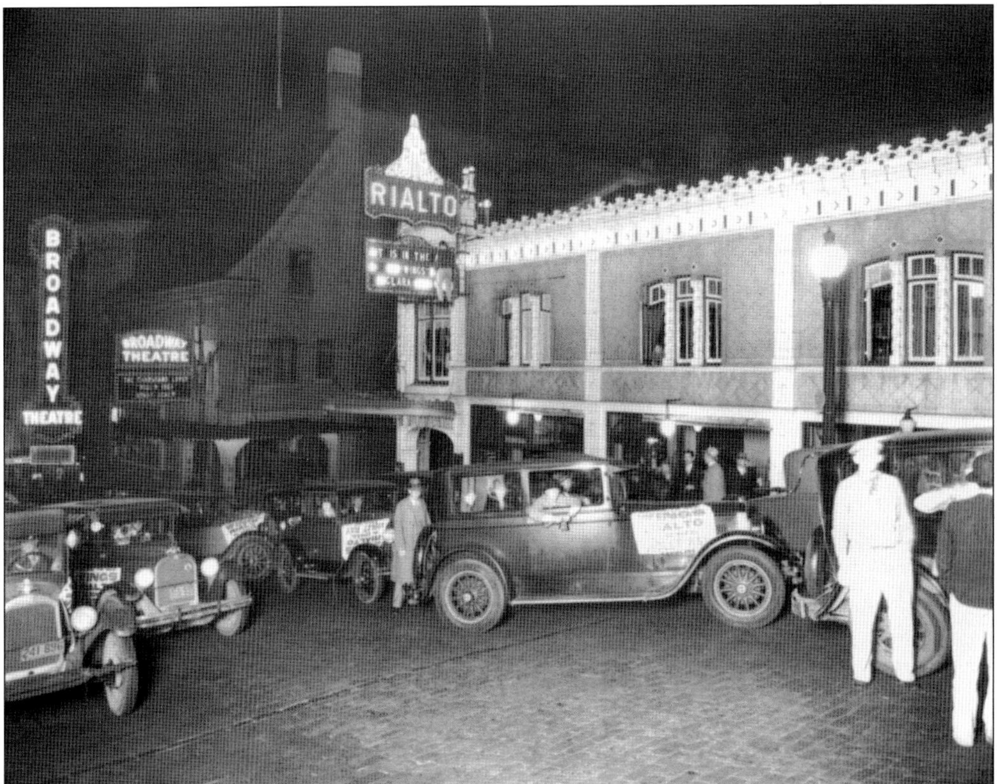

In October 1928, a parade of trucks and cars owned by General Service Station owners comes to an end outside the Rialto Theater, where the hit film *Wings* was showing. Four model planes were being given away by the *Tacoma Daily Ledger* and Sam Allen, president of Allen Lubricating Co., for the best 50-word essays on the motion picture. (Courtesy of the Tacoma Public Library.)

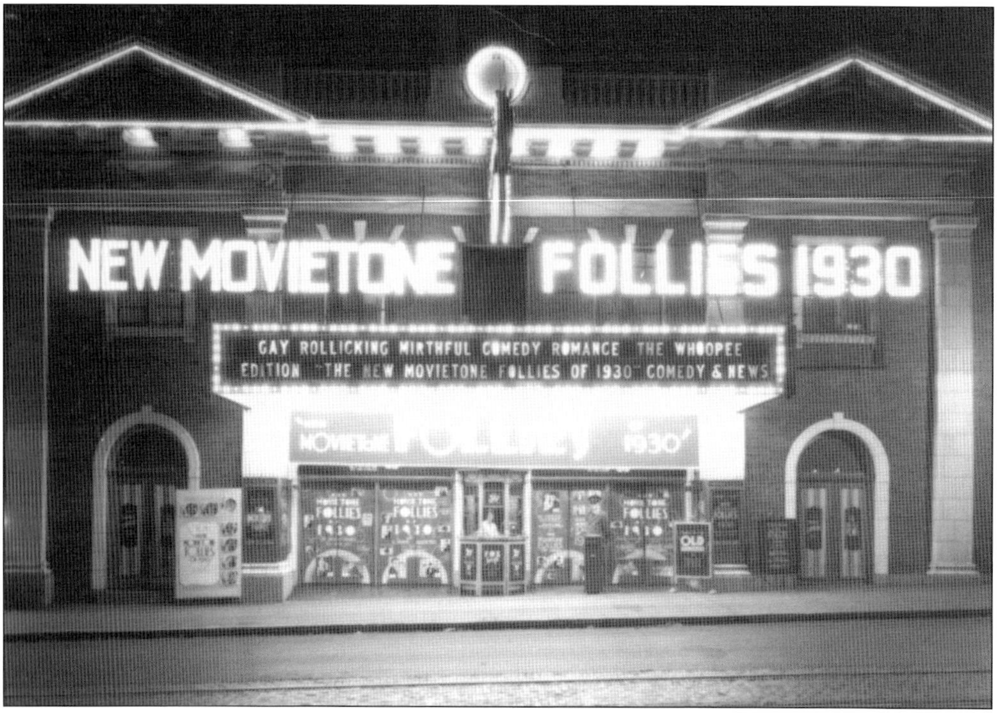

Bright lights advertising the *New Movietone Follies 1930* shine into the night from the front of the Colonial Theater, 916 Broadway. The 1930 musical film featured sequences filmed in multicolor, an early color process which enjoyed brief success in early sound pictures from 1929 to 1932. (Courtesy of the Tacoma Public Library.)

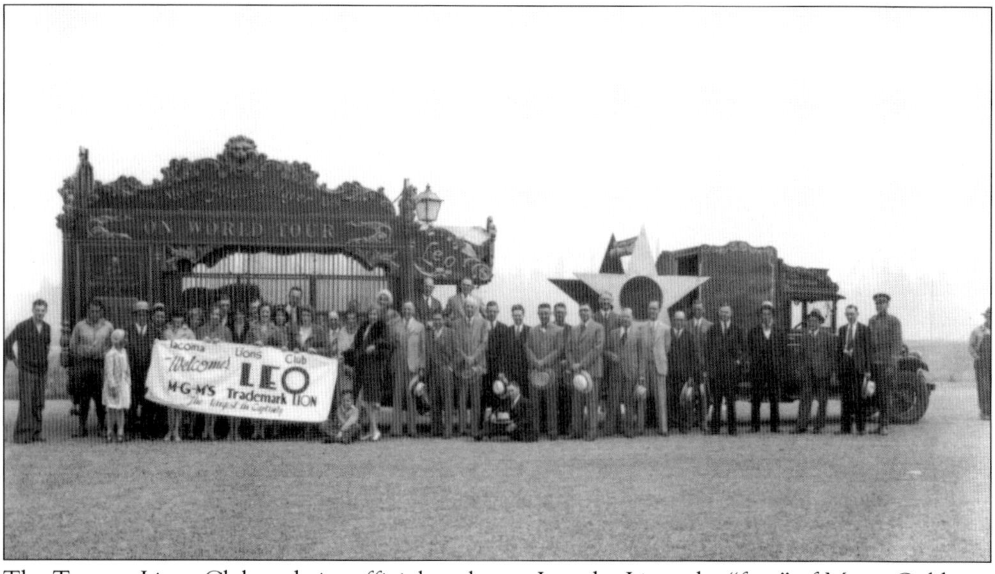

The Tacoma Lions Club and city officials welcome Leo the Lion, the "face" of Metro Goldwyn Mayer (MGM) films, when he arrived in Tacoma in August 1930 during the highly promoted "Leo's World Tour." Leo's roar had been trademarked and marked the start of MGM motion pictures for decades. While in town, the MGM lion performed in front of the Broadway and Rialto Theaters. (Courtesy of the Tacoma Public Library.)

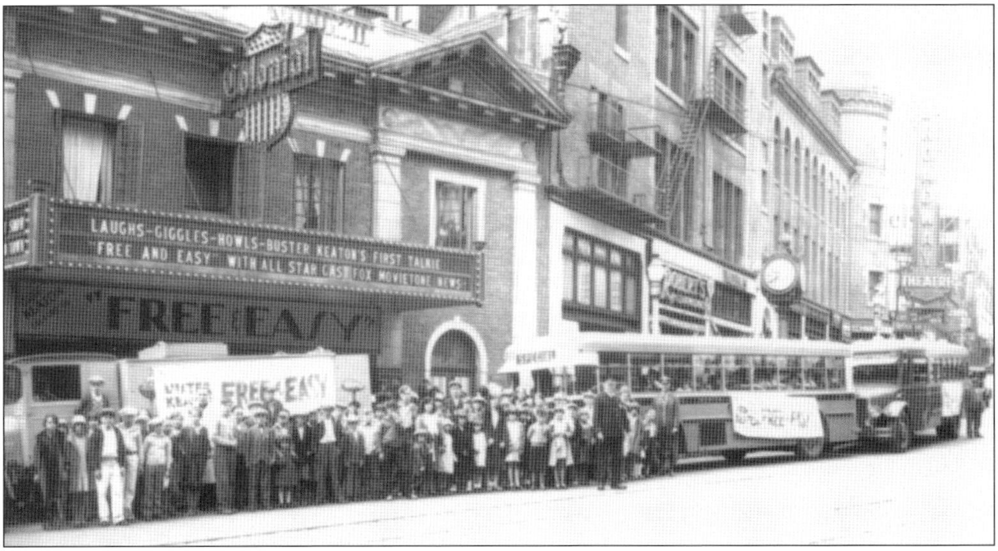

A large crowd of schoolchildren gathered at the Colonial Theater on Broadway to see, and hear, Buster Keaton's first talkie, 1930's *Free and Easy*. Famous from his many years in vaudeville and self-directed silent films, Keaton was one of the stars who successfully transitioned to talking films and, later, television. (Courtesy of the Tacoma Public Library.)

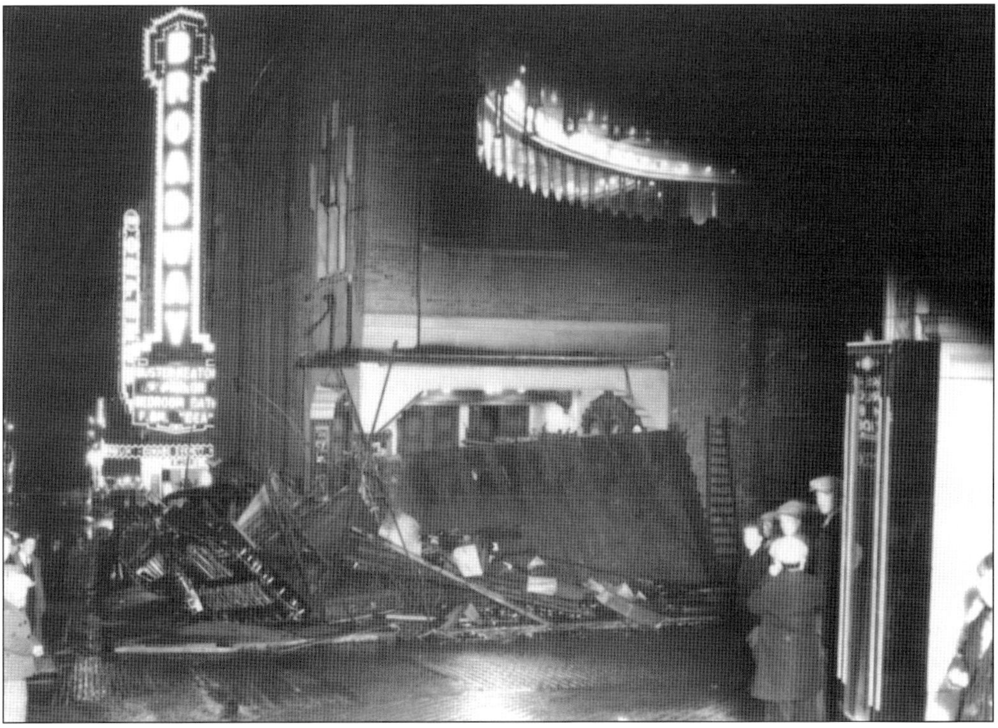

On the evening of March 10, 1931, the iron canopy at the Broadway Theater collapsed. The canopy, which hung over the theater's entrance at Ninth Street and Court C, was in the process of having new electric lights installed. Luckily, no one was injured when the weight of the workmen and the new lights proved too much for the old canopy to support. (Courtesy of the Tacoma Public Library.)

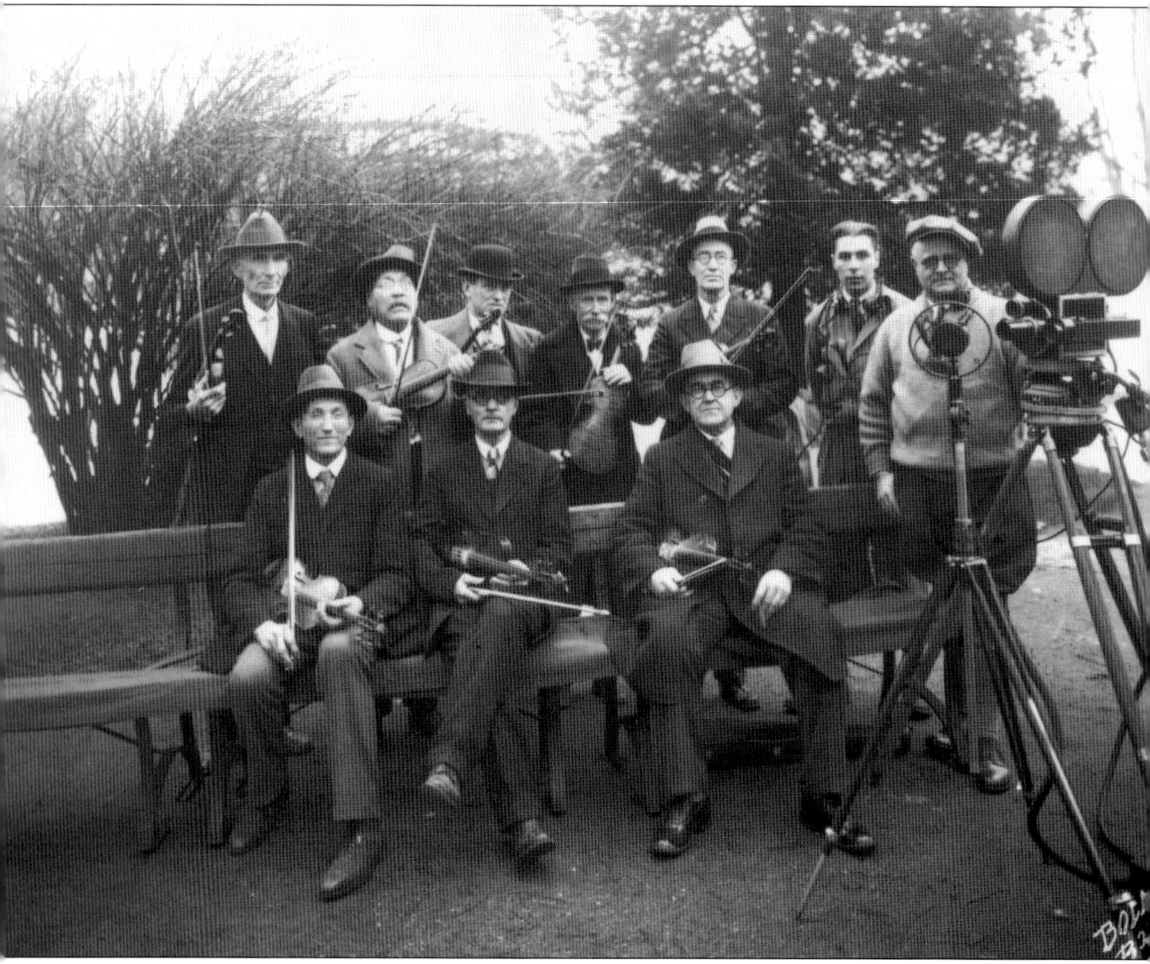

In February 1930, the RKO Pantages Theater and the *News Tribune* sponsored a contest to choose the best "Old-Time Fiddler" in the Tacoma/Pierce County region. The contestants were filmed by Pathé News to appear on a newsreel that would be shown throughout the United States. Charles Kahana of the Puyallup tribe was judged the winner, receiving a prize of $25 and special recognition on the newsreel. This photograph of the contestants with their instruments was taken on February 14, 1930, in Tacoma's Wright Park, just under a mile from the Pantages Theater. Kahana, the contest winner, is standing second from left. The two men standing at far right are members of the Pathé newsreel crew. (Courtesy of the Tacoma Public Library.)

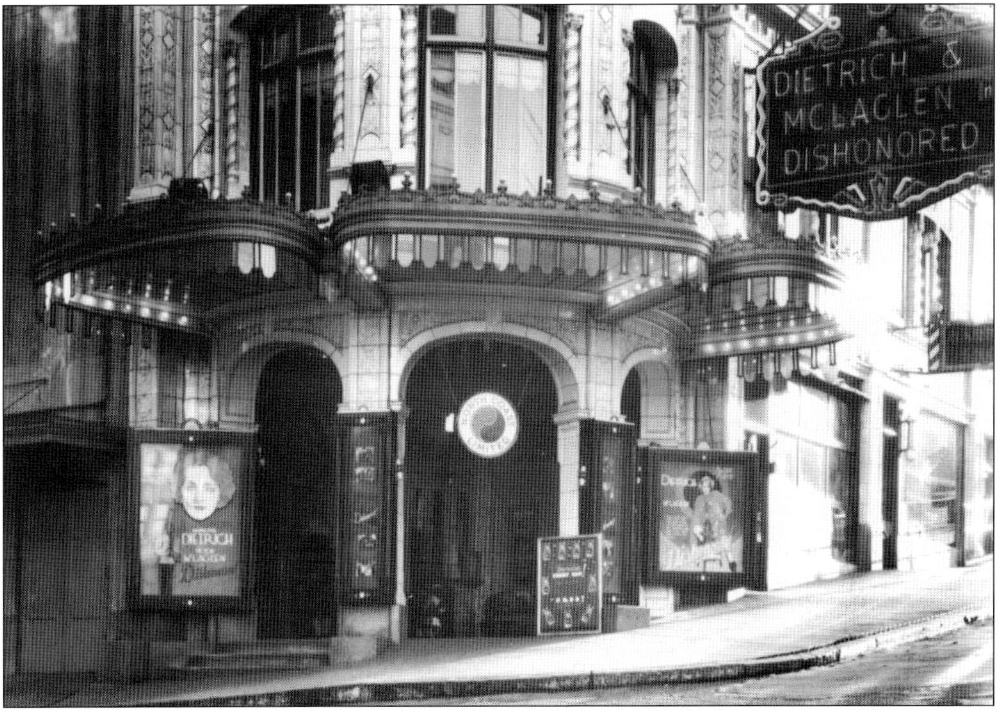

In April 1931, the Rialto Theater displayed a North Coast Limited sign, to coincide with the showing of *No.1*. The first transcontinental trip to be filmed in sound, *No.1* took viewers from Chicago to Tacoma, including scenes of the Rockies and the Cascades. Scheduled to play in every major city in the United States, the film provided Tacoma with nationwide exposure. (Courtesy of the Tacoma Public Library.)

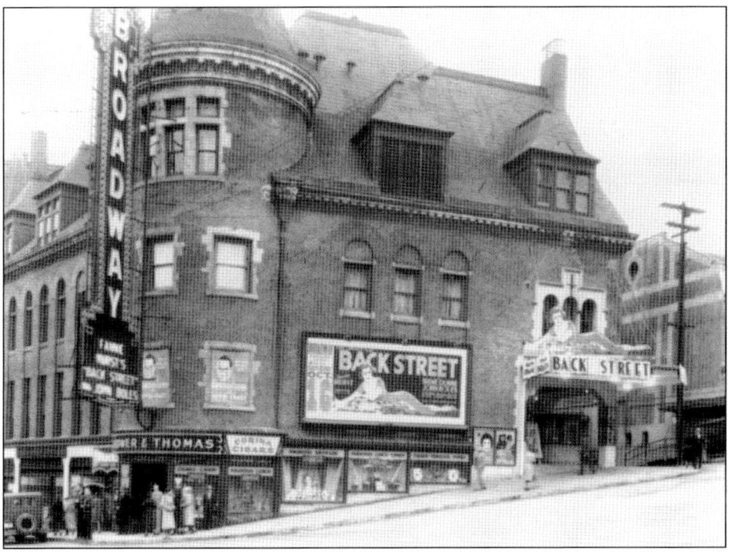

The 1932 film *Back Street*, starring Irene Dunne and John Boles, was heavily advertised on multiple signs and marquees when it appeared at the Broadway Theater. The film told the story of a woman whose love and devotion to a married man resulted in her being relegated to the "back streets" of his life. (Courtesy of the Tacoma Public Library.)

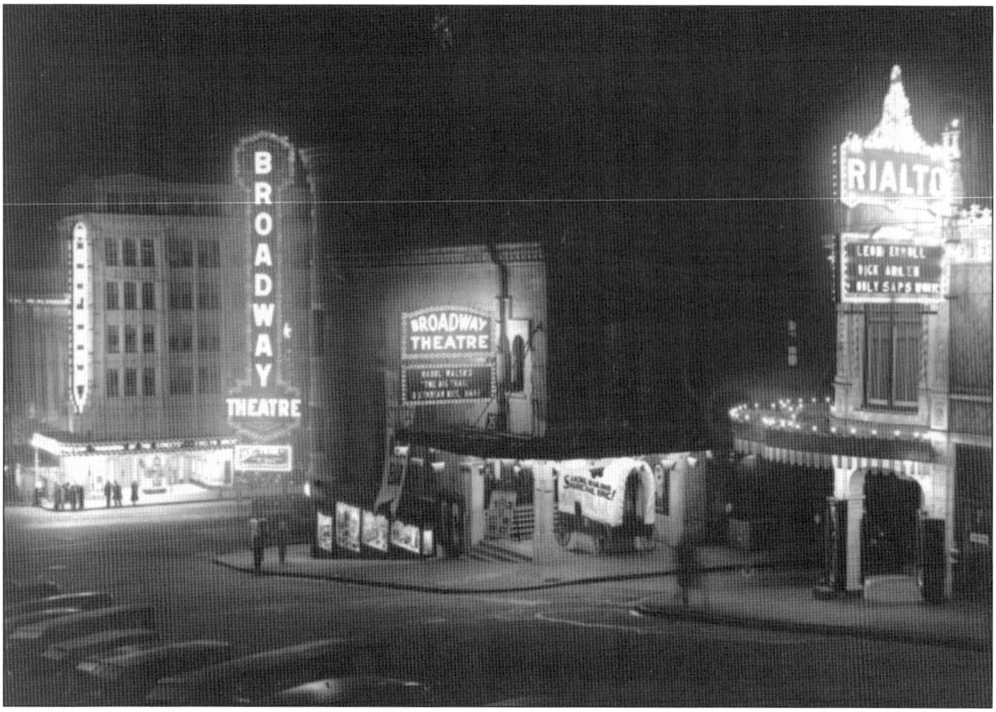

The marquees of the Rialto, Broadway, and Orpheum Theaters light up the night sky on an evening in 1930. Showing at the Orpheum is the talking remake of the silent classic *Madonna of the Streets*. The Broadway was featuring *The Big Trail*, which provided John Wayne his first starring role. At the Rialto was *Only Saps Work*, the talkie debut for Leon Erroll. (Courtesy of the Tacoma Public Library.)

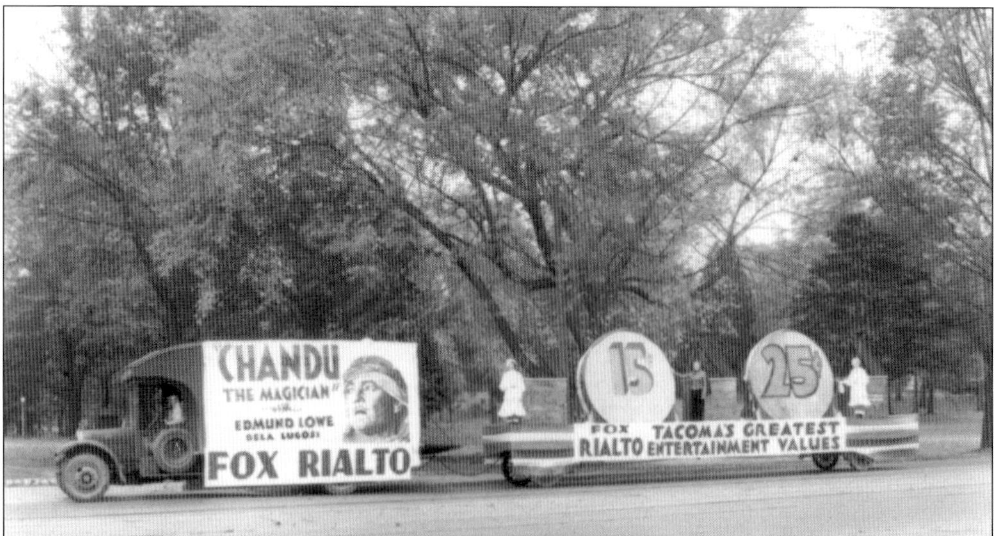

Advertising for the latest film to appear in Tacoma was not limited to a theater's marquee. The Rialto took its message on the road in 1932, promoting both the film *Chandu the Magician* and the Rialto's 15¢ and 25¢ admission rates with this truck-and-trailer contraption, seen here passing by Wright Park. (Courtesy of the Tacoma Public Library.)

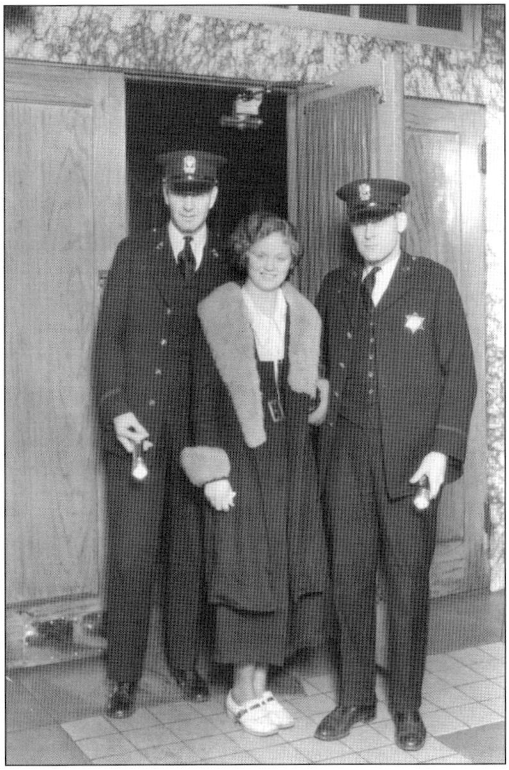

In November 1932, the Blue Mouse Theater (1131–1133 Broadway) was showing *White Zombie*, the first Hollywood zombie film, starring Bela Lugosi. As a publicity stunt, the theater offered $10 to any woman who would sit through a midnight preview on November 3, alone and without screaming—18-year-old Marjorie Yonk took on the challenge. According to newspaper accounts, she was taken by police car, sirens blaring, to Dr. F.J. Hansen's office to determine the strength of her heart and then to the theater. Prior to the start of the film, she posed for a photograph with her police escorts, Officers E.J. Schutz (left) and J.F. White. From the look in her eyes when she emerged from the theater at the film's conclusion, Yonk certainly earned her $10. (Both, courtesy of the Tacoma Public Library.)

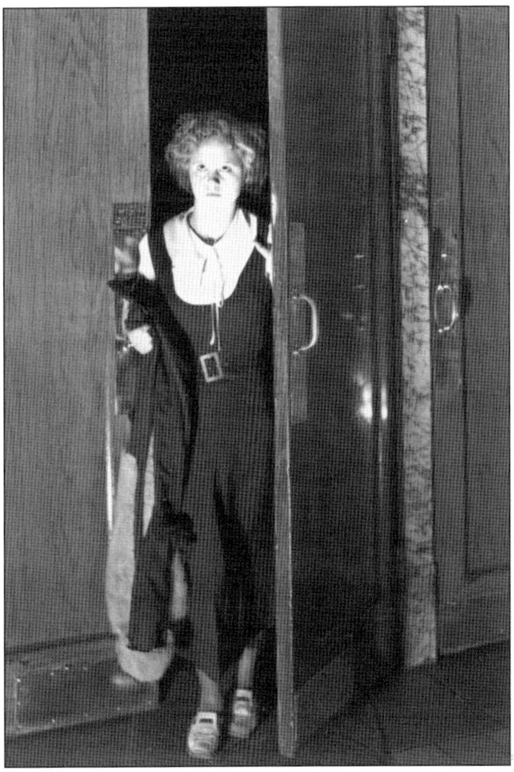

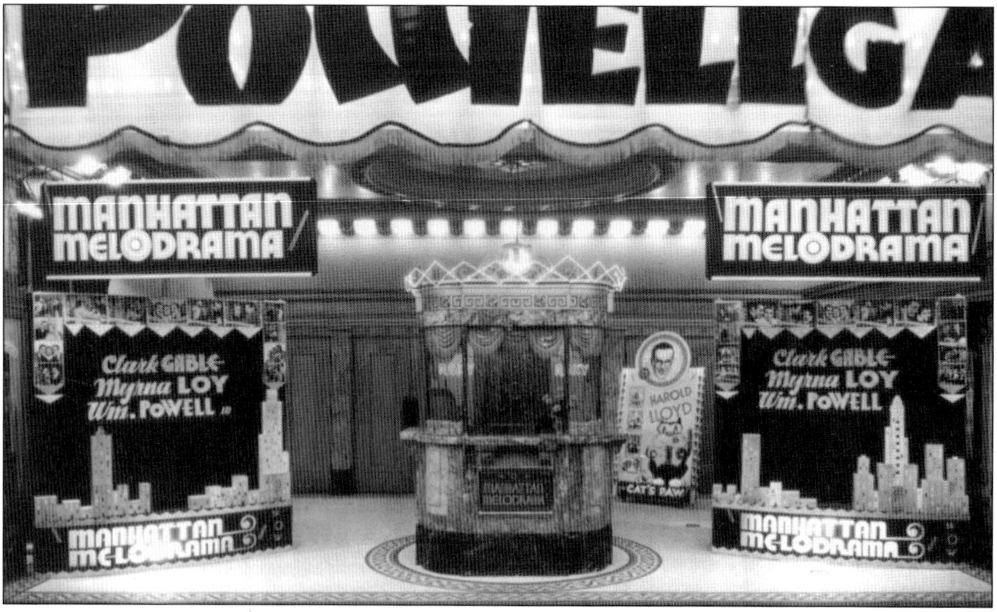

The exterior foyer and box office of the Roxy Theater (formerly Pantages and Orpheum) were heavily decorated for the arrival of the 1934 film *Manhattan Melodrama*, starring Clark Gable, Myrna Loy, and William Powell. In the background is a poster promoting Harold Lloyd in *The Cat's Paw*, also released in 1934. (Courtesy of the Tacoma Public Library.)

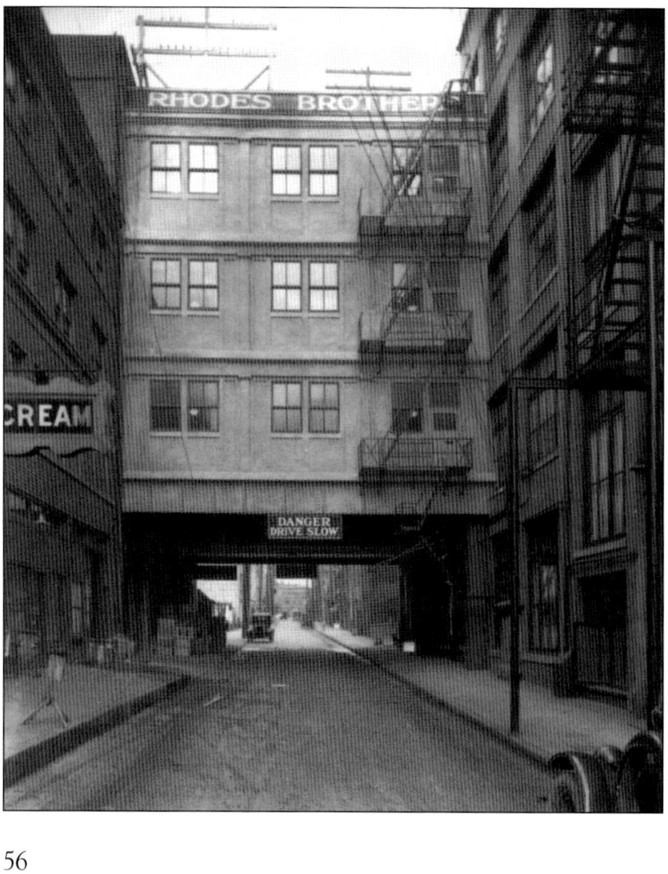

Three floors of the Rhodes Brothers department store span over the Court C alley behind the 900 block of Broadway. At left is the Olympic Ice Cream shop, 954 Court C, managed by Aaron Robbins. Aaron's son Irv, who worked in this shop as a teenager, would go on to found the Baskin-Robbins chain with partner and brother-in-law Burt Baskin. (Courtesy of the Tacoma Public Library.)

The 1936 film *Prisoner of Shark Island* is the feature at the Music Box Theater (formerly the Broadway) at the corner of Ninth Street and Broadway. Looking up the hill along St. Helens Avenue, past the longtime fixture Caswell Optical Co., the 17-story Medical Arts Building, which opened in 1930, dominates this view. (Courtesy of the Tacoma Public Library.)

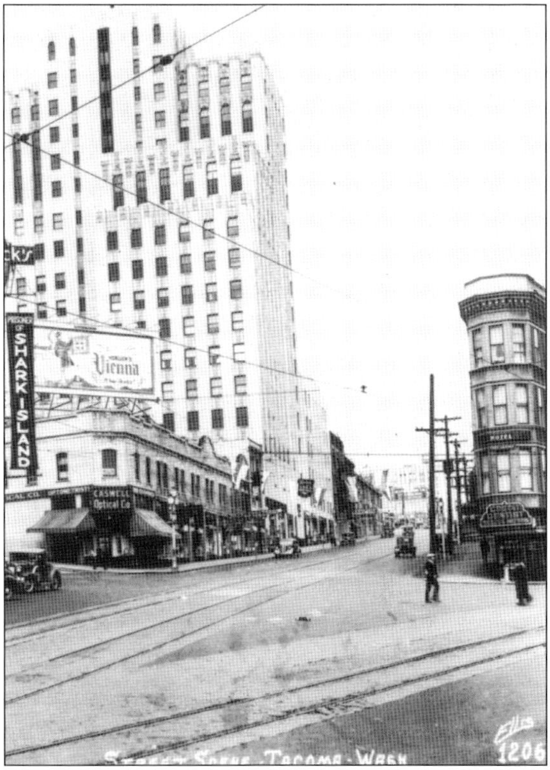

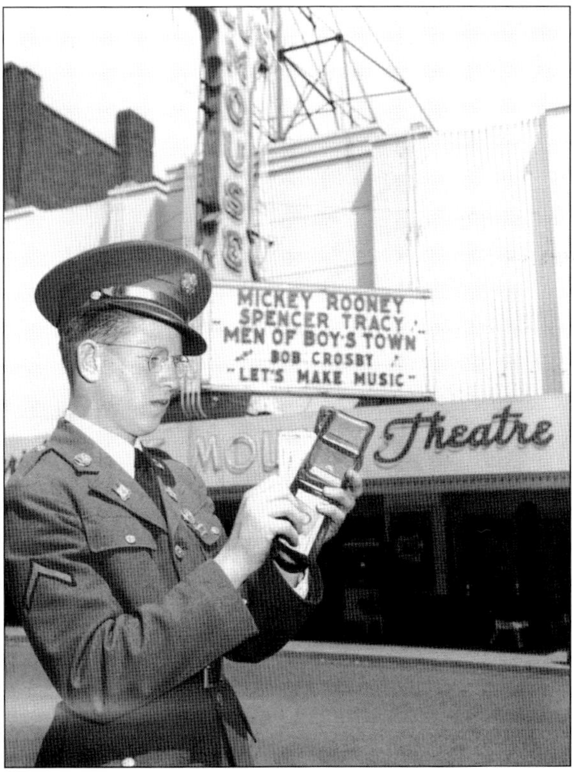

In May 1941, the *Tacoma Times* reported on Pfc. Kenneth E. Wilkinson, labeling him the "Army's biggest movie fan." The soldier from LaGrande, Oregon, went to the movies four to five nights per week and estimated that he had seen nearly 250 feature-length films since enlisting in October 1940. In this photograph, he counts the cash in his wallet, checking to see whether he has enough for a ticket at the Blue Mouse. (Courtesy of the Tacoma Public Library.)

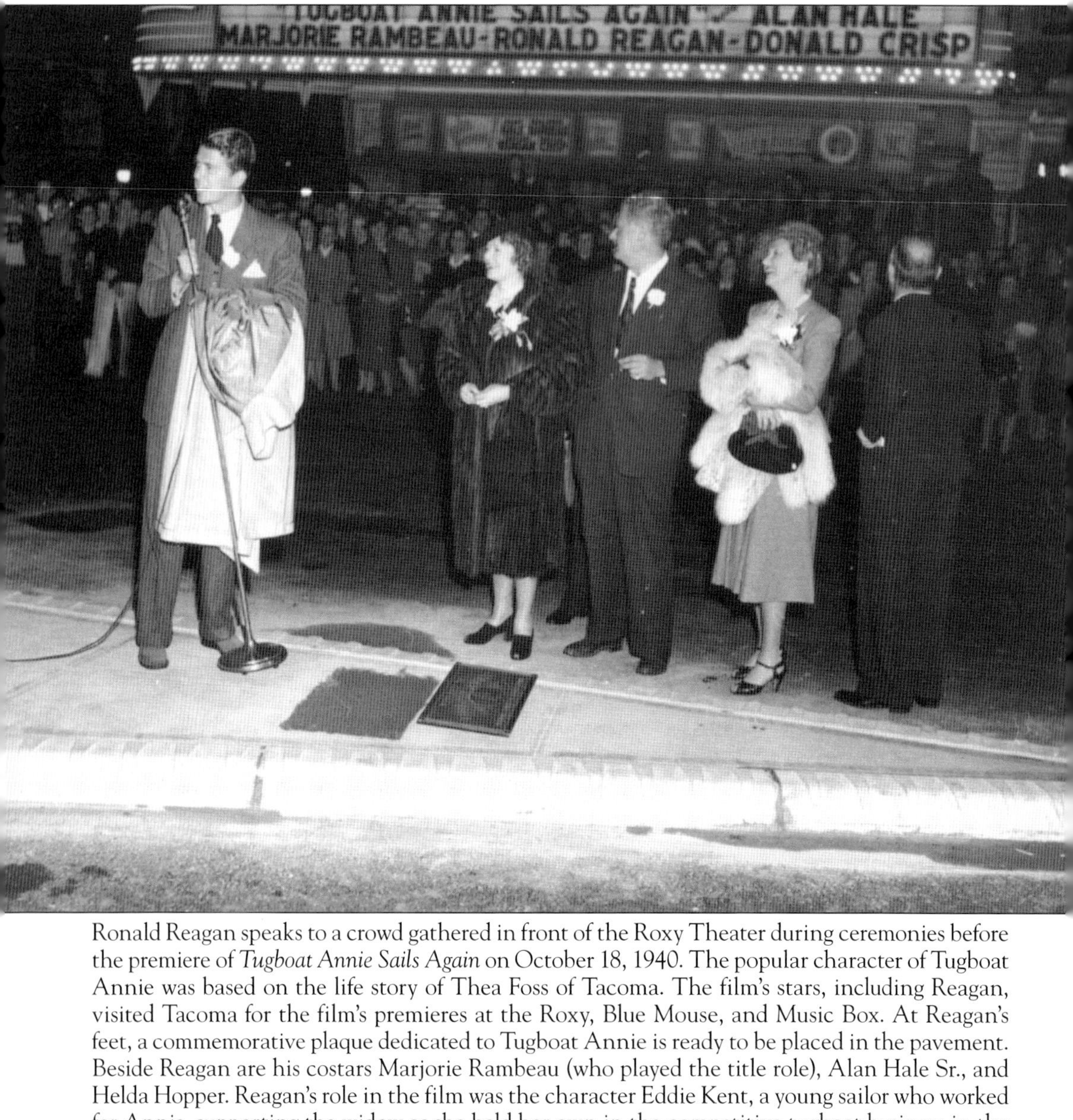

Ronald Reagan speaks to a crowd gathered in front of the Roxy Theater during ceremonies before the premiere of *Tugboat Annie Sails Again* on October 18, 1940. The popular character of Tugboat Annie was based on the life story of Thea Foss of Tacoma. The film's stars, including Reagan, visited Tacoma for the film's premieres at the Roxy, Blue Mouse, and Music Box. At Reagan's feet, a commemorative plaque dedicated to Tugboat Annie is ready to be placed in the pavement. Beside Reagan are his costars Marjorie Rambeau (who played the title role), Alan Hale Sr., and Helda Hopper. Reagan's role in the film was the character Eddie Kent, a young sailor who worked for Annie, supporting the widow as she held her own in the competitive tugboat business in the fictional port of Secoma. (Courtesy of the Tacoma Public Library.)

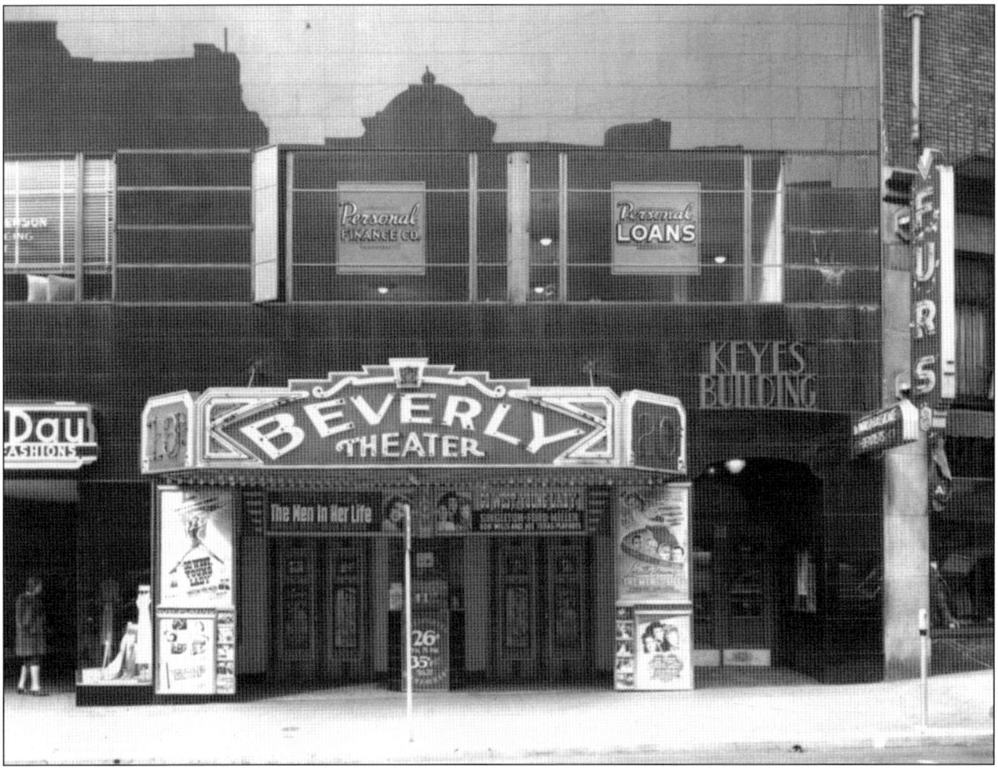

The Beverly Theater at 916–918 Broadway was named after the daughter of the theater's manager, Mike Barovic. The building, which was home to the Colonial Theater from 1914 until its closure in 1930, was completely remodeled in 1931, reopening as the Beverly in 1934 with a shiny black Vitrolite and nickel-silver exterior. (Courtesy of the Tacoma Public Library.)

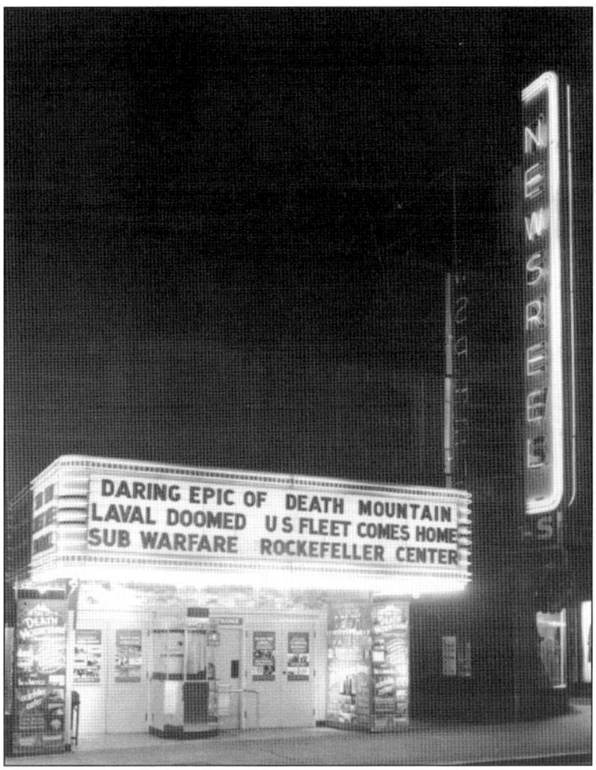

The dramatic neon marquee of the Telenews Theater (916–918 Broadway) lights up the night sky in November 1945. The Telenews, which opened after the Beverly Theater closed at the same location, operated for about five years, showing only newsreels, short travel films, and documentaries. (Courtesy of the Tacoma Public Library.)

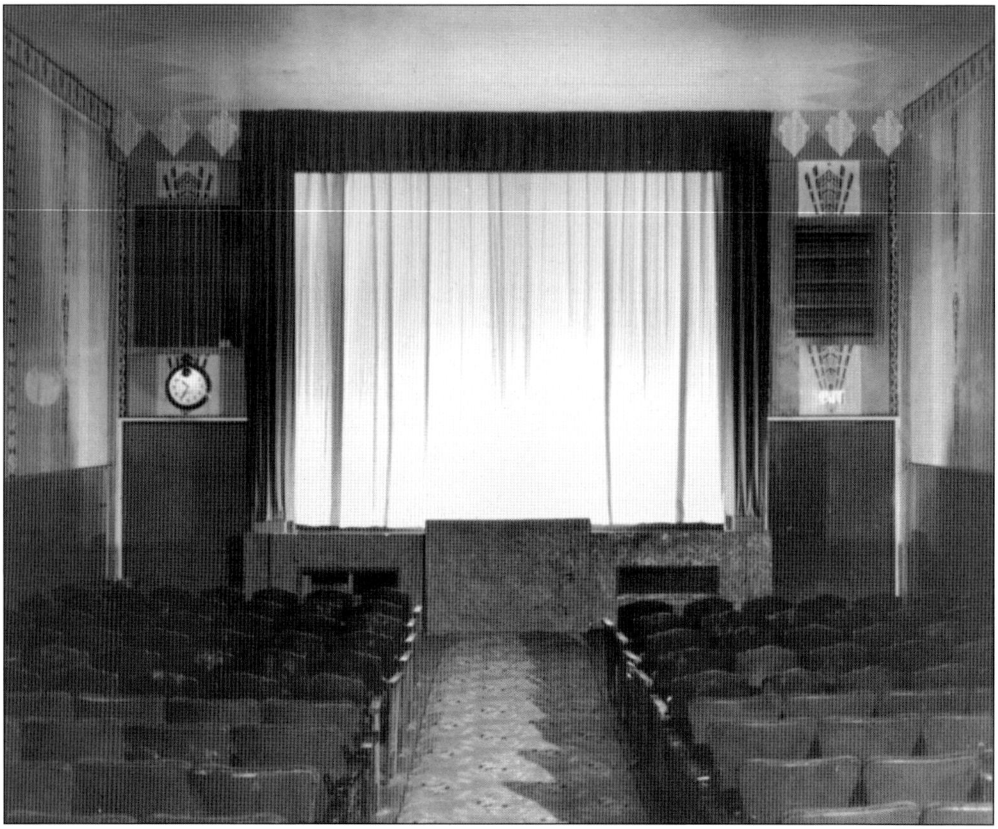

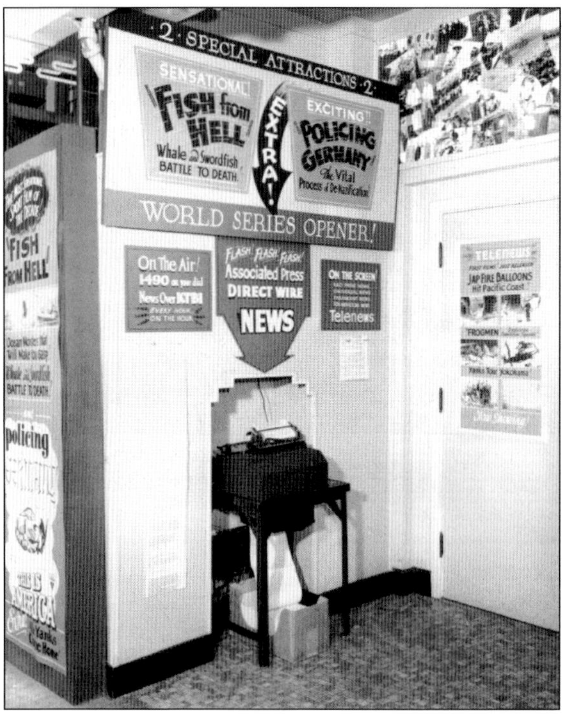

The interior of the Telenews Theater, 916–918 Broadway, is seen here a few weeks after its September 1945 grand opening, which drew an audience of 400. Patrons were invited to see "history in the making" as they viewed the news of the week. The theater was formerly known as the Colonial (1914–1930) and the Beverly (1934–1945). (Courtesy of the Tacoma Public Library.)

A Teletype machine brings the latest headlines to the lobby of the Telenews Theater in October 1945. In addition to war news from Germany and Japan and updates from baseball's World Series, Telenews patrons could view *Fish From Hell*, which was being advertised as "the most sensational sport film of the decade." (Courtesy of the Tacoma Public Library.)

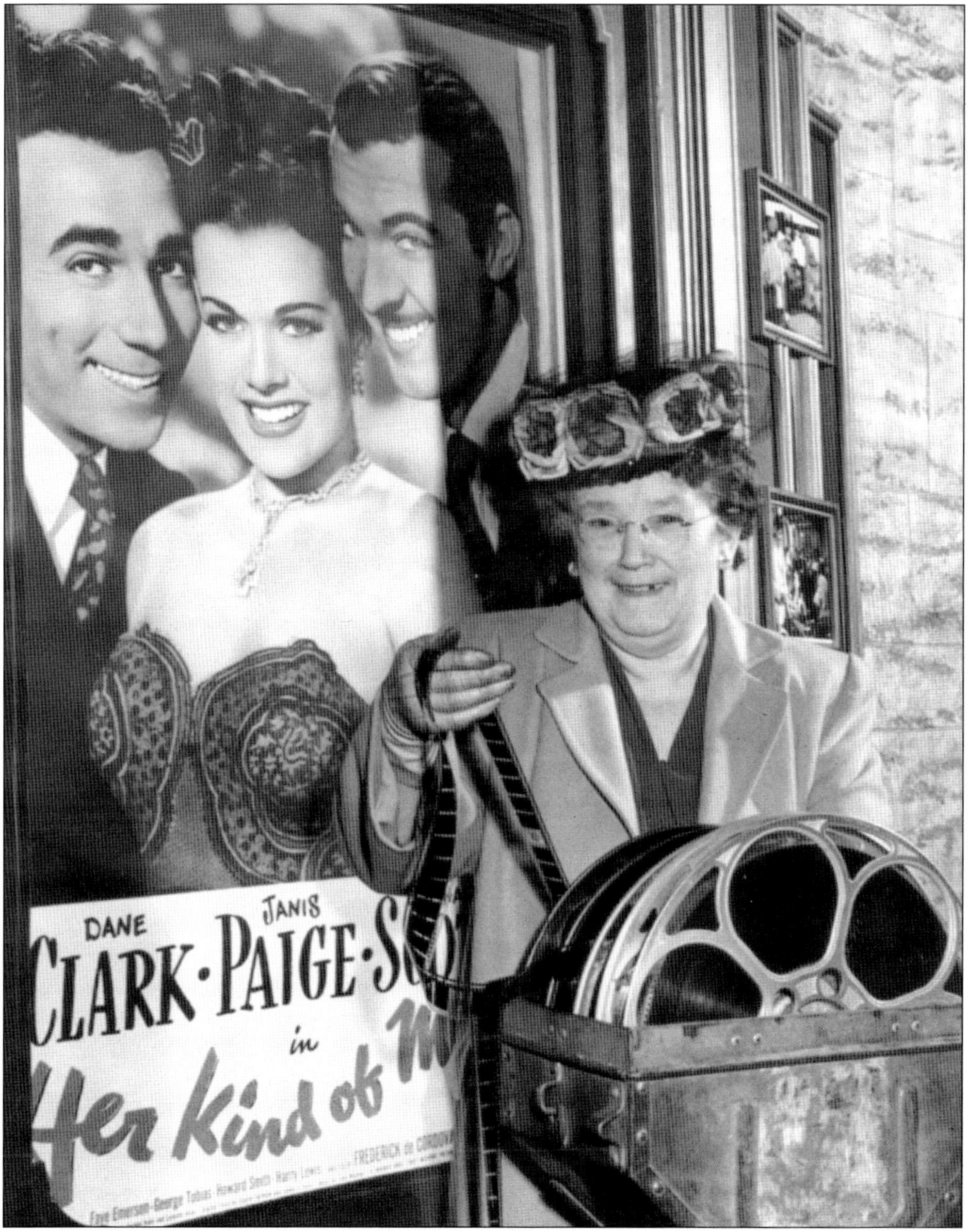

Julia Paige, the grandmother of the actress Janis Paige, was shown a special screening of the movie *Her Kind of Man* on Friday, May 3, 1946, at the Music Box Theater, 902 Broadway. Warner Brothers sent a special print of the film to Tacoma because the elder Paige had been seriously ill. Born as Donna Mae Tjaden in Tacoma in 1922, Janis Paige was singing in public by age five in local amateur shows. She moved to Los Angeles after graduating from Stadium High School and earned a job as a singer at the Hollywood Canteen during the war years. *Her Kind of Man* was her first feature film to be released, and she went on to appear in many more Hollywood films. Never quite finding her place in the studio system, Paige went on to find success on Broadway, as a touring cabaret singer, and on television. (Courtesy of the Tacoma Public Library.)

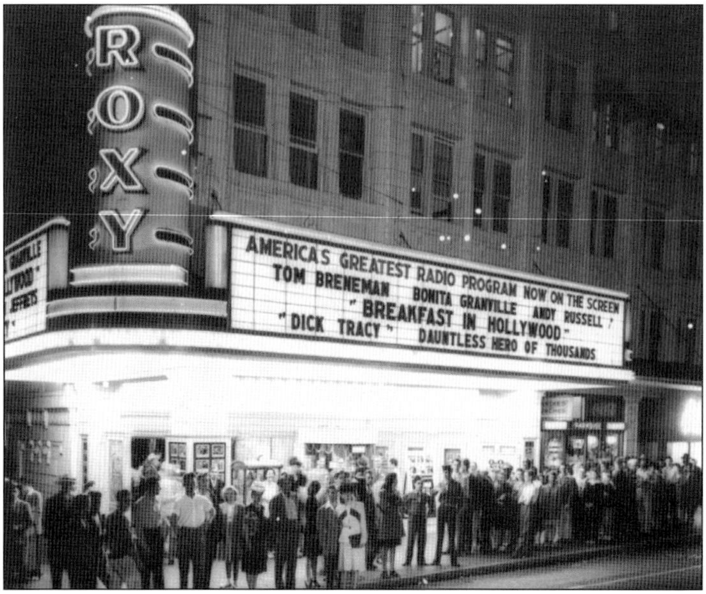

August 20, 1946, was opening night for Tom Breneman's *Breakfast in Hollywood Show* at the Roxy Theater. The movie was based on Breneman's popular radio show, which was broadcast locally on KJR. The film's director, Harold Shuster, provided nearly 100 extras and minor characters the chance to call out their names and hometowns on camera. (Courtesy of the Tacoma Public Library.)

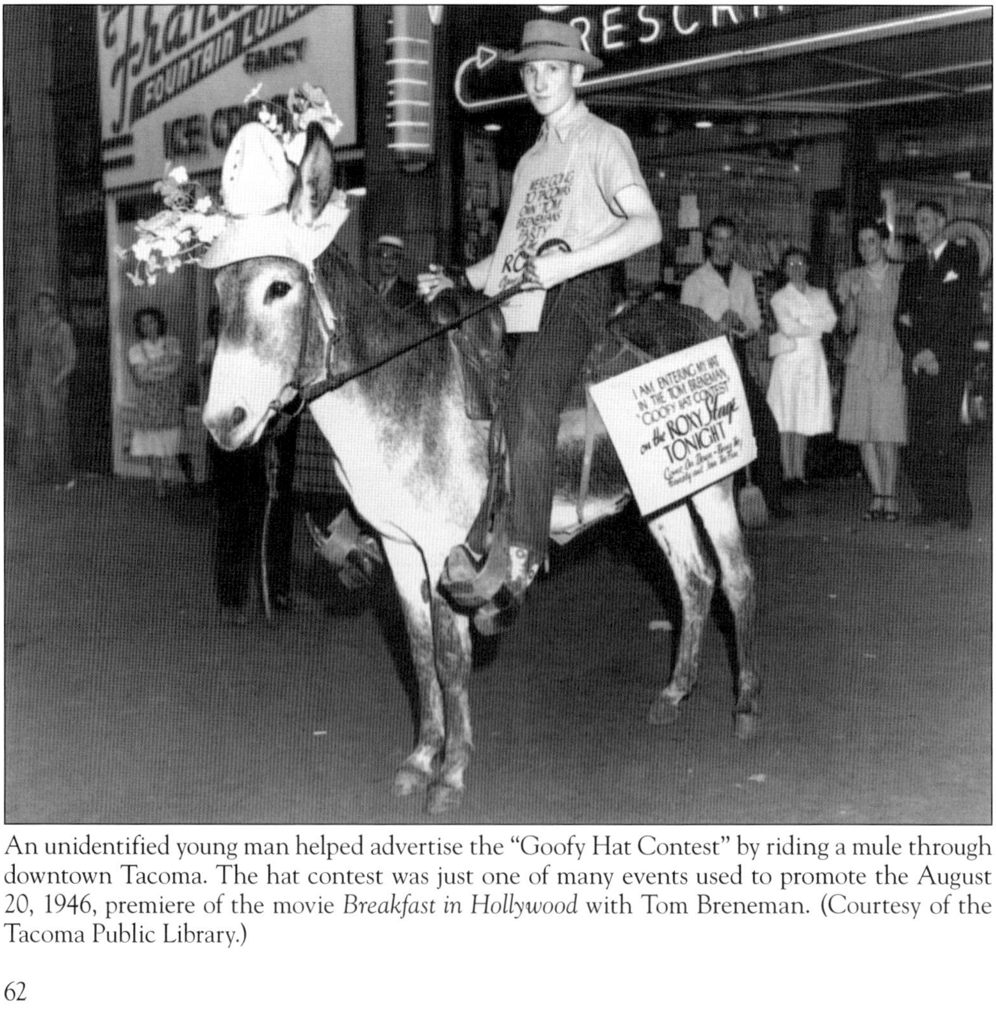

An unidentified young man helped advertise the "Goofy Hat Contest" by riding a mule through downtown Tacoma. The hat contest was just one of many events used to promote the August 20, 1946, premiere of the movie *Breakfast in Hollywood* with Tom Breneman. (Courtesy of the Tacoma Public Library.)

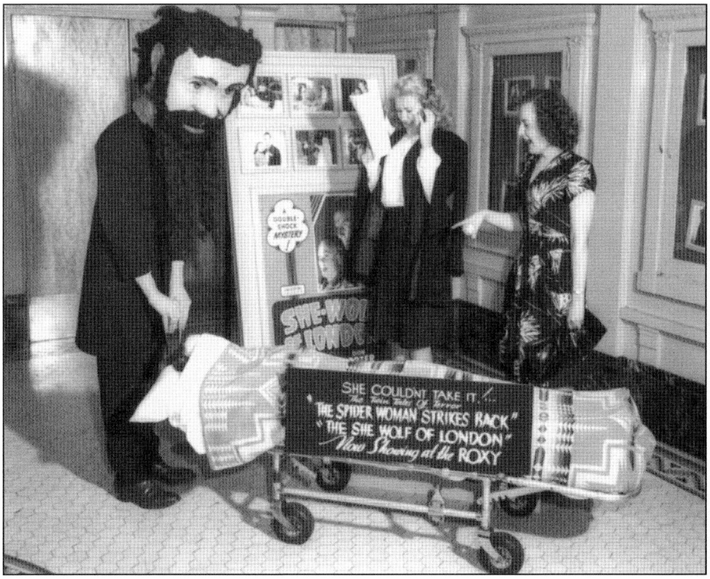

An unidentified man in a large mask, advertising the two terrifying films showing at the Roxy in September 1946, pulls a gurney with a woman who "couldn't take it" from the lobby while two other women look on, screaming. *Spider Woman Strikes Back* and *She-Wolf of London* were both 1946 productions of Universal Studios. (Courtesy of the Tacoma Public Library.)

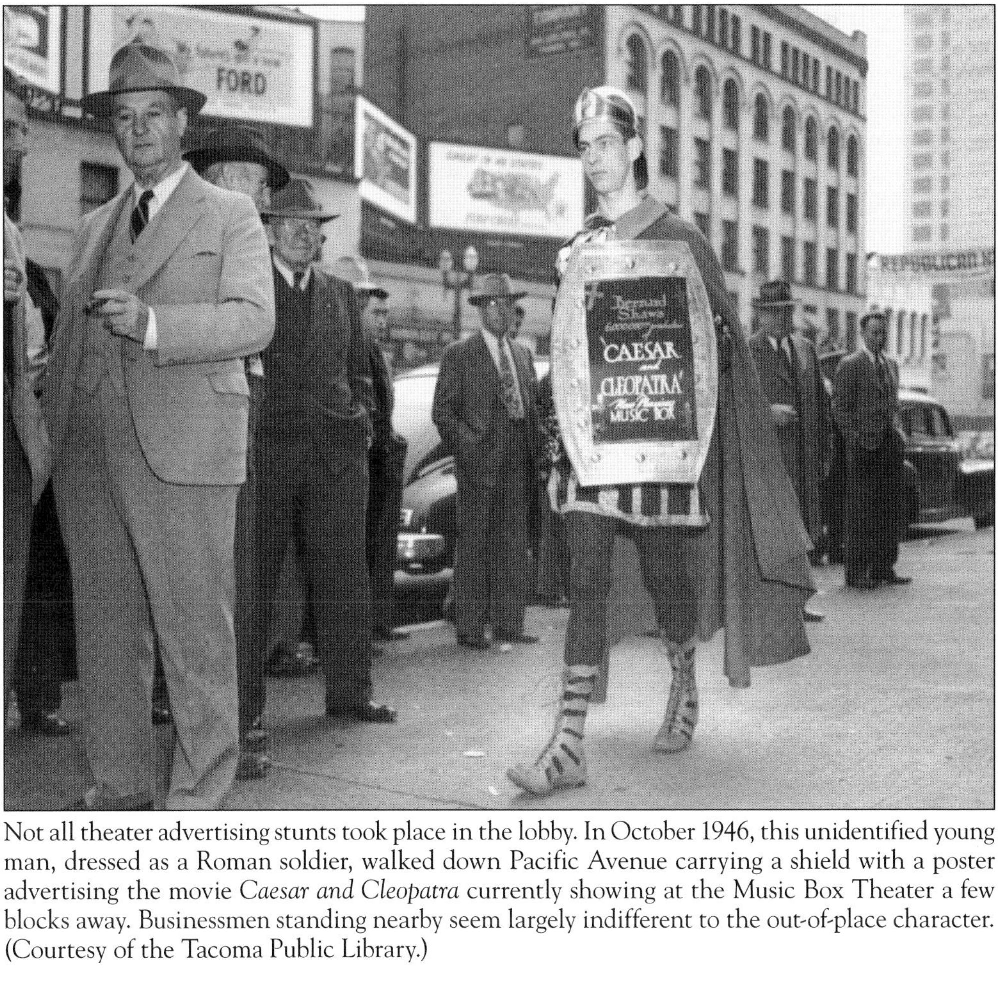

Not all theater advertising stunts took place in the lobby. In October 1946, this unidentified young man, dressed as a Roman soldier, walked down Pacific Avenue carrying a shield with a poster advertising the movie *Caesar and Cleopatra* currently showing at the Music Box Theater a few blocks away. Businessmen standing nearby seem largely indifferent to the out-of-place character. (Courtesy of the Tacoma Public Library.)

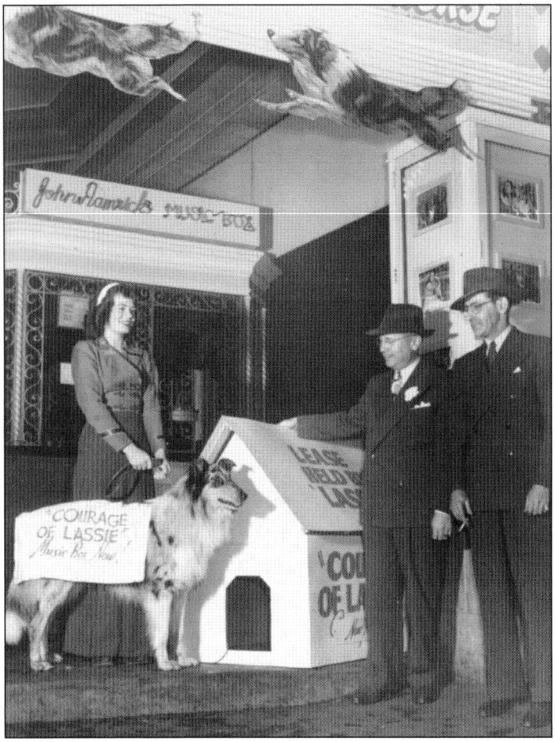

In December 1946, Lassie visited Tacoma to advertise the opening of *The Courage of Lassie* at the Music Box Theater. Just outside the box office, an usherette holds the leash while Lassie stands next to her doghouse. *The Courage of Lassie* was the third of seven Lassie films made by MGM between 1943 and 1951. (Courtesy of the Tacoma Public Library.)

For the February 27, 1947, opening of *The Dark Mirror*, a film featuring identical twins who both fall in love with the same man, the Rialto Theater held a special party, inviting any area twins over the age of 16. Approximately 106 (53 sets of twins) attended. From left to right, the youngest, 17-year-olds Deloris and Doris Johnson, and oldest, 60-year-olds Helen Barth and Lillian Hibbard, were photographed in front of the theater. (Courtesy of the Tacoma Public Library.)

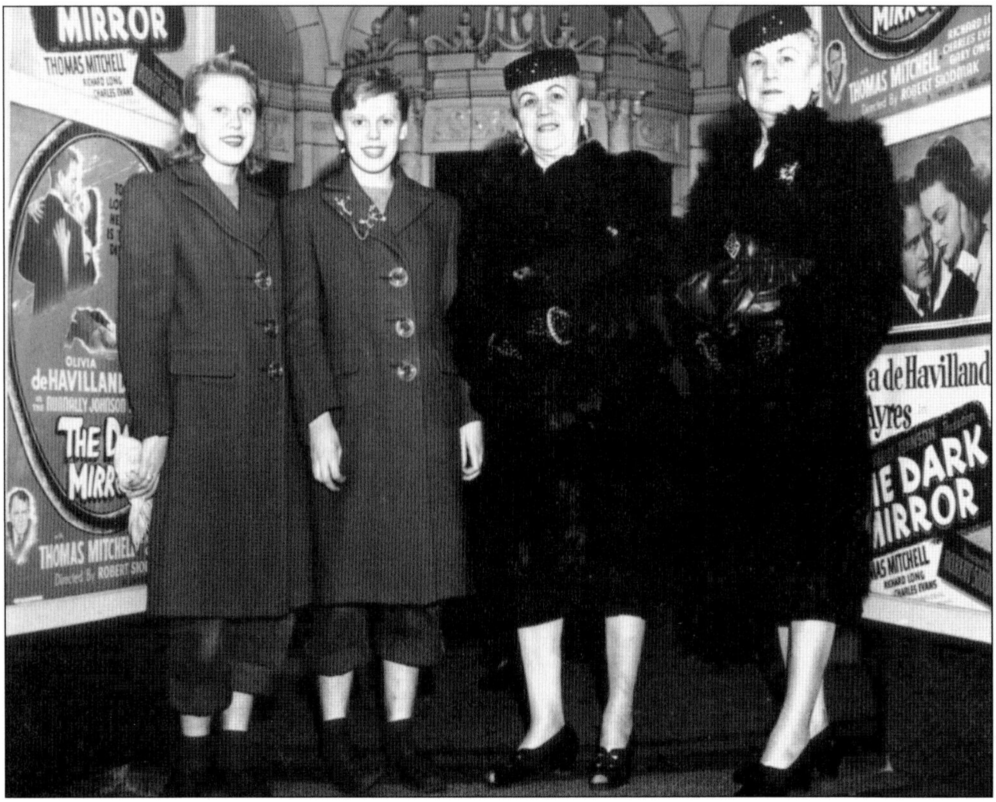

A new wood- and leather-trimmed candy bar was unveiled in 1947 at the Music Box Theater. The modern curves and neon signage of the new bar are juxtaposed with the stone and iron stairway of the historic theater, originally the Tacoma and then the Broadway. The identity of the candy girl posing next to her station is unknown. (Courtesy of the Tacoma Public Library.)

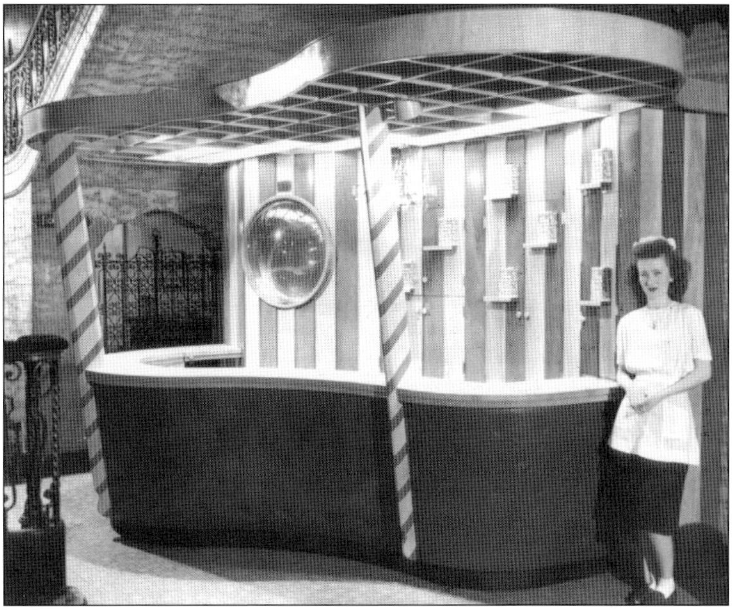

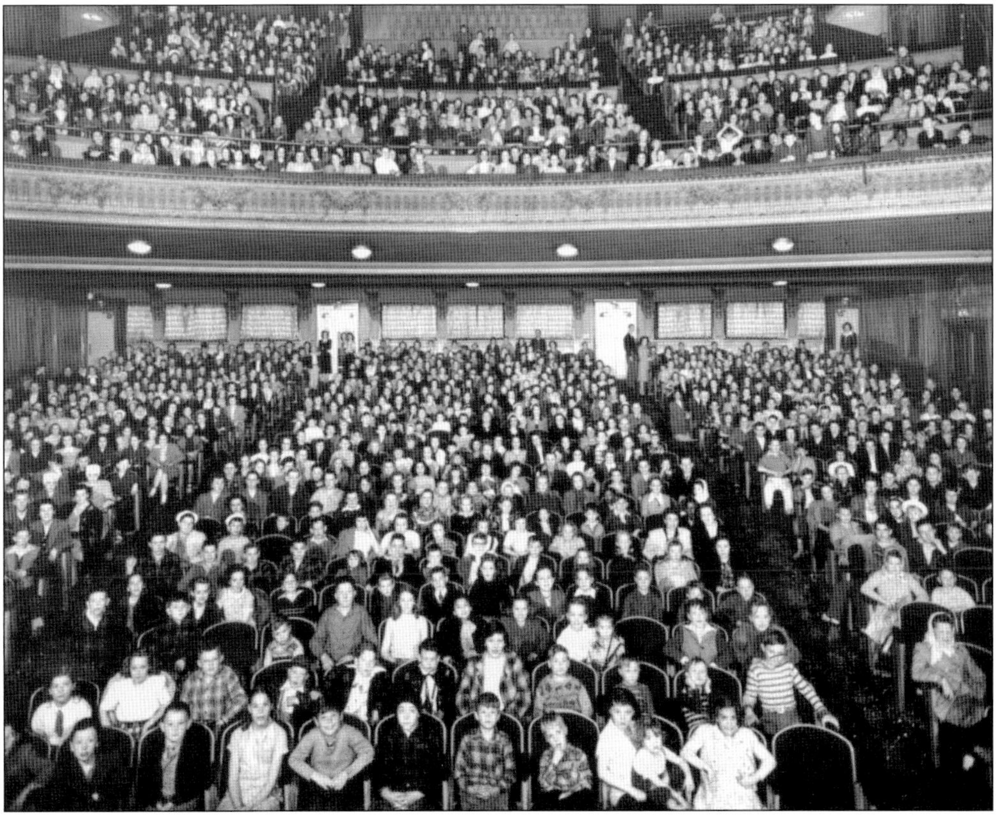

The Tacoma Council of Churches sponsored free admission to Cecil B. DeMille's *King of Kings* at the Roxy Theater (901 Broadway) in March 1948. The theater was nearly full, and the audience included a large number of young children for the showing on March 26, when this photograph was taken. (Courtesy of the Tacoma Public Library.)

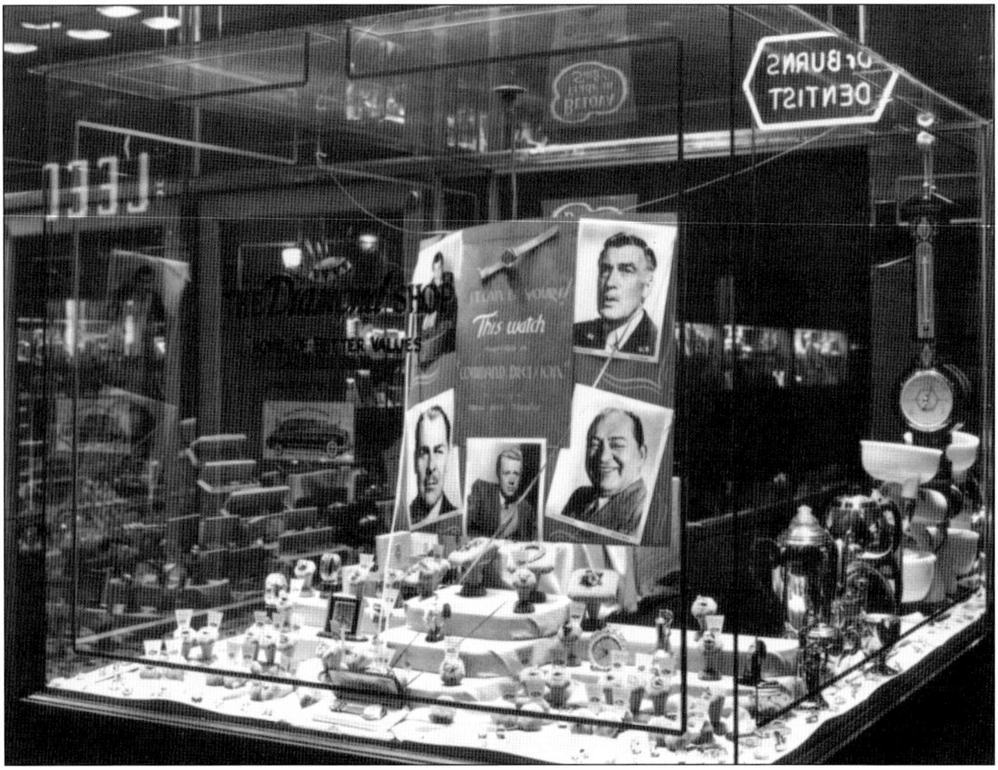

Businesses in the theater district often organized display windows around the films currently showing in neighboring theaters. In March 1949, with the Music Box Theater showing MGM's *Command Decision*, the Diamond Shop at 937 Broadway featured a watch worn by actors in the film along with the sales pitch, "It can be yours!" (Courtesy of the Tacoma Public Library.)

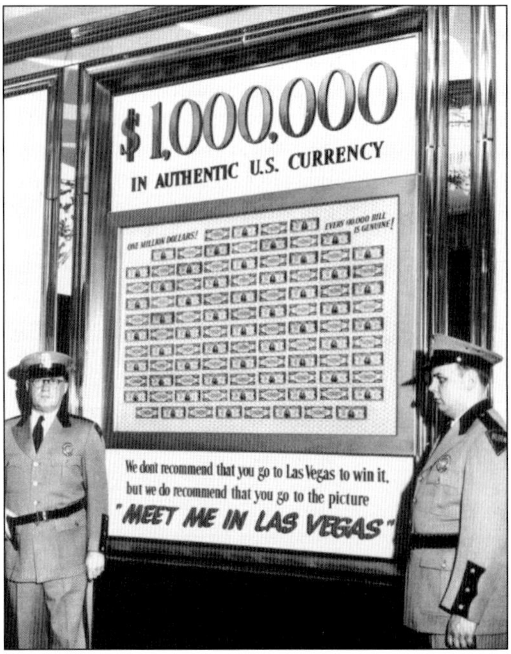

As promotion for the film *Meet Me in Las Vegas*, showing at the Music Box Theater in April 1956, $1 million in US currency was on display. The million-dollar display in $10,000 bills was guarded by two uniformed officers from Burns Security. The money appears to be blocked from contact by metal screening and glass. (Courtesy of the Tacoma Public Library.)

Four

A Place for Community

Stage and screen entertainment are not the only events that have drawn crowds to Tacoma's theater district over the decades. The district has also, throughout its existence, been at the center of community gatherings such as parades, holiday celebrations, and speeches by visiting dignitaries. When US president Benjamin Harrison visited Tacoma in 1891, a parade in his honor concluded in a reception at the intersection of Ninth Street and Broadway. Just shy of 60 years later, a speech by President Truman would be witnessed by thousands at the same location. During World War II, the streets outside the Pantages and Music Box Theaters played host to military parades, war-bond sales, troop enlistments, and scrap-metal drives.

Generations of Tacoma residents visited the theater district on a Saturday in April to watch the annual Daffodil Parade, cheering on floats and marching bands as they proceeded north on Broadway, turned at Ninth Street in front of the Pantages, and then continued south on Pacific Avenue. Another of Tacoma's oldest traditions, the lighting of a holiday tree, also calls the intersection of Ninth Street and Broadway home. In an era before the existence of facilities such as the Tacoma Dome or the convention center, several organizations held gatherings in the theater district, staging parades on the surrounding streets and utilizing facilities such as the Hotel Winthrop and the theaters themselves.

In addition to these specific events, the theater district was for many decades the heart of downtown Tacoma's shopping district. Major department stores, automobile dealerships, jewelers, clothiers, public markets, and specialty shops were located, amongst the theaters, in a few-block radius of Ninth Street and Broadway. As the photographic record demonstrates, the wide range of businesses sharing this relatively small area created a vibrant commercial center for downtown Tacoma. This shopping district thrived from the late 19th century until finally succumbing to shifts in population and the development of shopping malls outside the city center in the 1960s.

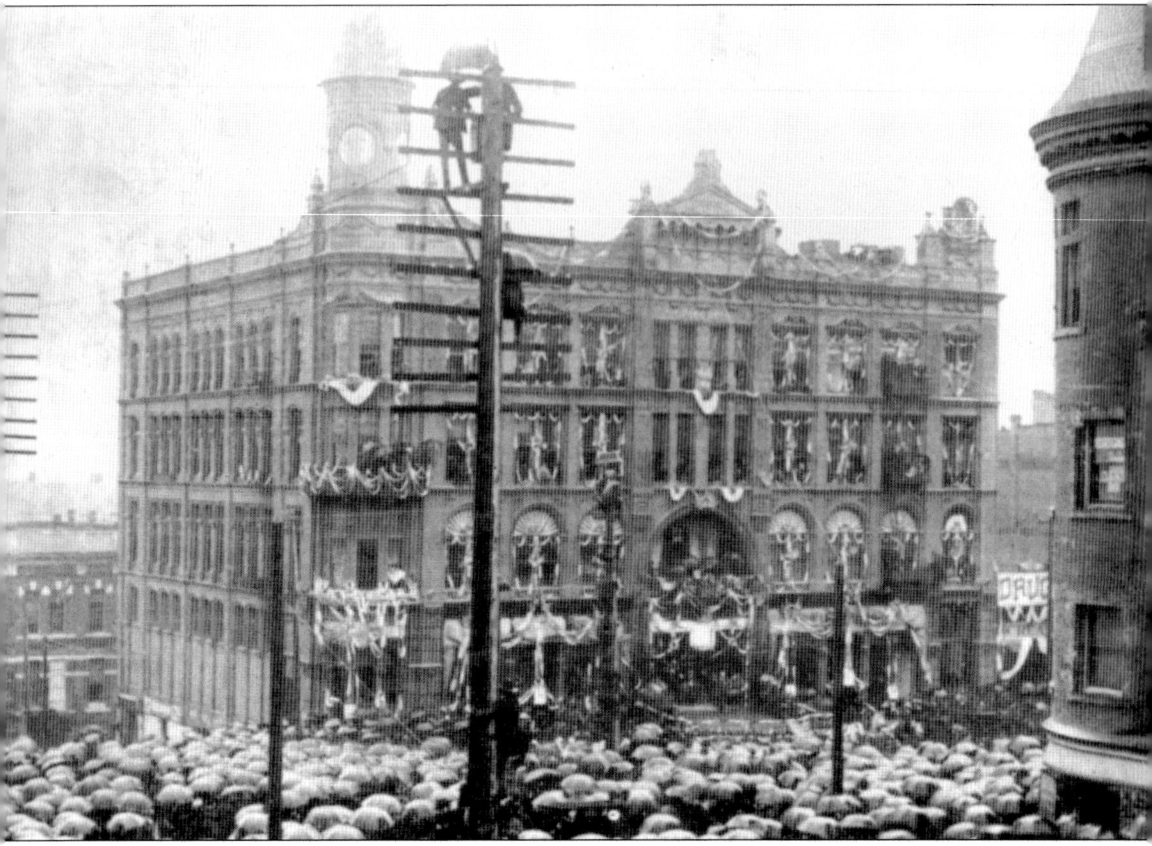

On May 6, 1891, a large number of Tacoma residents filled the intersection of Ninth Street and Broadway as they awaited the arrival of Pres. Benjamin Harrison. In addition to the hundreds huddled under umbrellas at street level, a few brave souls climbed tall poles in order to get a better view. A parade that included military and civic organizations was scheduled to march up C Street and weave through residential areas on Tacoma, Yakima, and Division Avenues before returning back to the intersection pictured here for a public reception in the president's honor. The Gross Bros. department store, which occupies much of this view, was just one of many downtown Tacoma businesses decorated with bunting for the president's visit. The Tacoma Theater, which had opened at the beginning of 1890, can be seen at far right. (Courtesy of the Tacoma Public Library.)

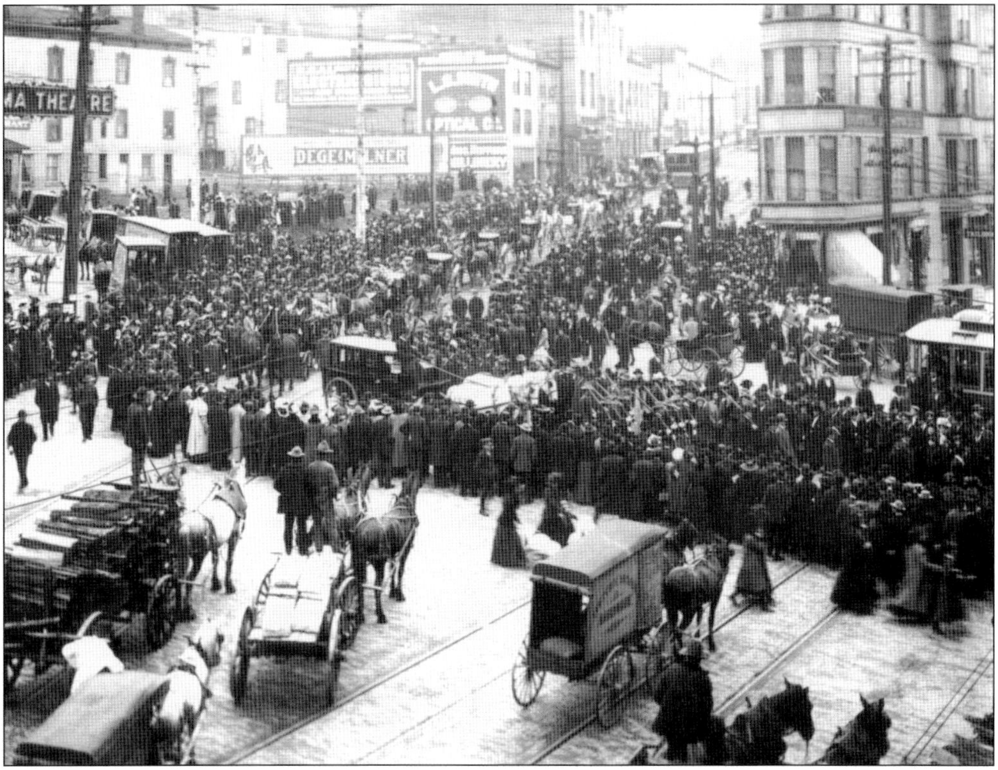

Thousands of Tacoma residents gathered on February 27, 1908, to pay tribute to Tacoma fireman Lt. George Hill, who had been killed on February 24 while fighting a fire at the Davis Smith & Co. building at 1754 Pacific Avenue. Signage for the Tacoma Theater can be seen at far left, while the Hotel Bostwick is at right. (Courtesy of the Tacoma Public Library.)

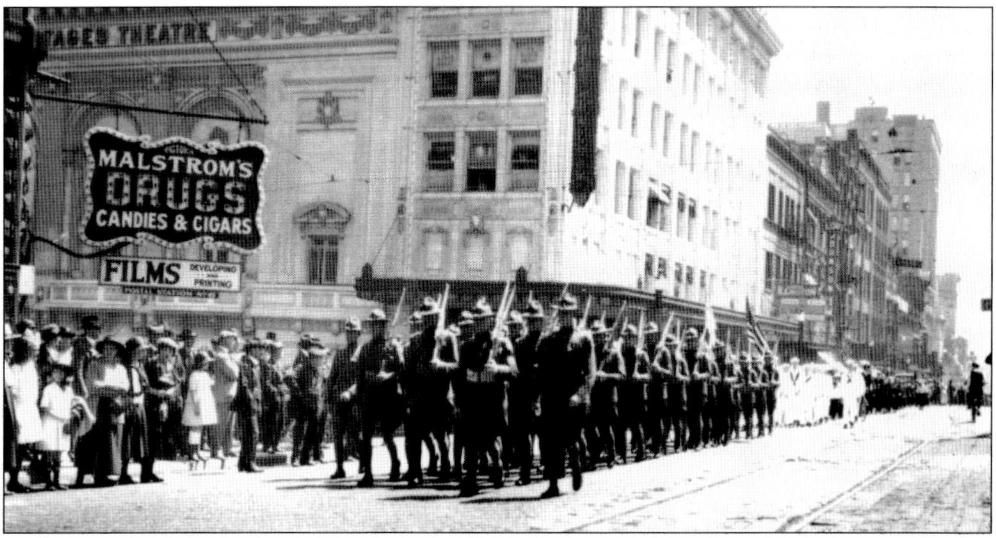

The still-new Pantages Theater provides a beautiful backdrop for this photograph of a parade down Broadway on May 21, 1921. US Army soldiers are followed by a group from the US Navy in their dress whites as the parade progresses north on Broadway past the intersection with Ninth Street. (Courtesy of the Tacoma Public Library.)

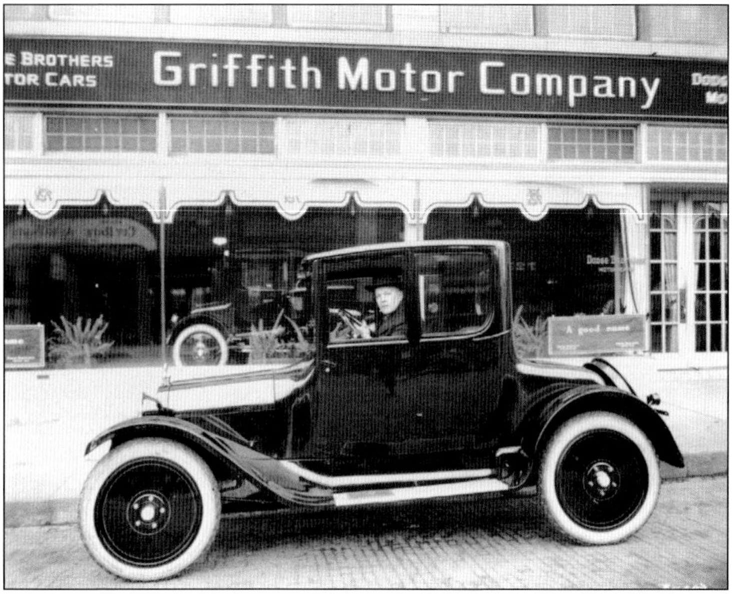

A new Dodge coupe is parked on the brick street outside Griffith Motor Company (728–730 Broadway) on February 11, 1922. A new car purchase was still a relative rarity at this date, and local newspapers frequently ran photographs of happy customers—in this case, Tacoma businessman H.J. Salmela—at the wheel of their new vehicles. (Courtesy of the Tacoma Public Library.)

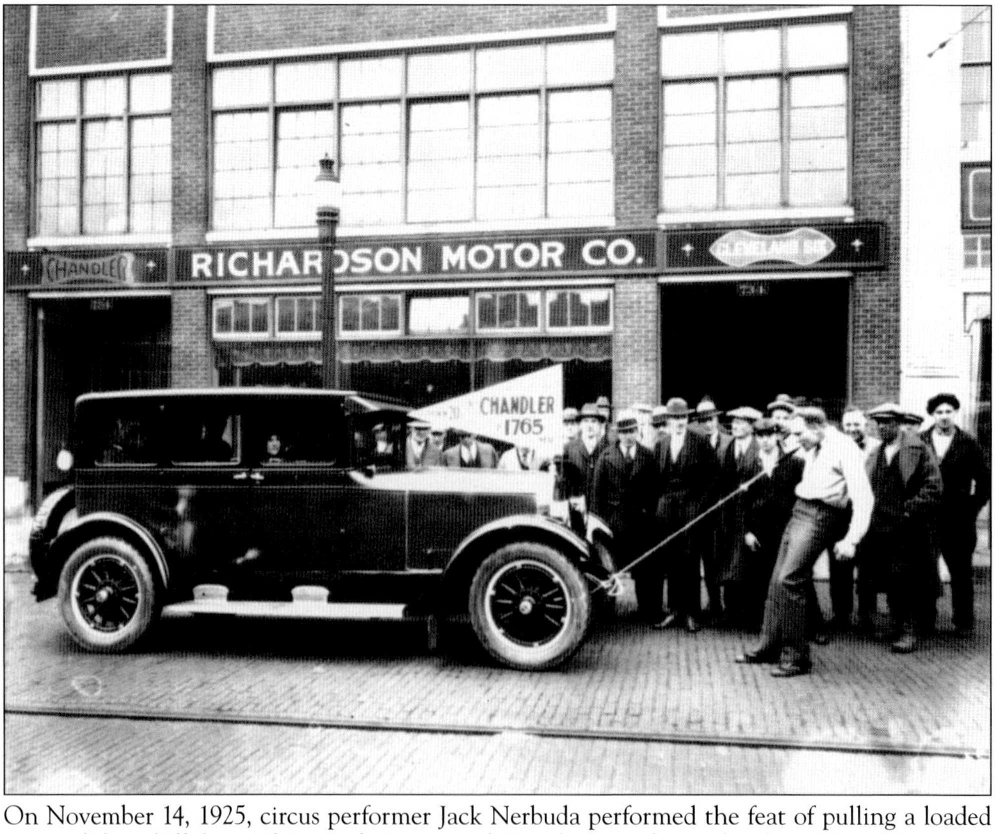

On November 14, 1925, circus performer Jack Nerbuda performed the feat of pulling a loaded automobile uphill from Thirteenth Street and Broadway to the Richardson Motor Company (734 Broadway) with his teeth. Nerbuda was reported to have completed the task without losing a single tooth. The publicity stunt was staged to advertise the new Chandler four-door sedan. (Courtesy of the Tacoma Public Library.)

On March 28, 1924, Thomas L. Hofto, a violin maker, poses with one of his works in progress in his workshop at 917 ½ Broadway. Completed instruments, as well as many of the tools of his trade, are visible on the workbenches and hanging on the wall. Hofto lived in Tacoma for 40 years, building scores of instruments, until his death in 1951 at the age of 65. (Courtesy of the Tacoma Public Library.)

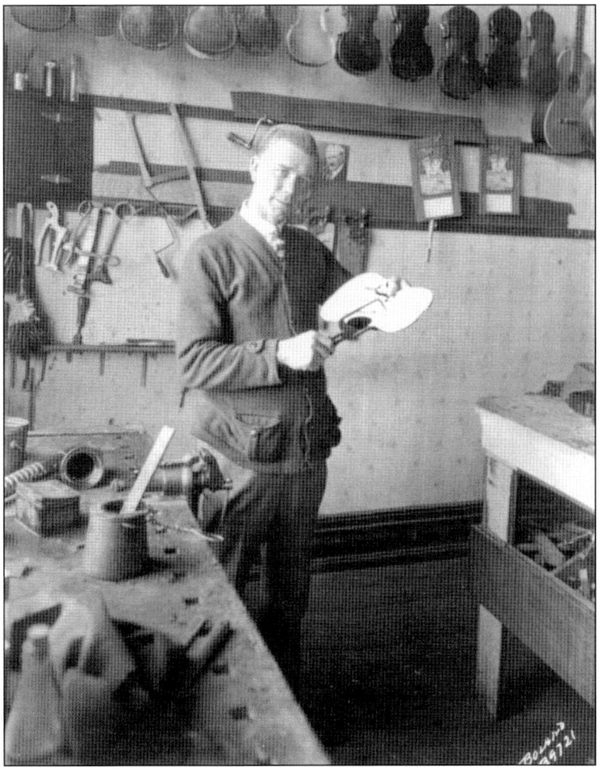

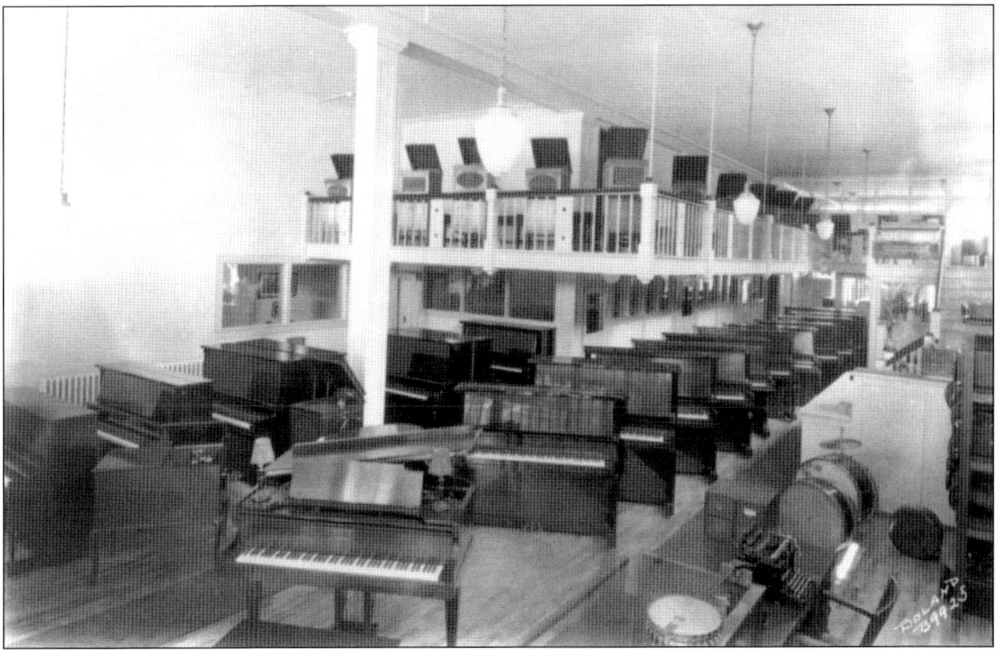

Over the decades, the theater district has been home to many shops selling musical instruments and supplies. This photograph from April 1924 shows the interior of Silvers Piano Co., located at 1155–1157 Broadway. The main level of the shop is filled with many upright pianos, while the upper-level features a display of Brunswick phonographs. (Courtesy of the Tacoma Public Library.)

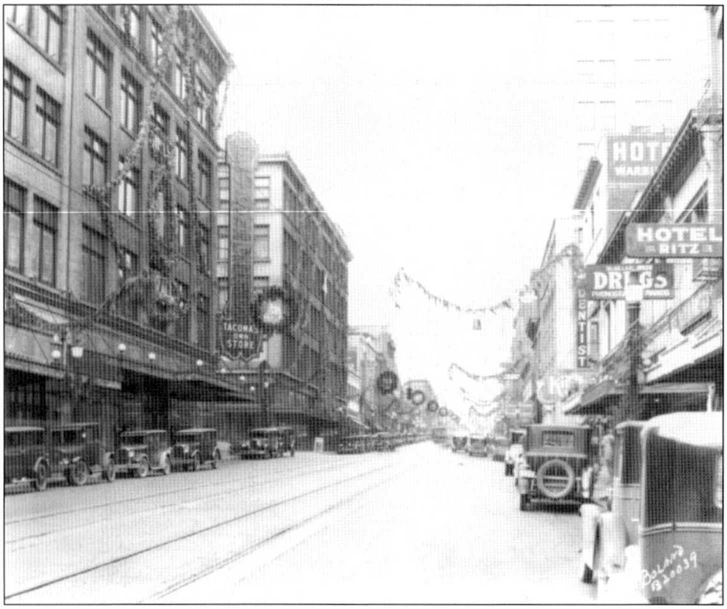

Broadway is decorated for the holidays in this view, looking north from the 1100 block, in December 1928. Fisher's, "Tacoma's Own Store," and Rhodes Brothers department store are at left, and signage for a wide variety of businesses can be seen at right. Just visible in the distance left of the center is the unique shape of the Bostwick Building. (Courtesy of the Tacoma Public Library.)

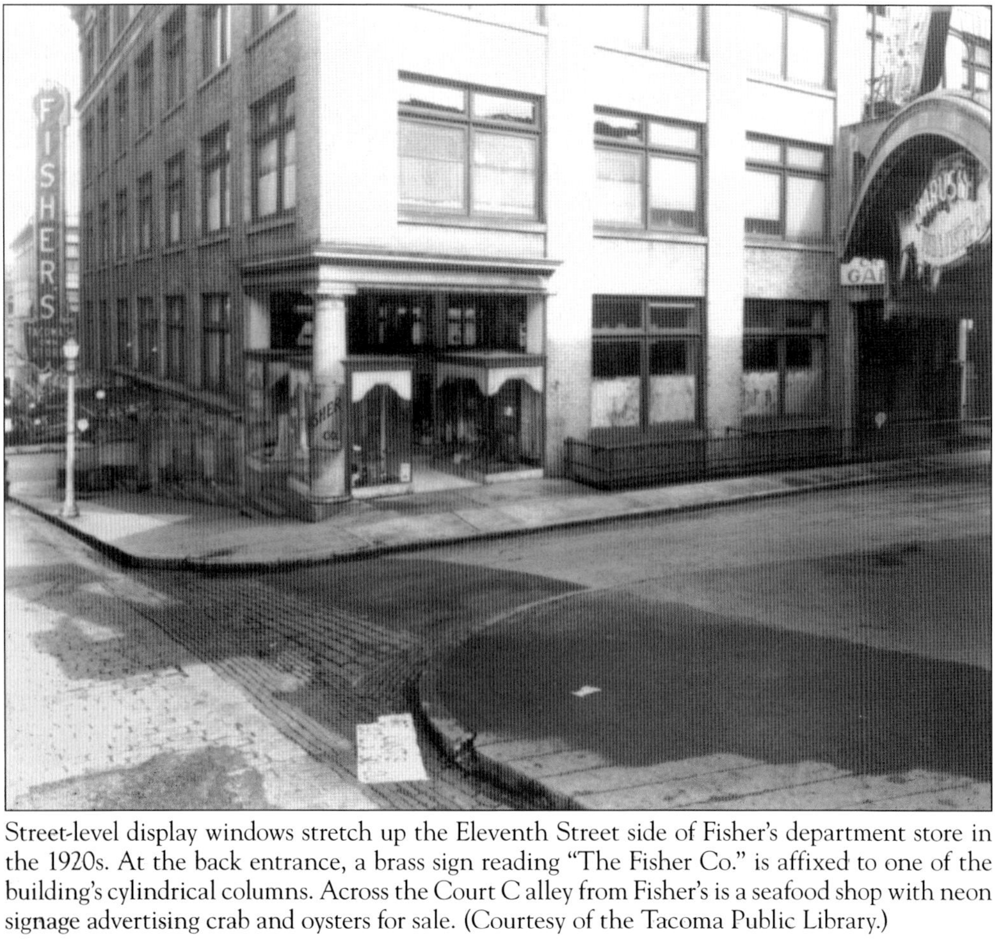

Street-level display windows stretch up the Eleventh Street side of Fisher's department store in the 1920s. At the back entrance, a brass sign reading "The Fisher Co." is affixed to one of the building's cylindrical columns. Across the Court C alley from Fisher's is a seafood shop with neon signage advertising crab and oysters for sale. (Courtesy of the Tacoma Public Library.)

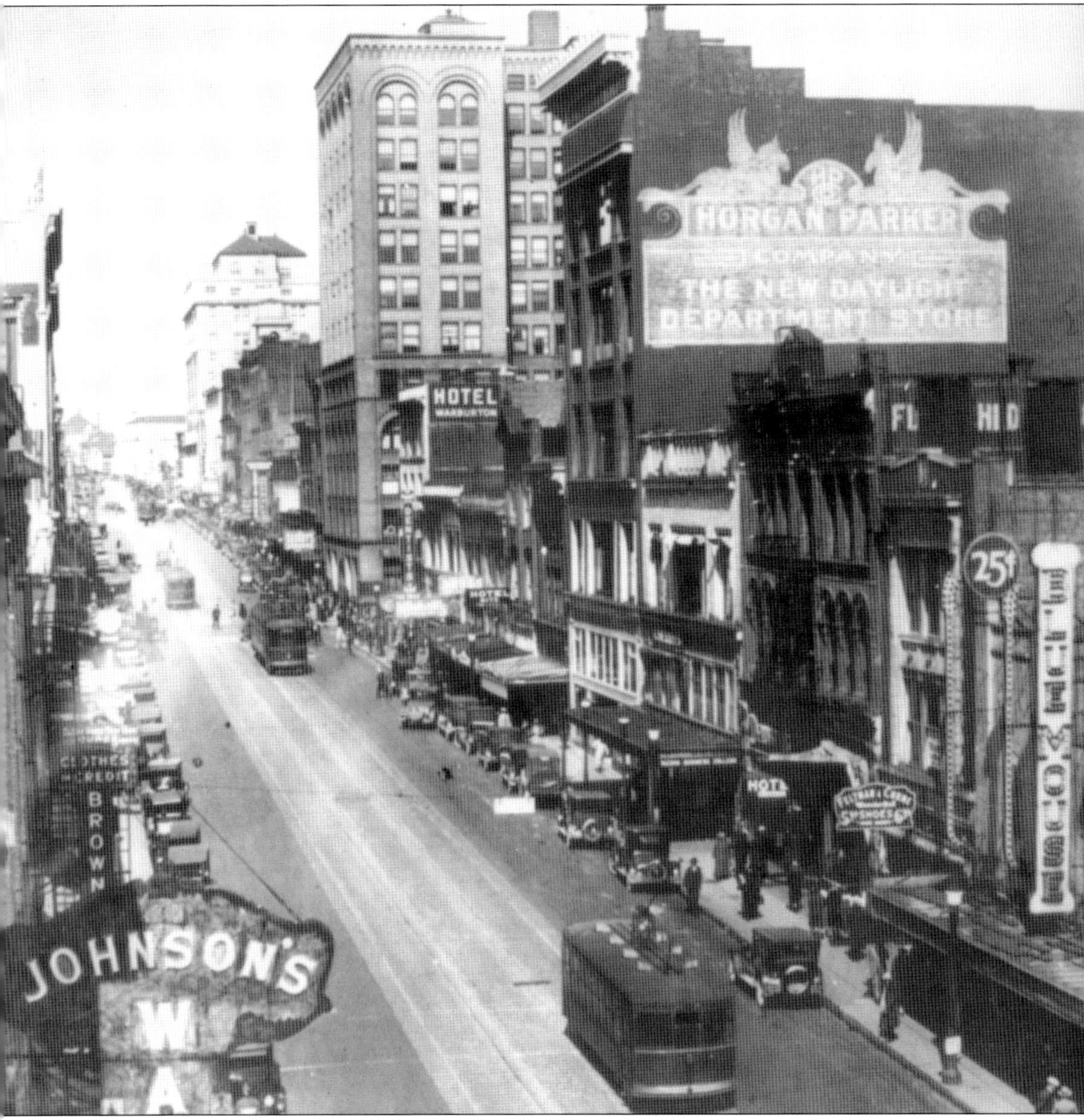

By the late 1920s, Broadway was firmly established as the heart of a lively theater and shopping district. A wide range of establishments can be seen in this view, taken about 1928, looking north from the middle of the 1100 block of Broadway. At far right is the Blue Mouse, advertising 25¢ tickets. Sharing the right side of the street with the Blue Mouse are Feltman & Curme (shoes), the Tacoma Business College, Kimball's (sporting goods), and the Hotel Ritz and Hotel Warburton. The Fidelity Building, situated at the northeast corner of Eleventh Street and Broadway, appears largest in this view, although the Hotel Winthrop, located another block in the distance, is actually a more massive structure. During this era, Tacomans utilized various means of transportation to visit downtown; multiple streetcars can be seen traveling Broadway, but there are also a large number of automobiles parked outside businesses and a substantial amount of pedestrian traffic. (Courtesy of the Tacoma Public Library.)

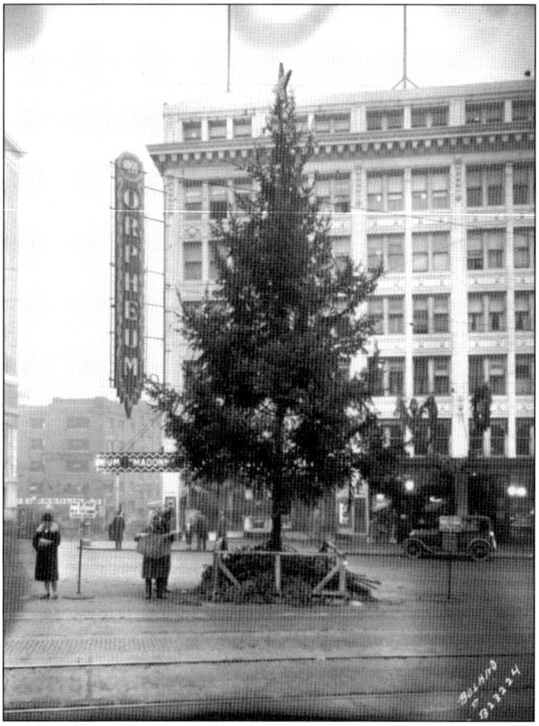

On December 10, 1930, a handful of people wait for the streetcar at the corner of Ninth Street and Broadway. A few days earlier, on the evening of December 6, the City of Tacoma had erected this 50-foot Christmas tree decorated with lights and topped with a large star. The Pantages Theater (known in 1930 as the RKO Orpheum) can be seen behind the tree. (Courtesy of the Tacoma Public Library.)

Shops in the theater district, especially the large department stores, were known for their festive displays during the holiday season. In this photograph from about 1930, Rhodes Brothers is adorned with garlands covering much of the Broadway side of the building, as well large lighted letters spelling out "Merry Christmas." (Courtesy of the Tacoma Public Library.)

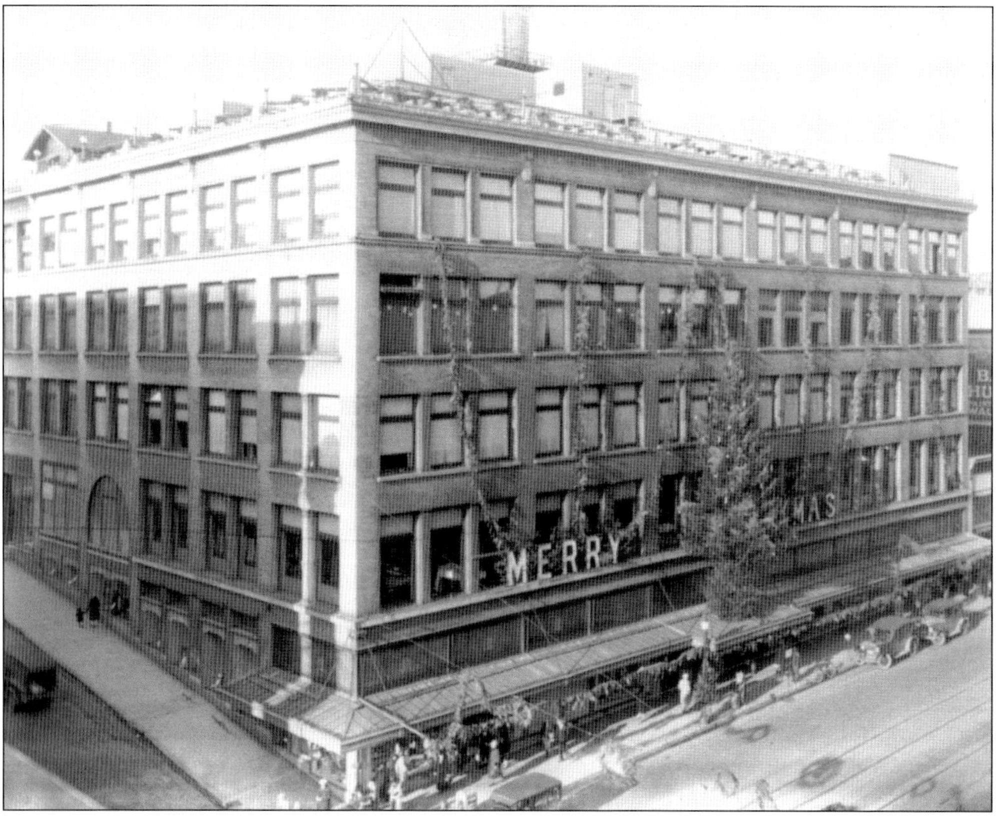

Burnett Bros. Jewelers, a long-standing Broadway business, is seen here in about 1930. Their ornate clock and neon sign occupy a significant amount of space outside their 932 Broadway storefront. One neighboring business advertises Victor records, pianolas (player pianos), and player rolls. The building also houses the Puget Sound Nursery Co., as well as Sunday services for Unity Truth Church. (Courtesy of the Tacoma Public Library.)

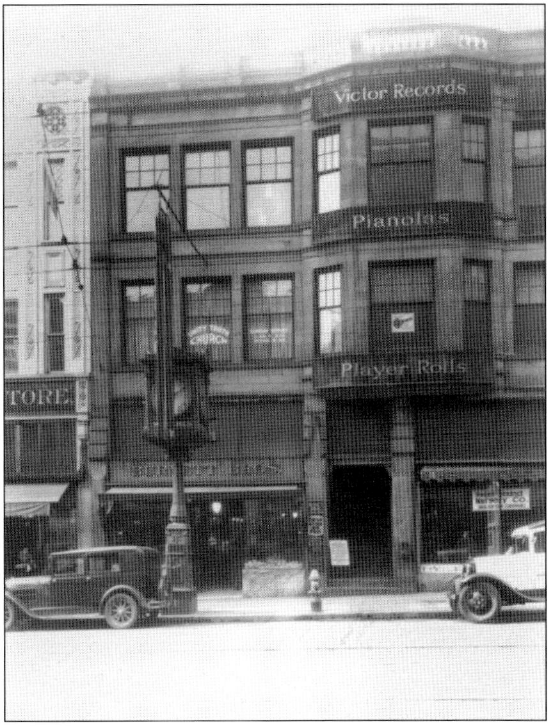

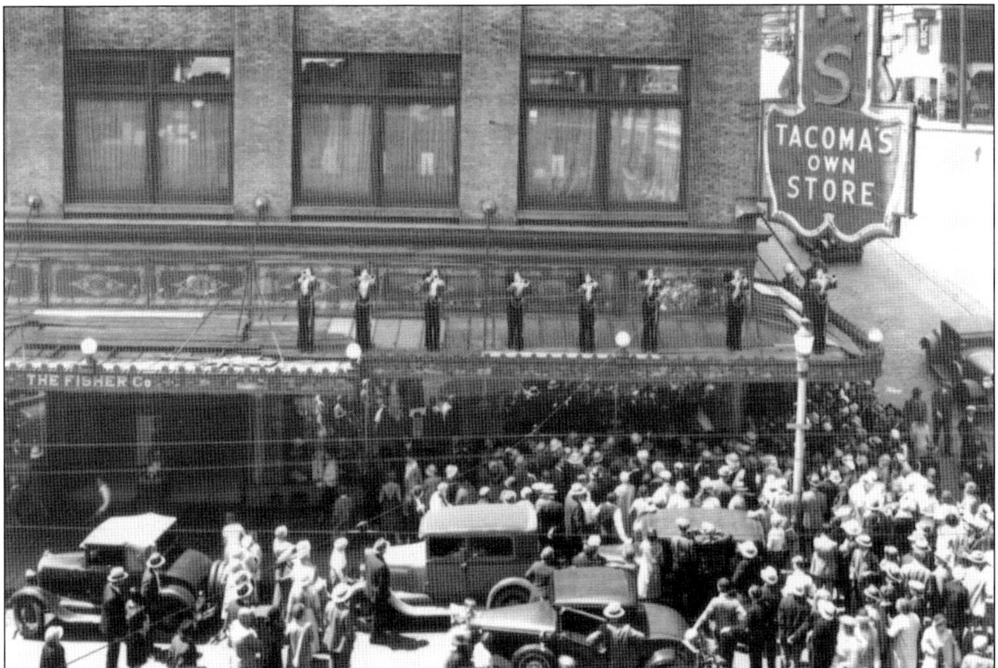

A crowd gathers outside Fisher's department store, 1104 Broadway, in June 1931. A vaudeville act was in the street-level display window, and young women in matching costumes are stand atop the store's awning, holding trumpets. The photograph was taken for the Broadway Theater. (Courtesy of the Tacoma Public Library.)

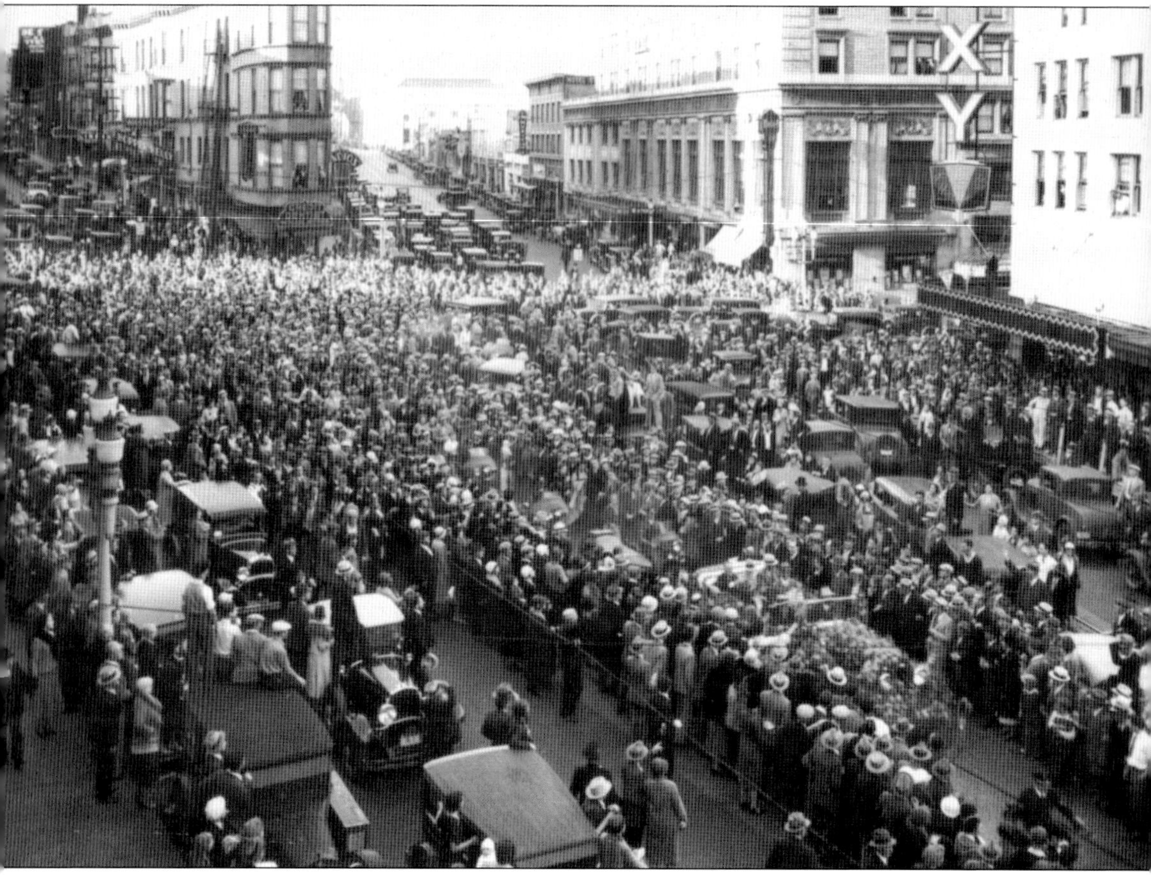

Thousands gather at Ninth Street and Broadway to catch a glimpse of presidential candidate Franklin Delano Roosevelt as his motorcade passes through downtown Tacoma on September 20, 1932. The candidate's open vehicle (bottom right) is led and followed by police officers on motorcycles. Roosevelt, then governor of New York, had just delivered a speech to thousands at the Puyallup Fairgrounds. According to newspaper reports of the event, Roosevelt's motorcade arrived in Tacoma about 30 minutes earlier than expected, so hundreds of people missed their chance to see him. In addition to the crowds at street level, several people have climbed on top of cars seeking a better view. There are also many looking out of windows of neighboring buildings: the Brant Hotel in the Bostwick Building at left, the Hotel Winthrop right of center, and the Roxy Theater at right. (Courtesy of the Tacoma Public Library.)

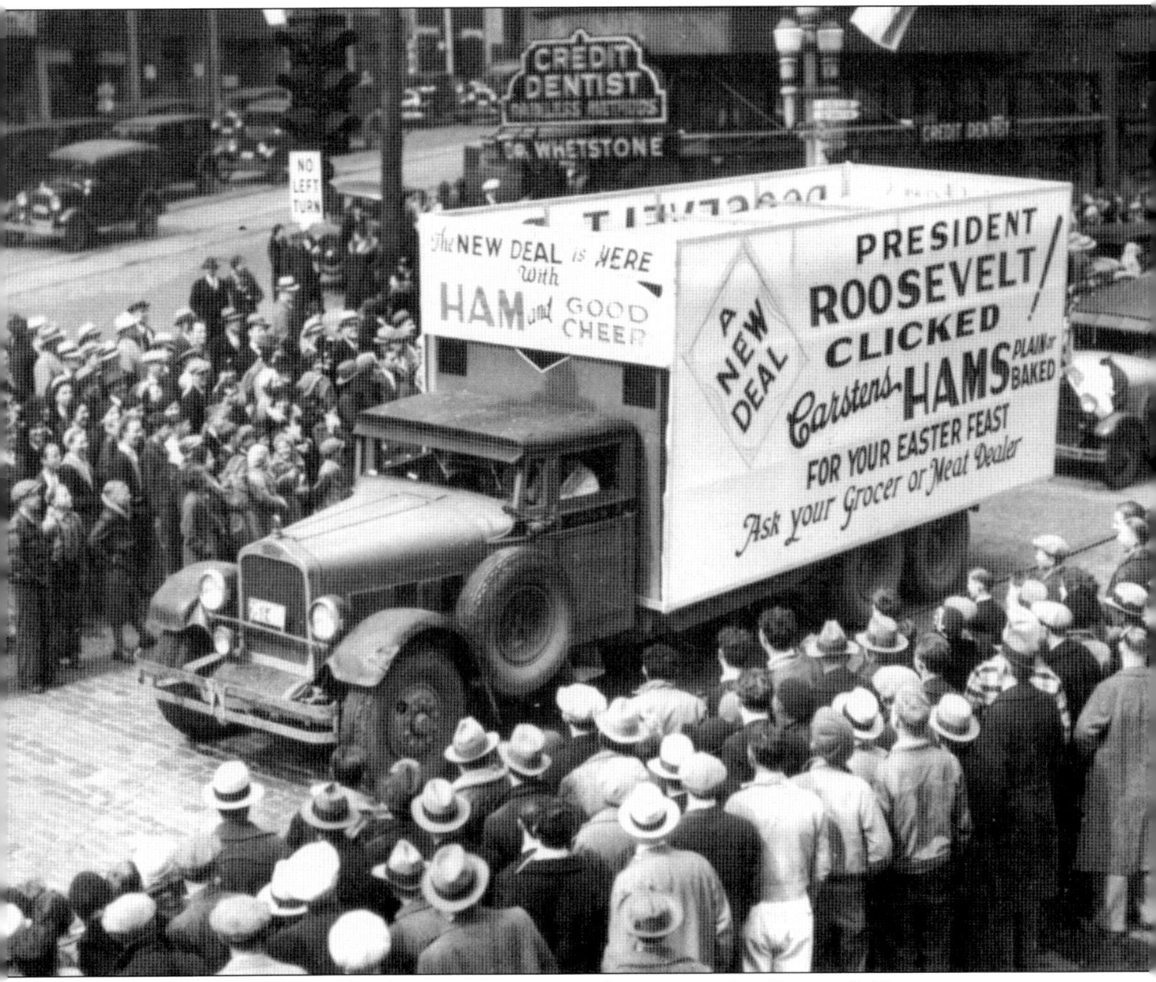

April 8, 1933, was declared by the Tacoma mayor and city council as Roosevelt Day in recognition of the new president's leadership during a time of economic crisis. Roosevelt was honored with a large downtown parade that included participation from the military, local businesses, and civic groups. Citizens are lined up several rows deep along the parade route, which here is passing by Dr. Whetstone's dental clinic in the Bostwick Building on the corner of Ninth Street and Broadway. Carstens, a large meat-packing firm in Tacoma, took advantage of the event to advertise their products with a play on Roosevelt's New Deal slogan: "The New Deal is here with Ham and Good Cheer." Easter was just over a week away, and Carstens was promoting their hams as an economical choice for a traditional Easter dinner. (Courtesy of the Tacoma Public Library.)

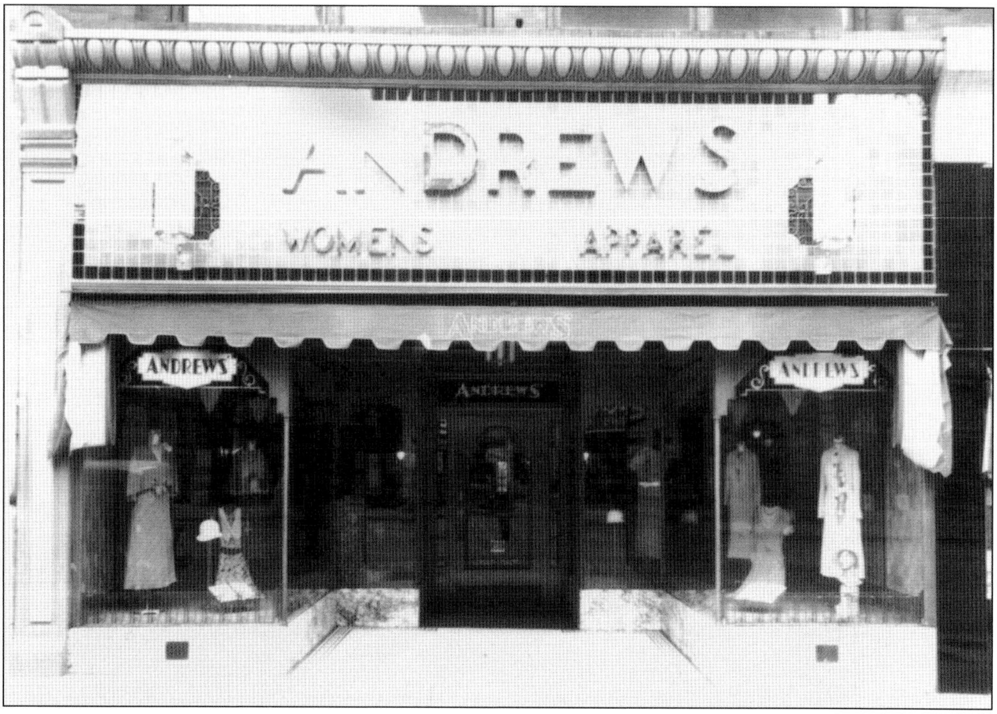

Andrews Women's Apparel opened in 1920 at 923 Broadway and is seen here in June 1932 after undergoing a major remodel in 1930. Owned and operated by Samuel A. Andrews, the store focused on dresses, suits, and hats for a discerning clientele. (Courtesy of the Tacoma Public Library.)

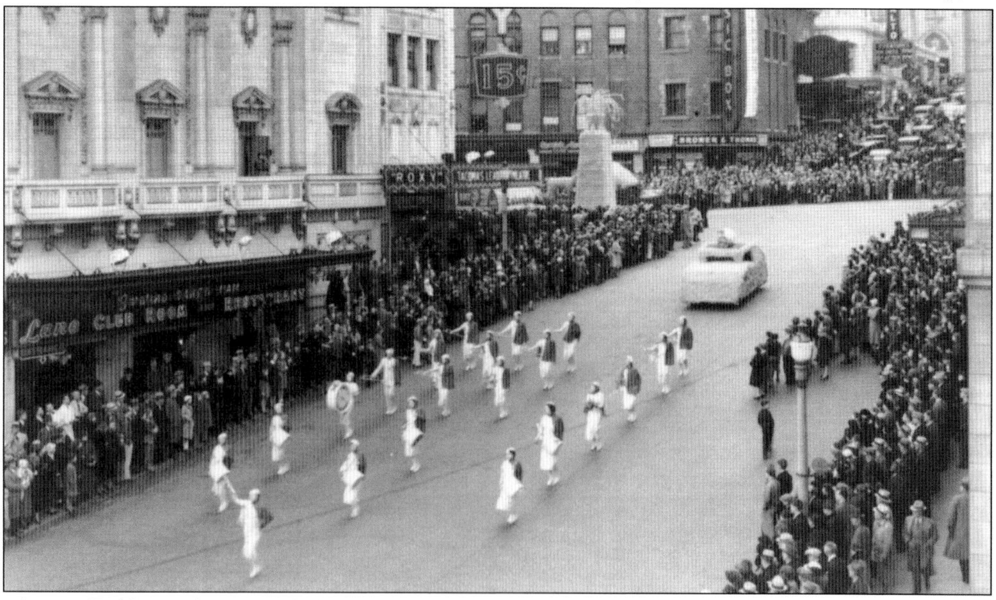

The Daffodil Parade proceeds down Ninth Street on March 23, 1935. The Roxy, Music Box, and Rialto Theaters provide a backdrop to the action. The Girls' Drum & Bugle Corps of the John R. Thompson Post of the United Spanish War Veterans is followed by daffodil-covered vehicle. Also visible, just below the Roxy marquee, is the 25-foot daffodil fountain, the royal viewing stand. (Courtesy of the Tacoma Public Library.)

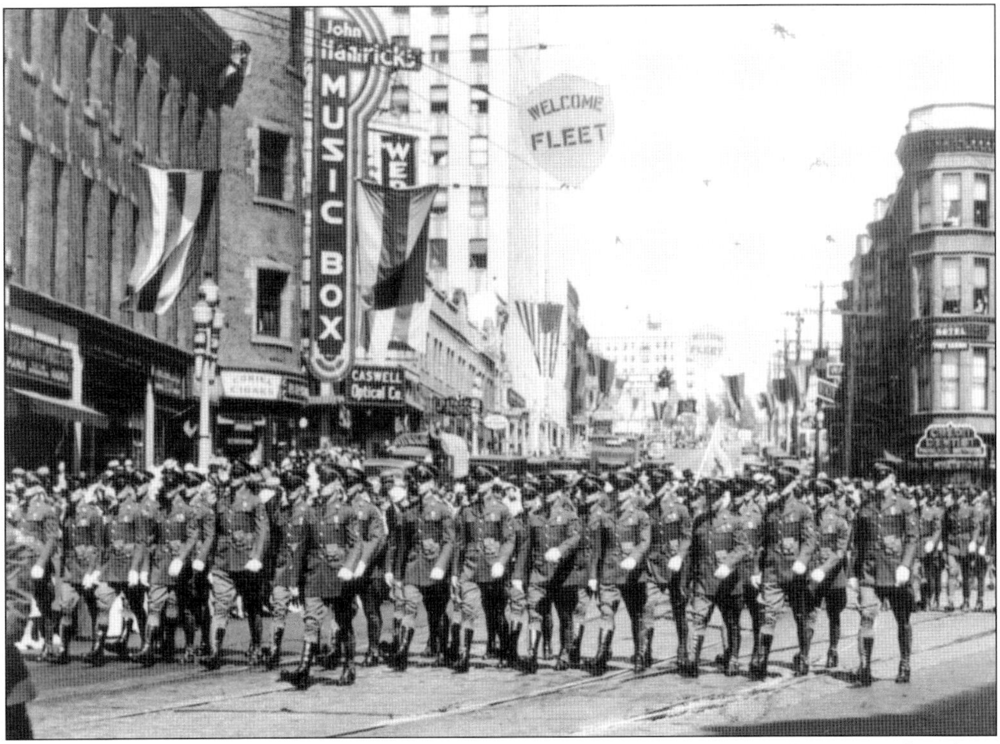

On July 18, 1935, thousands of Tacomans turned out for the Fleet Week military parade. There were 1,700 sailors and marines and 2,500 Fort Lewis soldiers, ROTC, and Citizens' Military Training Camp troops marching in the four-mile parade. A variety of flags, as well as signs reading, "Welcome Fleet," hang above the street. Reserve officers from Fort Lewis march down Broadway past the Bostwick Building (right) and the Music Box Theater (left). The reviewing stand for officials was set up just a bit farther down Broadway, in front of the Pay Less Drug Store. Tacoma mayor George Smitley is in the back row, second from left. Also on the stand are Adm. J.M. Reeves (far left), Brig. Gen. Otho B. Rosenbaum (second from the right), Brig. Gen. Charles M. Bundel, and Rear Adm. S.W. Bryant. (Both, courtesy of the Tacoma Public Library.)

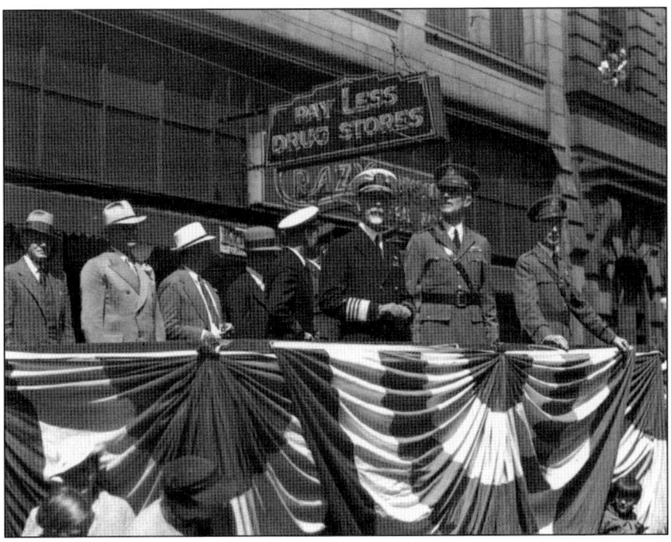

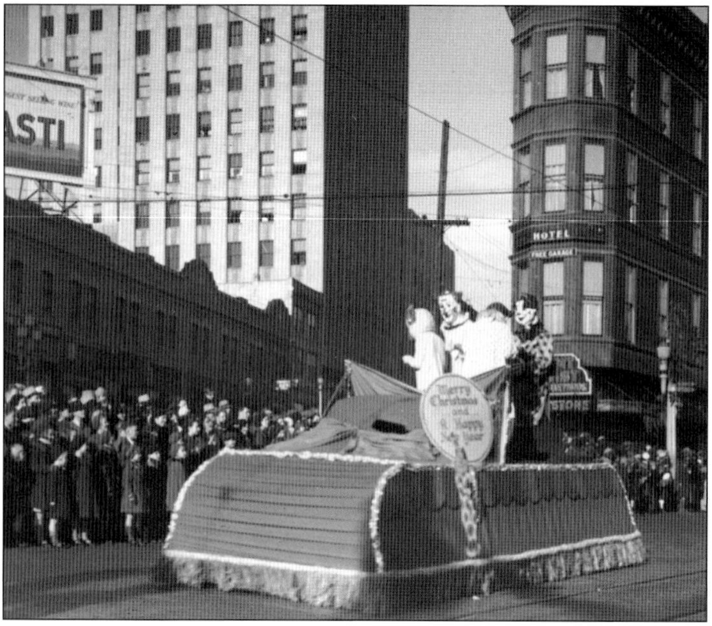

A crowd of spectators, including many young children, watch as a float passes through the intersection of Ninth Street and Broadway during the Fairyland and Christmas parade on the day after Thanksgiving, November 29, 1935. Four clowns are atop the float, which also includes a sign reading "Merry Christmas and a Happy New Year." (Courtesy of the Tacoma Public Library.)

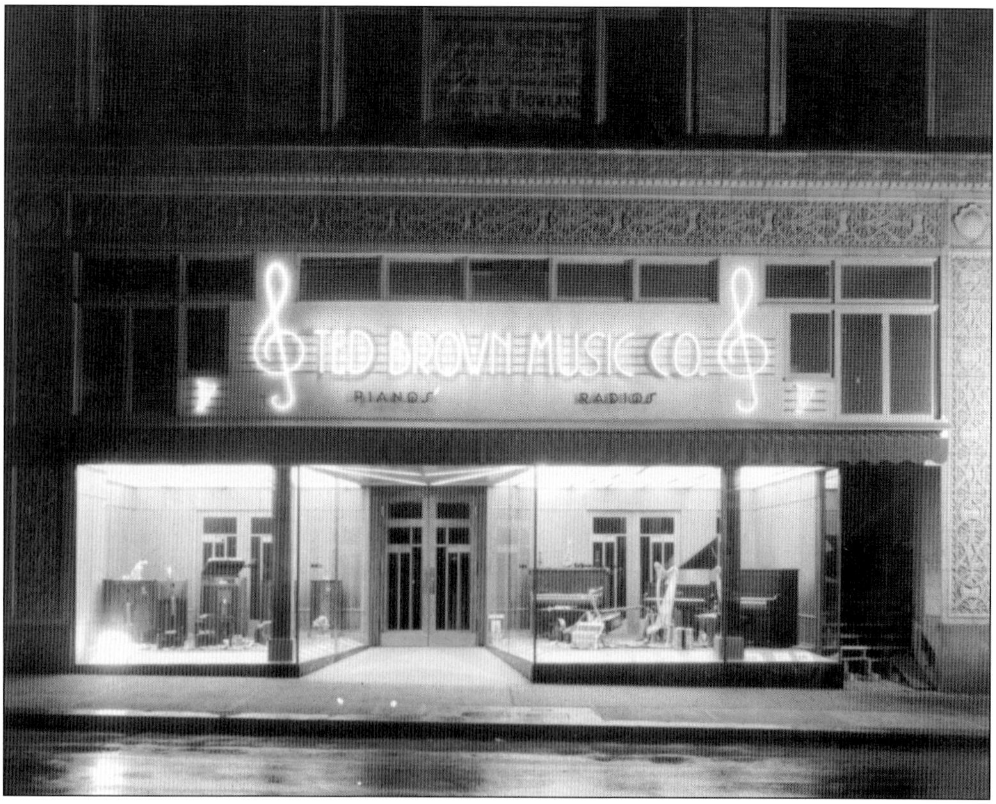

Ted Brown Music Company operated at this location on the 1100 block of Broadway from 1934 until leaving downtown in 2001. This photograph from 1935 reflects Ted Brown's early focus on pianos and radios, with several examples of each on view in the lighted storefront windows. (Courtesy of the Tacoma Public Library.)

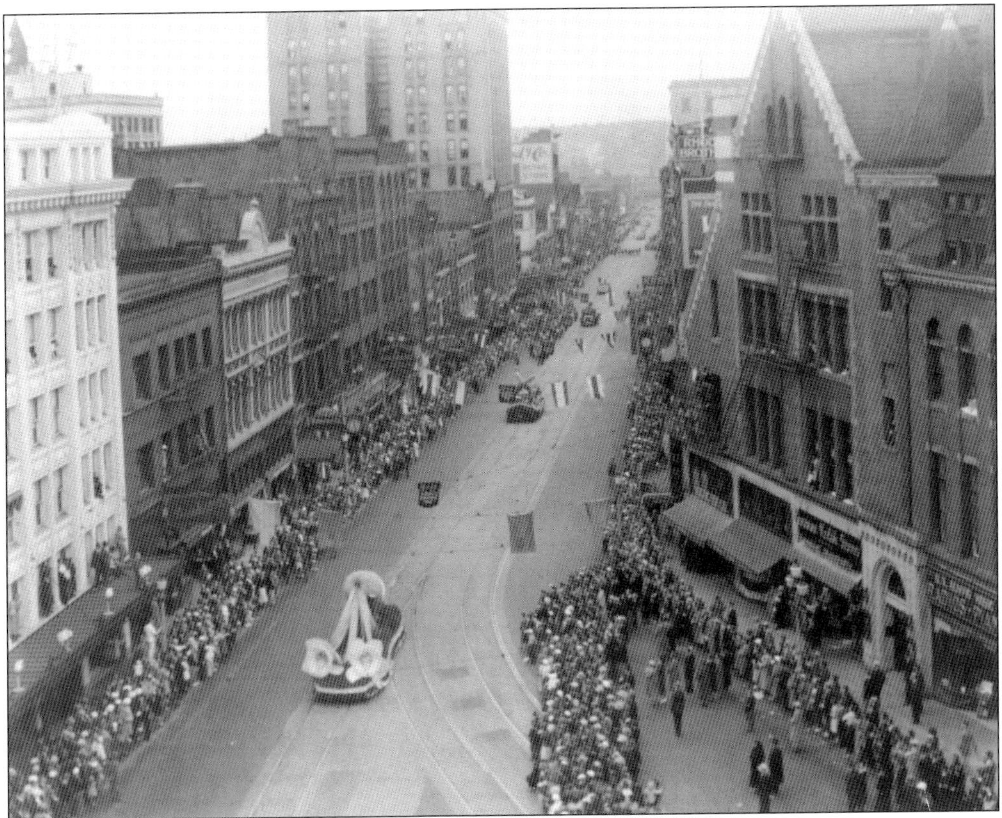

This photograph of the 1936 Daffodil Parade also provides an excellent view of the 900 block of Broadway as it appeared at the time. The chamber of commerce float, depicting oversized daffodils spilling out of a tipped vase, is in the lead. Thousands of people line Broadway for several blocks, and there are many people viewing the parade from windows of neighboring buildings. (Courtesy of the Tacoma Public Library.)

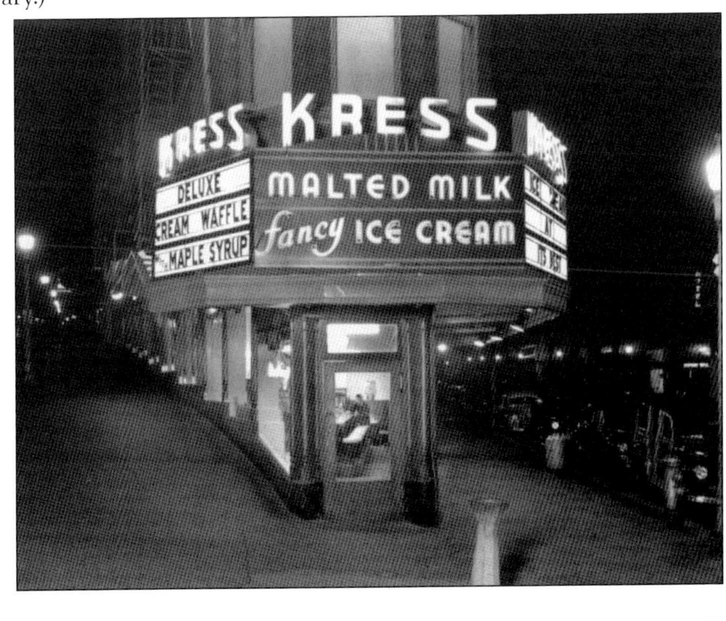

John "Lee" Kress opened this malt shop, his first in Tacoma, in the Bostwick Building at the corner of Ninth Street and Broadway in June 1937. Kress had already opened two ice cream shops in Olympia. The new Tacoma shop could seat 40 customers at the counter and in booths. (Courtesy of the Tacoma Public Library.)

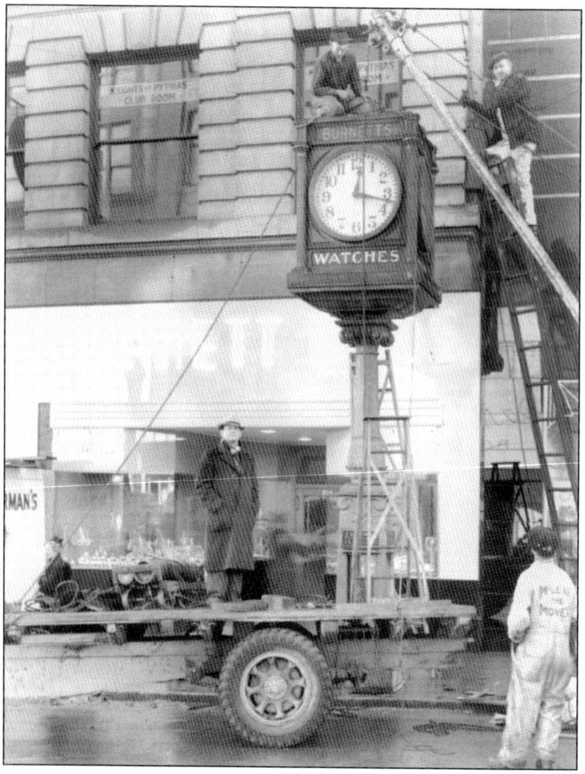

In February 1937, Burnett Brothers moved from 932 Broadway, where it had done business for more than 25 years, a few doors down to 924 Broadway. Owner L.H. "Louie" Burnett, standing on the truck bed, personally oversaw the move of the Burnett Brothers clock, while watch-repair specialist Fred E. Beckwith was also on hand to lend technical support. The clock weighed five tons and therefore required a large crew and specialized equipment to be moved. The new location called for a new neon sign, which can be seen glowing above the entrance. The interior view shows glass display cases with walnut finish resting on marble bases. The walls and ceiling are primarily white but with hand-painted accents. (Both, courtesy of the Tacoma Public Library.)

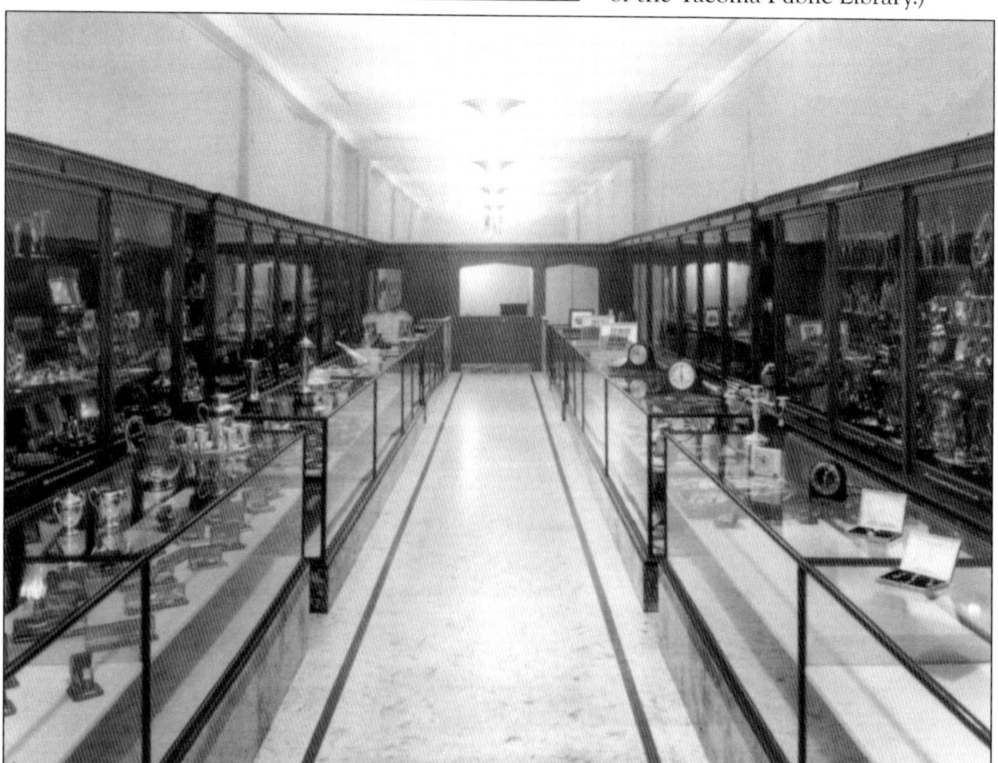

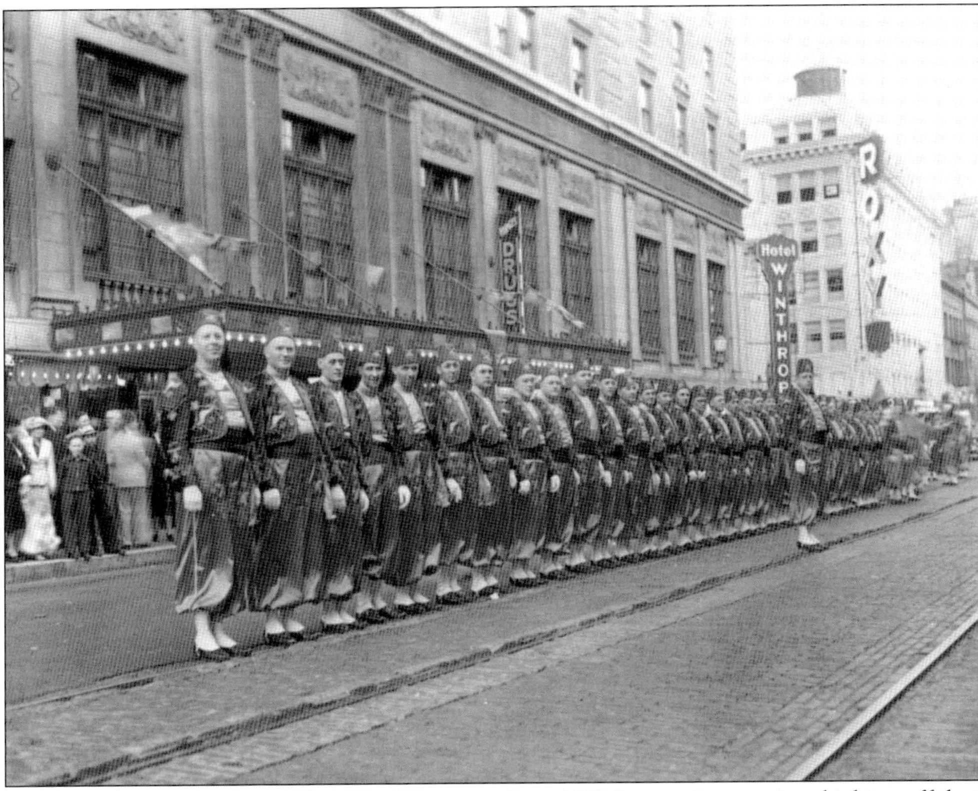

More than 1,000 Shriners gathered in Tacoma in June 1937 for a spring reunion, kicking off their gathering with a parade. Here, a long line of Shriners wait behind their drill leader for the parade to begin. The Hotel Winthrop provides a backdrop for the row of men, while the Roxy Theater features prominently in the background. (Courtesy of the Tacoma Public Library.)

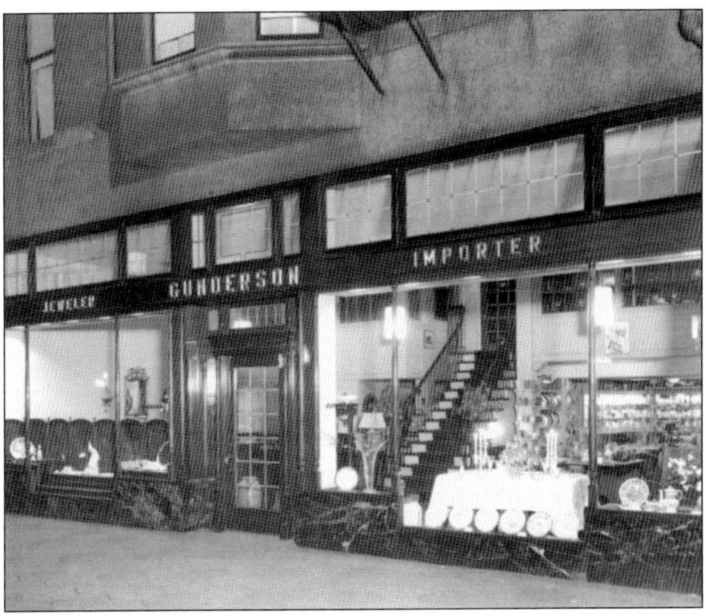

Gunderson's Jewelers, seen here in a photograph from March 1938, was a presence in the theater district for more than 60 years. This particular location, at 764 Broadway in the Bostwick Building, opened in 1937; it provided frontage on both St. Helens Avenue and Broadway and offered enough space for several departments, including a silver room. (Courtesy of the Tacoma Public Library.)

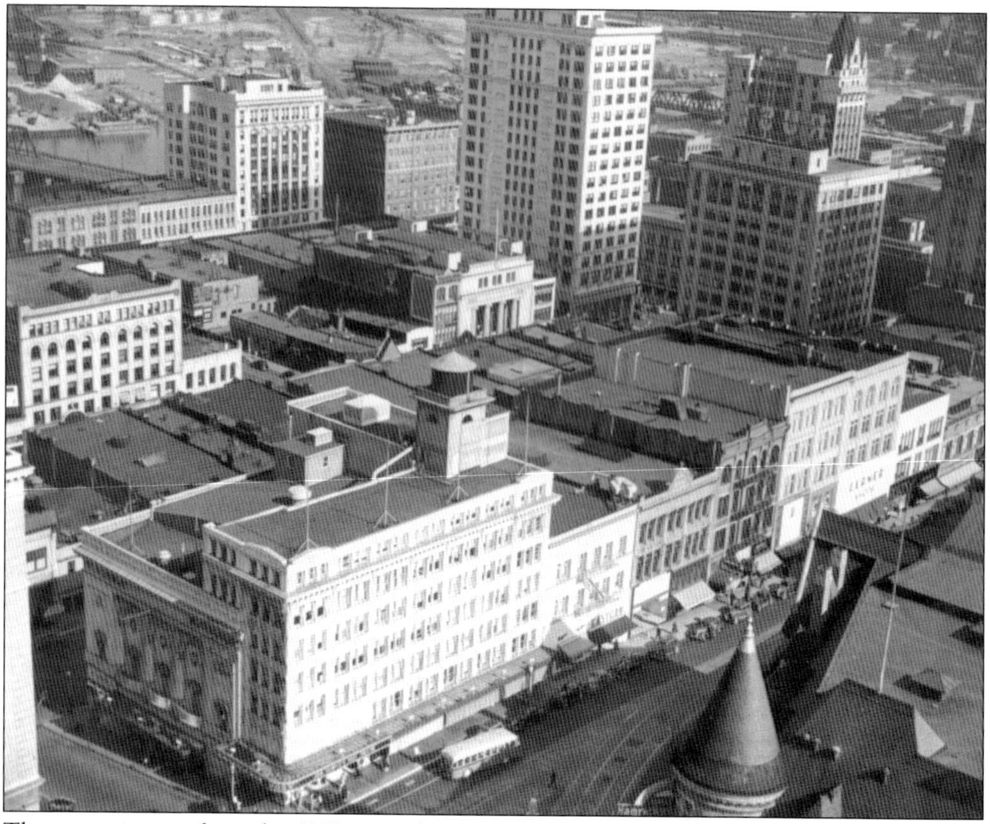

These two images from the 1930s provide an excellent view of the heart of the theater district at Ninth Street and Broadway in the context of the larger downtown Tacoma area. Both images were taken from the Medical Arts Building (747 Market). The daytime image, captured in May 1939, provides an excellent view of the Roxy (formerly Pantages) Theater at lower left, as well as the distinctive turret of the Music Box Theater at lower right. Also visible are several tall office buildings, bridges over the Thea Foss Waterway, and the Tideflats industrial area in the distance. The image captured after dark in about 1931 from a nearly identical angle puts the lights of the theater marquees and surrounding storefronts at center stage. (Both, courtesy of the Tacoma Public Library.)

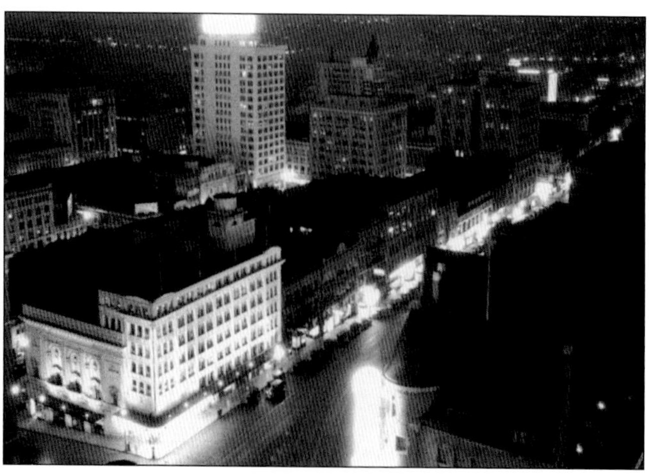

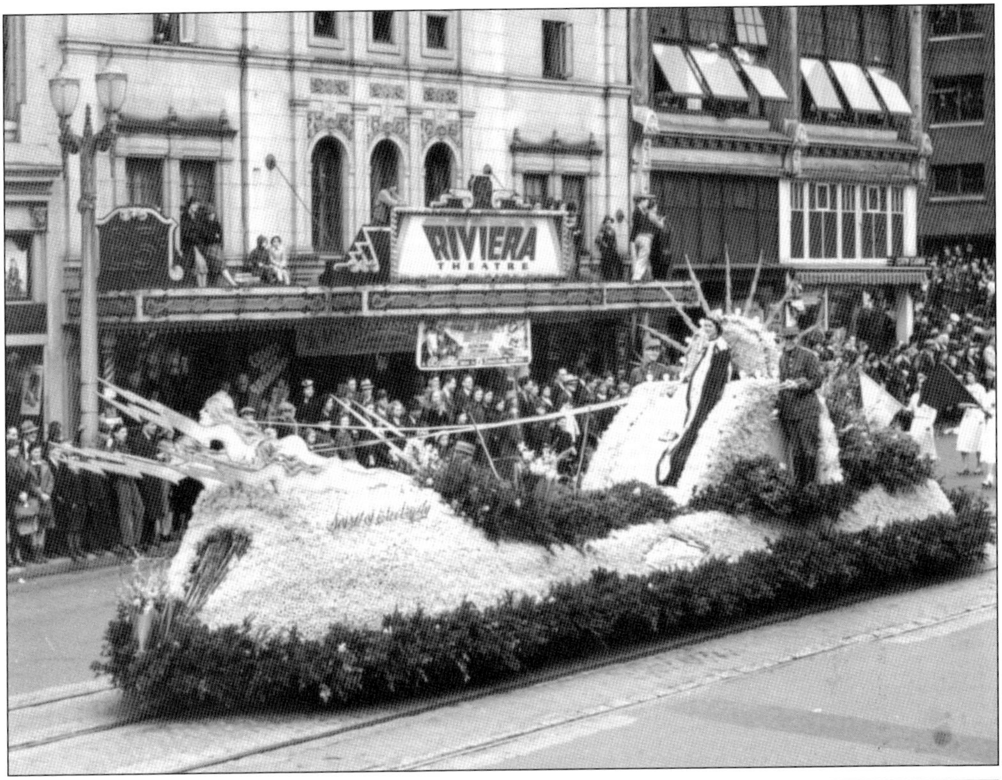

During the sixth annual Daffodil Parade on April 1, 1939, the "Spirit of Electricity" float moves past the Riviera Theater (or Theatre, as seen on the sign) at 906–908 Pacific Avenue. Hundreds of spectators line the streets, and several people—adults and children alike—have chosen the Riviera's marquee as a good vantage point for watching the parade. (Courtesy of the Tacoma Public Library.)

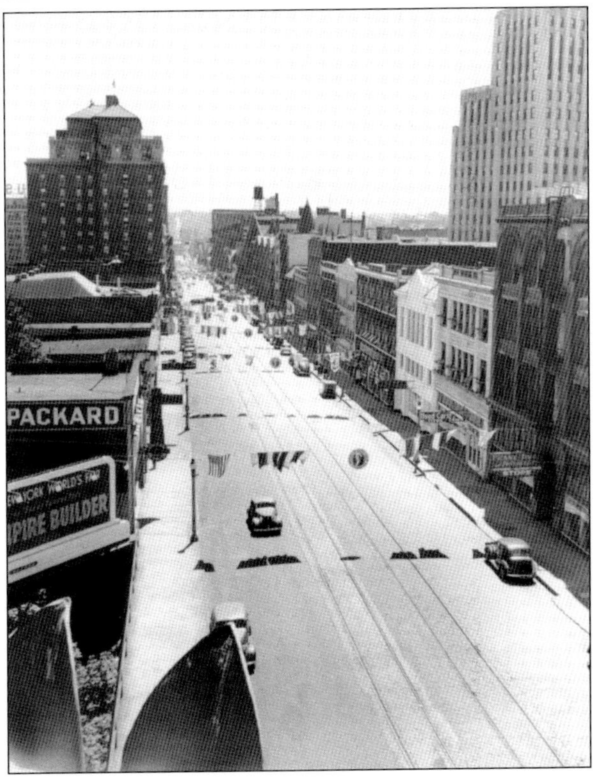

In July 1939, several blocks of Broadway were decorated with flags and banners in celebration of Washington State's 50th anniversary of statehood. This photograph of the 700 block of Broadway, with its many new and used car dealerships, was taken on July 22, the same day that a golden-jubilee parade was held. (Courtesy of the Tacoma Public Library.)

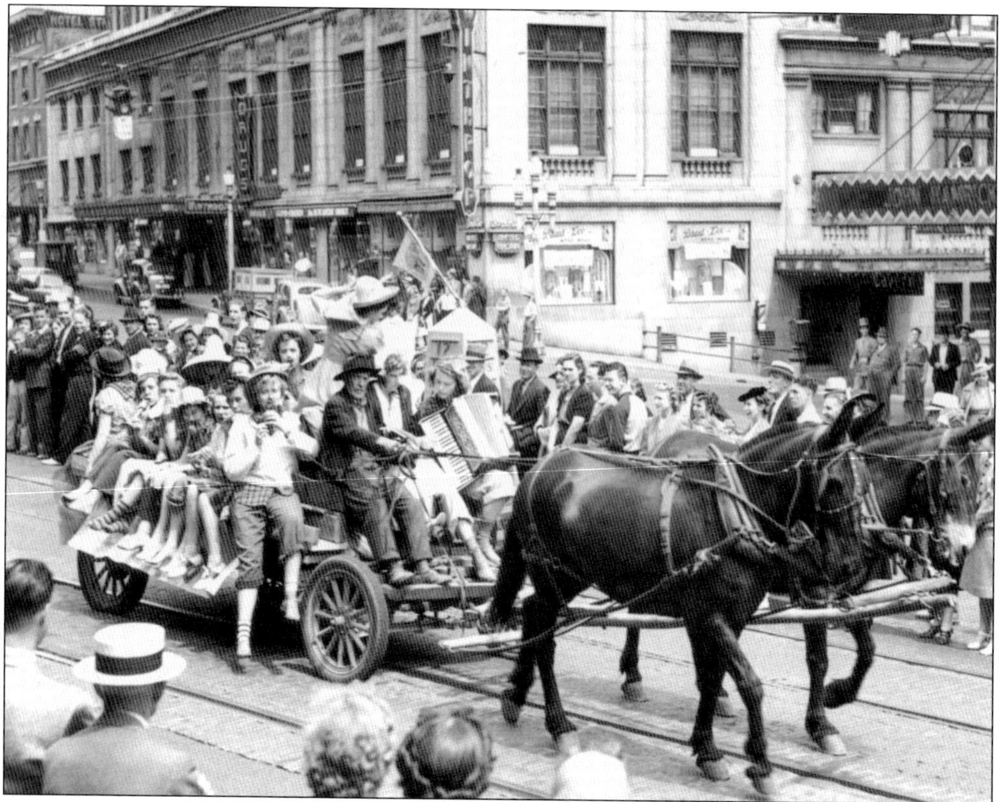

Nearly 1,200 representatives of the Rainbow Girls from around Washington met in Tacoma in July 1939 for their 13th annual Grand Assembly. On July 13, members met at the Masonic temple (47 St. Helens Avenue) and marched down St. Helens Avenue to Broadway. As these two photographs reveal, the parade included formal elements such as a group of Rainbow Girls in uniforms marching, as well as more casual elements, such as the group riding on a horse-drawn vehicle. The gathering concluded three days later with a picnic at Point Defiance Park. The Rainbow organization was founded in 1922 for young women whose fathers were members of the Masonic lodge and their friends. (Both, courtesy of the Tacoma Public Library.)

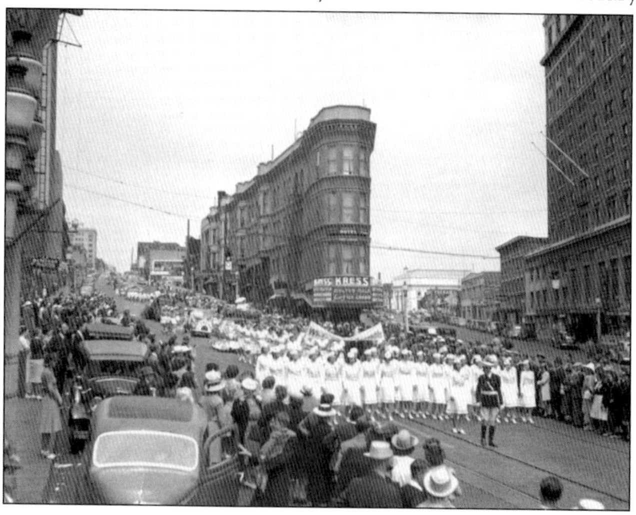

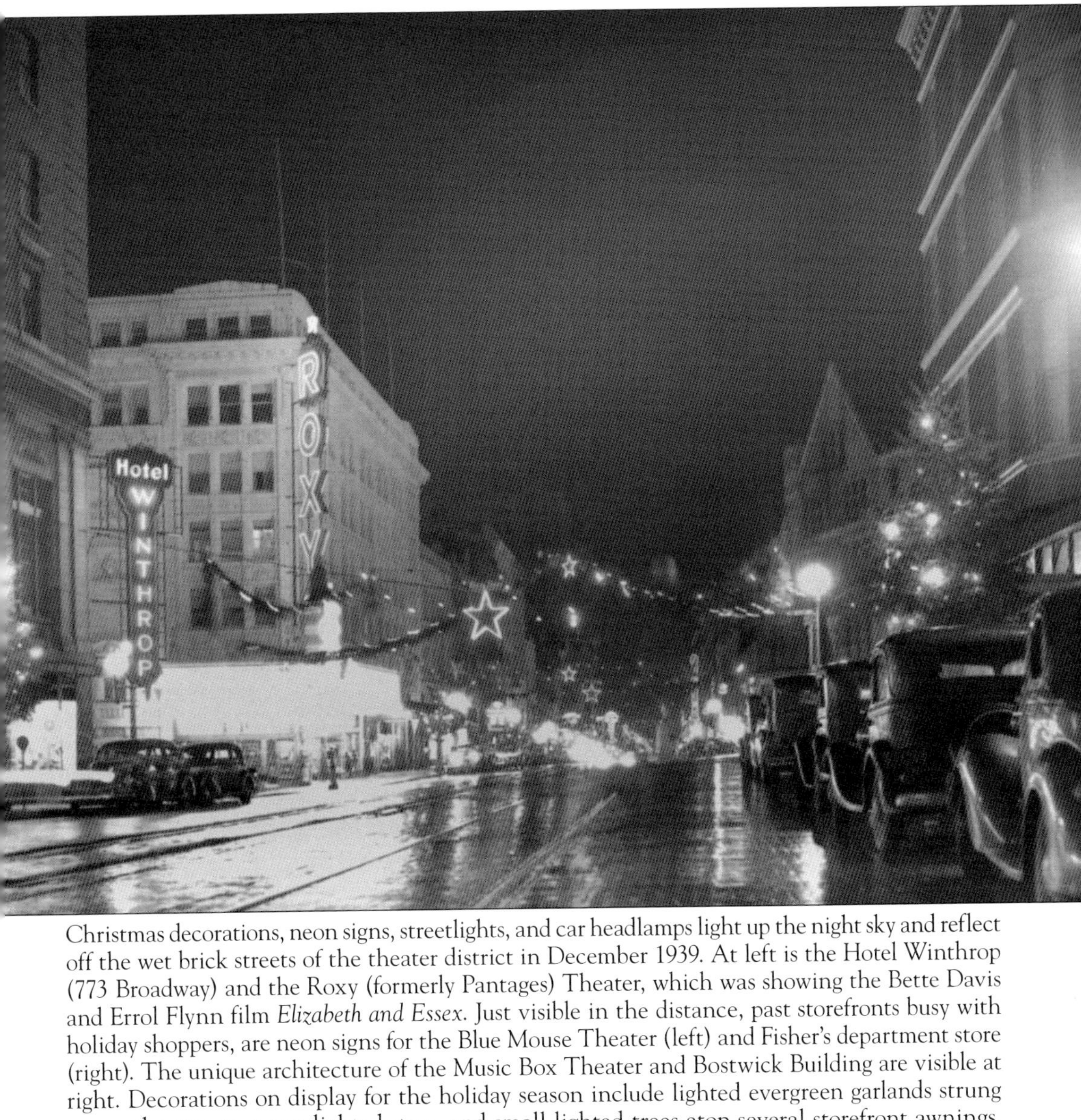

Christmas decorations, neon signs, streetlights, and car headlamps light up the night sky and reflect off the wet brick streets of the theater district in December 1939. At left is the Hotel Winthrop (773 Broadway) and the Roxy (formerly Pantages) Theater, which was showing the Bette Davis and Errol Flynn film *Elizabeth and Essex*. Just visible in the distance, past storefronts busy with holiday shoppers, are neon signs for the Blue Mouse Theater (left) and Fisher's department store (right). The unique architecture of the Music Box Theater and Bostwick Building are visible at right. Decorations on display for the holiday season include lighted evergreen garlands strung across the streets, many lighted stars, and small lighted trees atop several storefront awnings. (Courtesy of the Tacoma Public Library.)

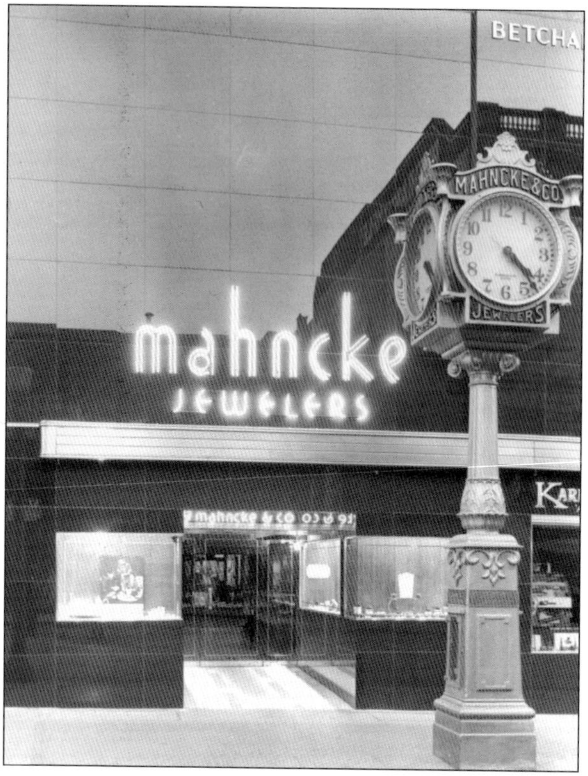

The Mahncke & Co. jewelry store (919 Broadway) was completely remodeled in early 1940, and these photographs of its exterior and interior were taken in May of that year to document the many updates. According to the newspaper reports of the time, every element of the store, save the large street clock, was given a completely new look. The entire facade was covered with wine-colored Carrara structural-glass tiles, which can be seen here reflecting the image of the Pythian temple from across Broadway. Employees pose amongst new wall cabinets and curved display cases. Frank Mahncke opened his first jewelry store in Tacoma in 1883, and the Mahncke store was taken over by Friedlanders in 1956. (Both, courtesy of the Tacoma Public Library.)

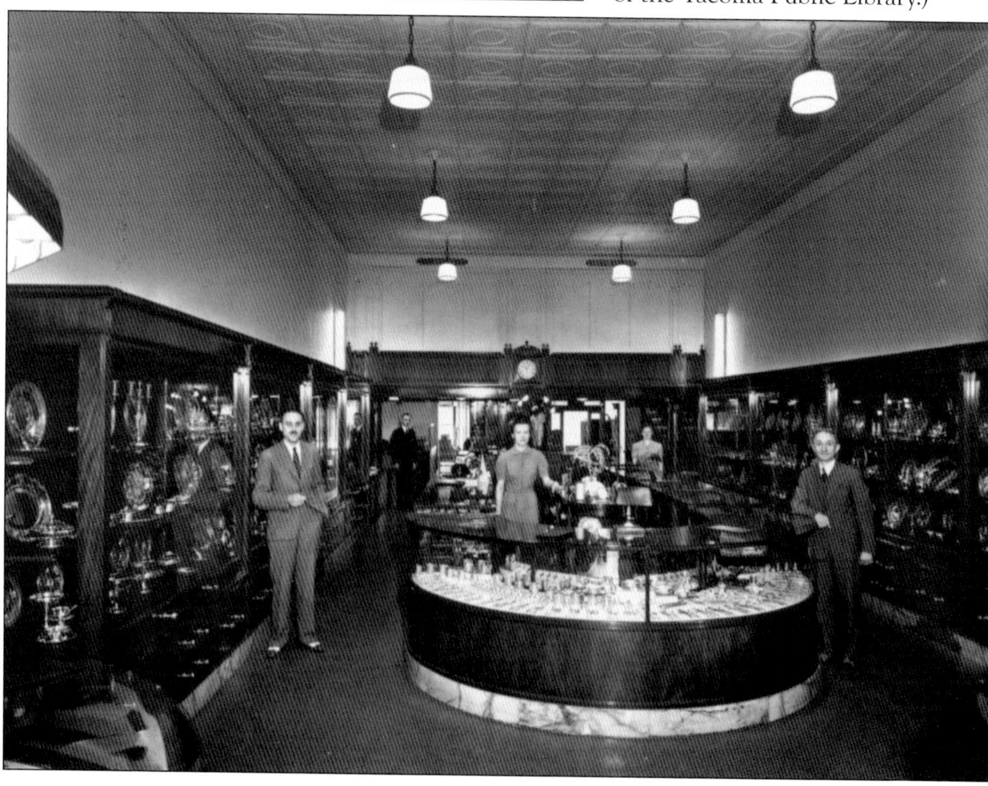

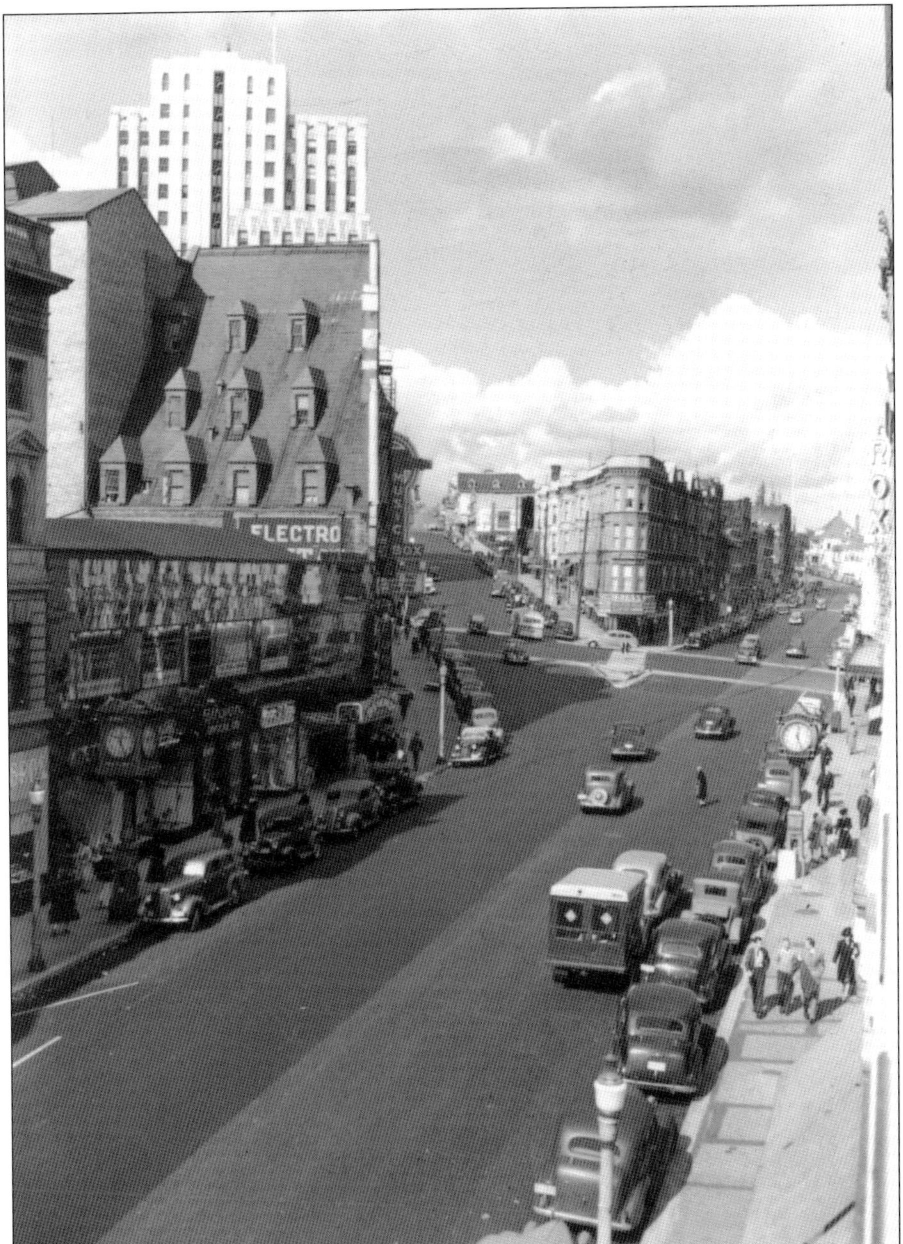

This view from 1940, looking northwest down the 900 block of Broadway, shows newly paved streets following the removal of streetcar lines. At far left is the Pythian temple (924–926 Broadway), the recently refaced Beverly Theater (916–918 Broadway), and the Music Box Theater, which was advertising *Boom Town*, starring Clark Gable and Spencer Tracy. The upper floors of the Medical Arts Building (747 Market) can be seen behind the multi-dormered roof of the Music Box. The distinctive Bostwick Building is at the center, as Broadway continues to the right and St. Helens Avenue up the hill to the left. The Roxy Theater sign is at far right. Although much about this view is similar to what would have been seen a few years earlier, the removal of the streetcar lines and replacement of brick streets with concrete are significant signs of changing times. (Courtesy of the Tacoma Public Library.)

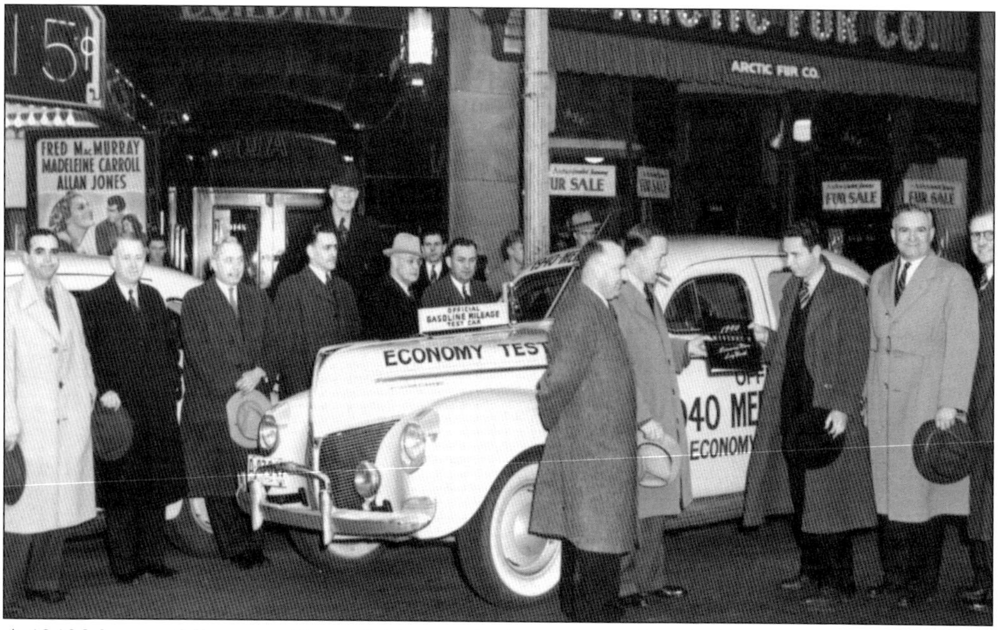

A 1940 Mercury-8 Economy Test vehicle is parked outside the Beverly Theater (914 Broadway) on January 5, 1940. The vehicle's run would cover 5,000 miles of roads in Washington and Oregon. J.J. Jaeger, second from left in front of the automobile, presents the logbook of the car's mileage to Bill Leith of the *Tacoma Times*, as representatives of local car dealerships look on. (Courtesy of the Tacoma Public Library.)

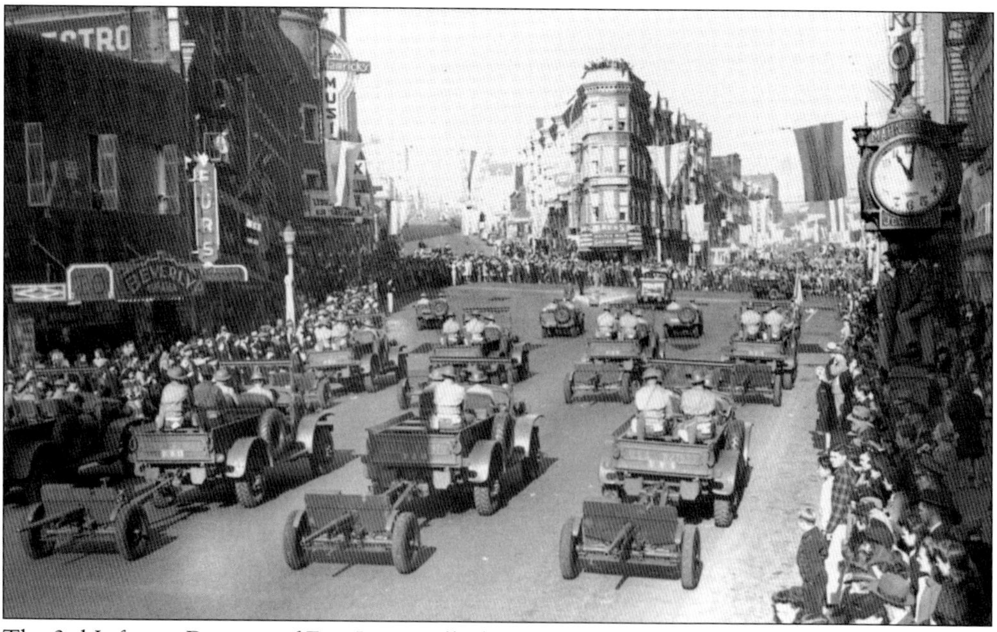

The 3rd Infantry Division of Fort Lewis rolls down Broadway past the Beverly, Music Box, and Roxy Theaters during a large military parade on October 30, 1941. Several hundred spectators, including many school-age children, line the streets to observe the festivities. The wartime film *Tanks a Million* is advertised on the marquee of the Music Box. (Courtesy of the Tacoma Public Library.)

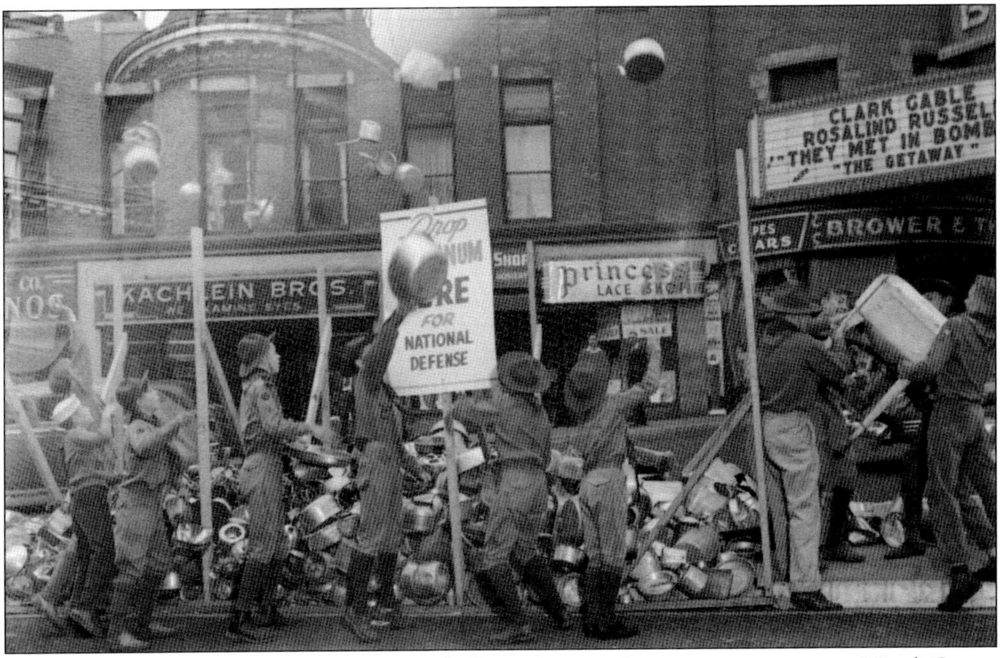

On July 23, 1941, a collection drive "corral" for gathering aluminum was set up at Ninth Street and Broadway; the metal was needed to build bombers for the Army Air Corp. The Boy Scouts of Troop 42, from the Larchmont area of southeast Tacoma, came downtown to contribute 135 pieces of scrap aluminum they had collected. Cole E. Oliver, owner of Oliver Taxi and Ambulance Company, also contributed, donating one of his company's ambulance vehicles, a Pierce-Arrow, which was made almost entirely of aluminum. Pictured around the vehicle, from left to right, are Oliver, Tommy Burns, Kenny Johnson, William Erickson, police officer Ross Mowre, and Russell Anderson, who was chairman of the aluminum drive. Anderson hoped to get 1,000 pounds of aluminum from the car. (Both, courtesy of the Tacoma Public Library.)

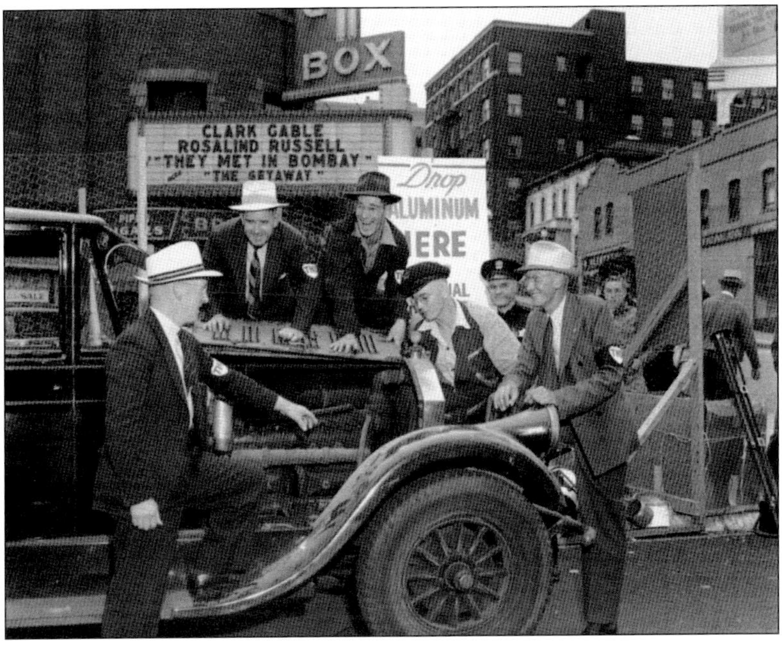

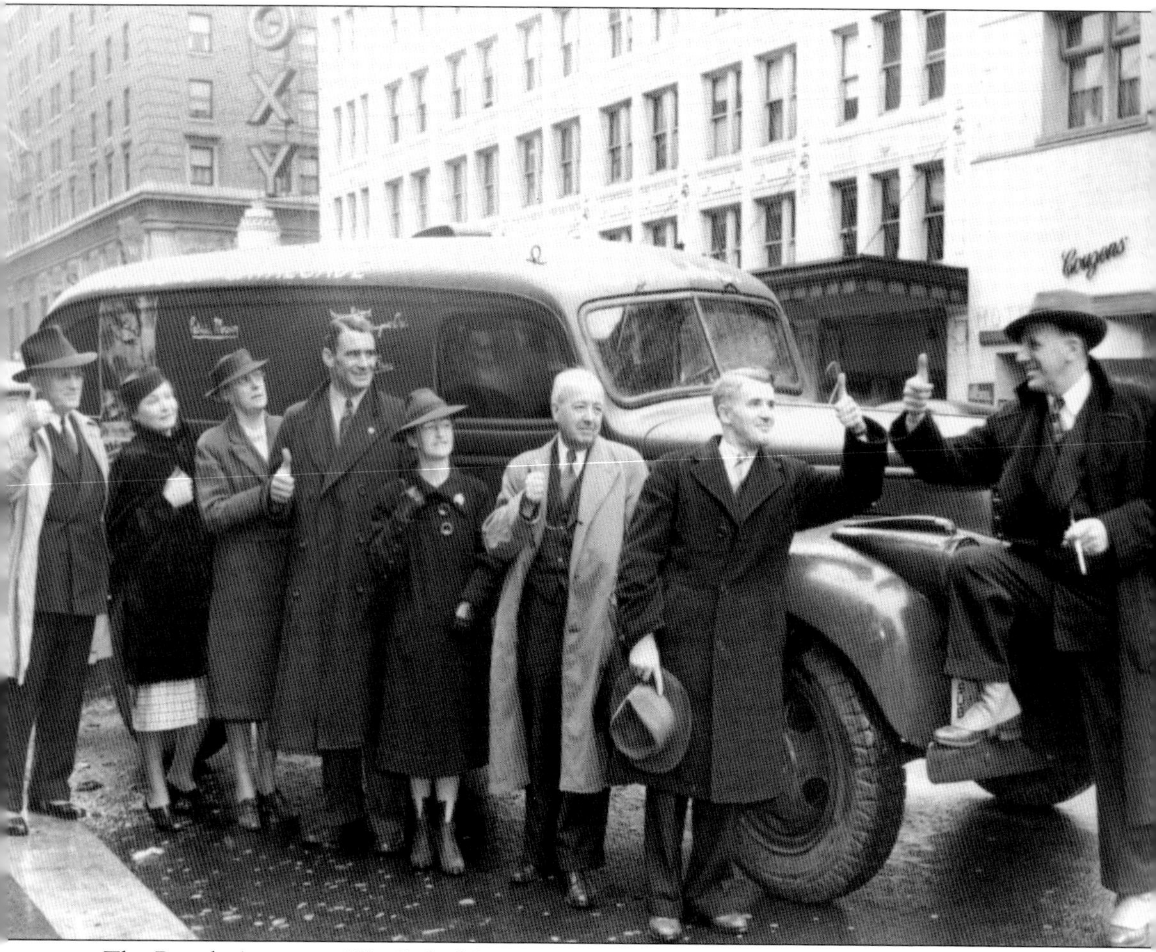

The British American War Relief Committee poses with a new ambulance in February 1941 outside their offices at 914 ½ Broadway. The Winthrop Hotel (left) and Roxy Theater (right) can be seen in the background. Doug Oldershaw, fourth from left, a professional football player with the New York Giants (1939–1941), was the driver of the ambulance as it traveled from Tacoma to San Francisco. The "Thumbs Up" Cavalcade of ambulances was on a three-month tour of the United States, with funds being raised during the tour to purchase airplane ambulances for the Royal Air Force. All five of the touring vehicles were driven by professional football players. After the tour, the ambulances were destined for service in Great Britain. (Courtesy of the Tacoma Public Library.)

Actress Lana Turner arrives at the Winthrop Hotel (773 Broadway) in a Titus Motor Company 1923 Lincoln Touring automobile during her June 1942 visit to Tacoma for a war bond rally. Mayor Harry P. Cain is standing between the actress and her mother in the rear of the vehicle. (Courtesy of the Tacoma Public Library.)

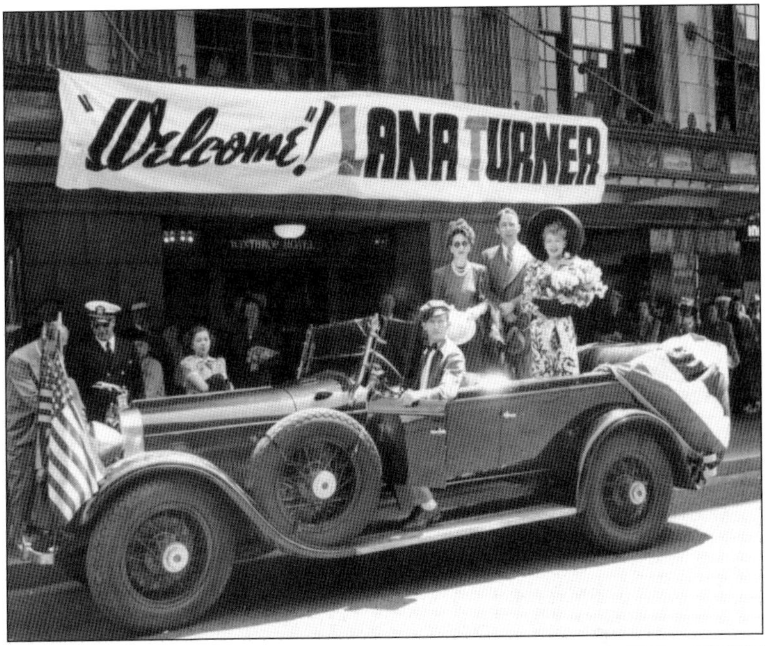

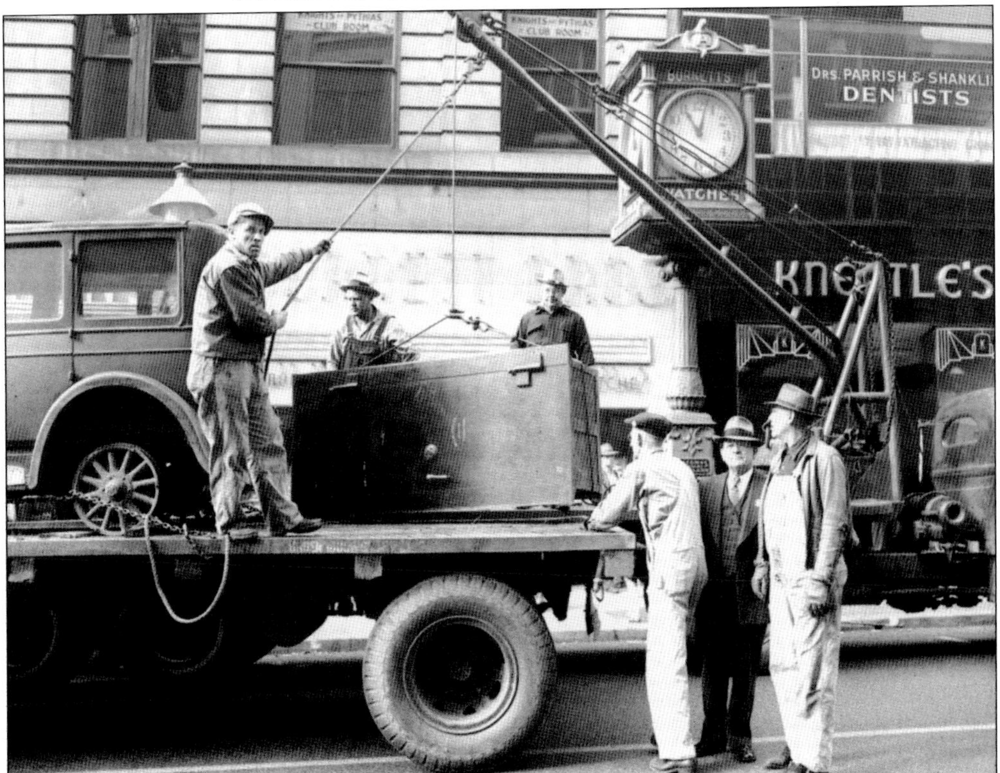

Scrap metal large and small was collected during a "Salvage for Victory" drive on November 1, 1942. One of the larger pieces was this 4,000-pound safe donated by Burnett Brothers Jewelers, which had seen 40 years of use in their business on Broadway. Over 2,000 tons, three times the expected amount, was collected in the drive. (Courtesy of the Tacoma Public Library.)

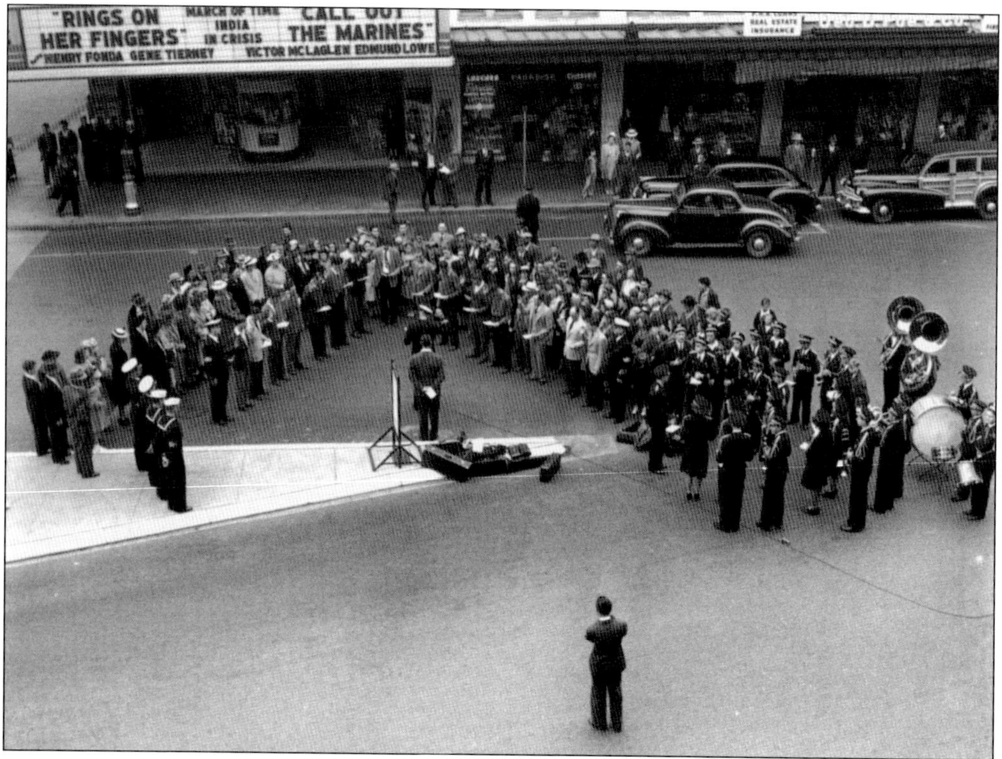

Several young men from around Tacoma and Pierce County were sworn into the US Navy at a special Avenge Pearl Harbor Day ceremony held on Sunday, June 7, 1942, at the corner of Ninth Street and Broadway. A military band was present for the formal ceremony, during which the participants were arranged in V-for-Victory formation. Following the event, the new recruits gather for a group photograph with a small child in a Navy uniform. The Roxy Theater, with wartime films and newsreels advertised on the marquee, provided a backdrop for the event. (Both, courtesy of the Tacoma Public Library.)

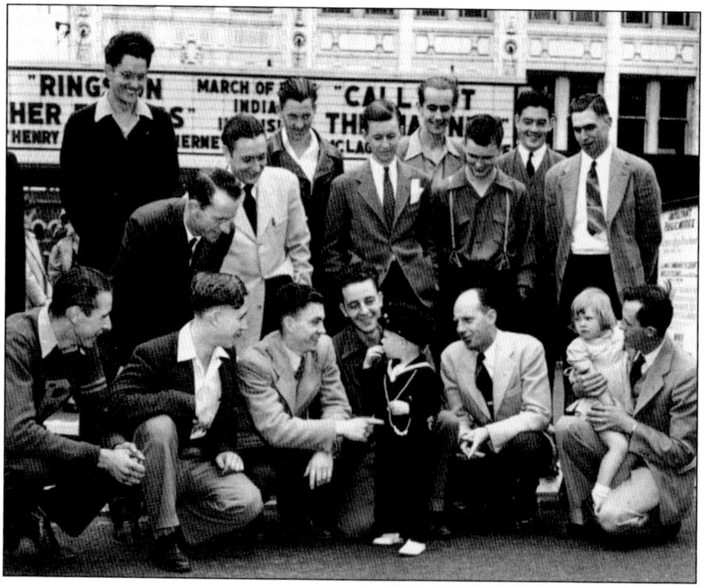

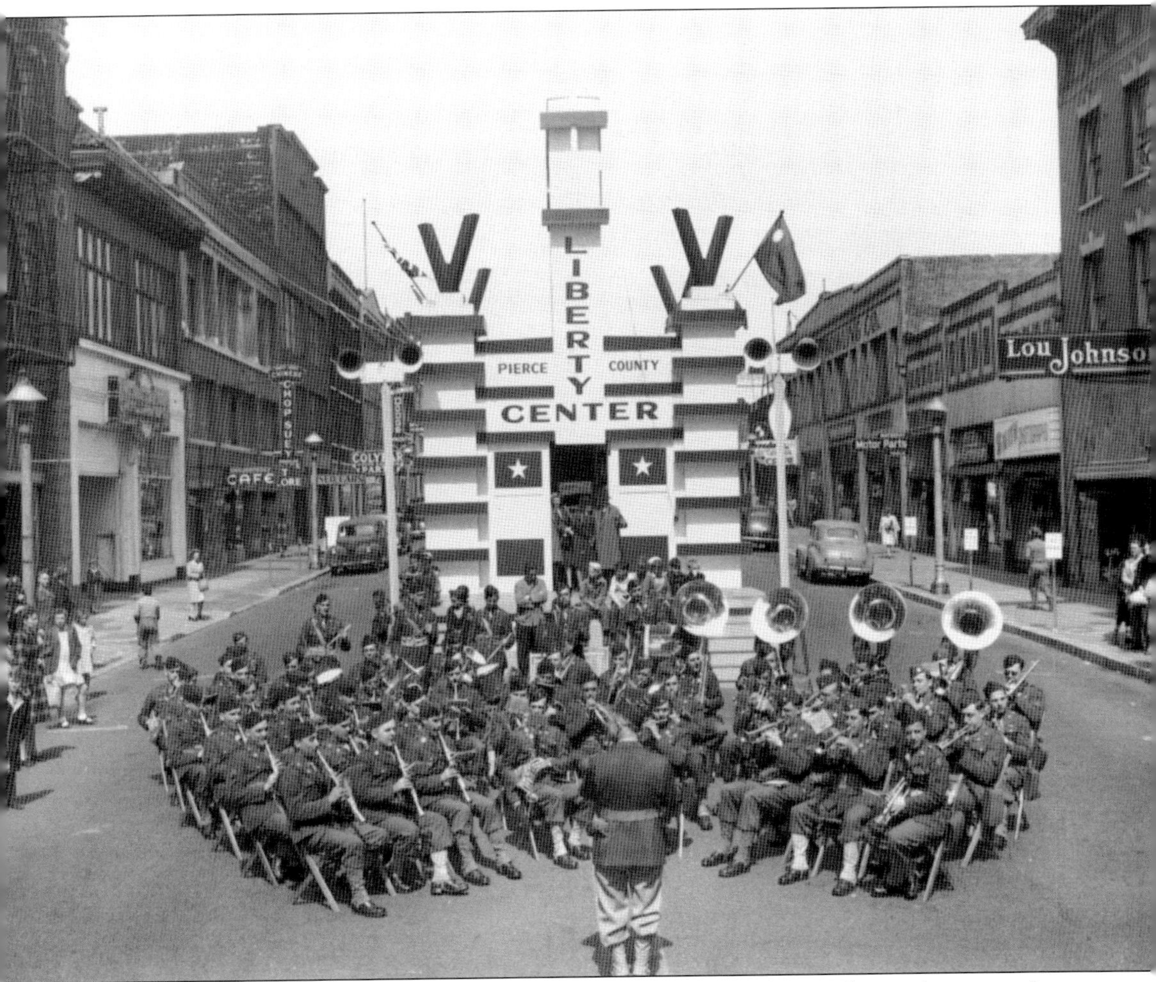

The Pierce County Liberty Center was first built in 1942 and moved twice during the war as the city tried to identify a central location for it that did not interfere with vital traffic. By 1943, the small building was located here, in the middle of Broadway just north of Ninth Street. In late April 1943, the citizens of Tacoma purchased $10,000 worth of war bonds at the center. During this huge bond sale, visitors were serenaded by two Fort Lewis bands, the artillery band under the leadership of chief warrant officer Joseph C. Hladik and the infantry band under the direction of warrant officer Seymour H. Magenheim. Broadway businesses visible in the background include several car dealerships and cafes as well as, at right, Lou Johnson (women's clothing), Smith Photographs, and the Broadway Bowling Co. (Courtesy of the Tacoma Public Library.)

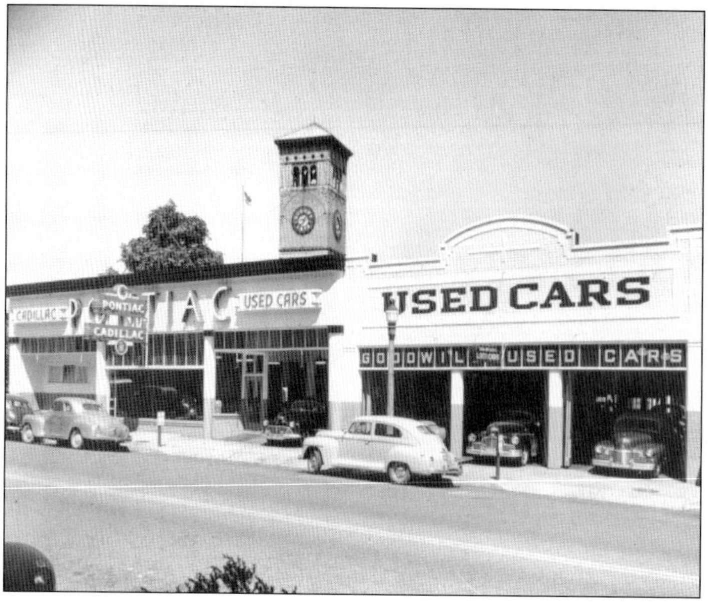

Tacoma Auto Sales Company, a dealer of Pontiac and Cadillac, was one of many automobile dealerships and garages on the 700 block of Broadway. In this photograph from July 11, 1947, the distinctive clock tower of the old city hall building can be seen in the background. (Courtesy of the Tacoma Public Library.)

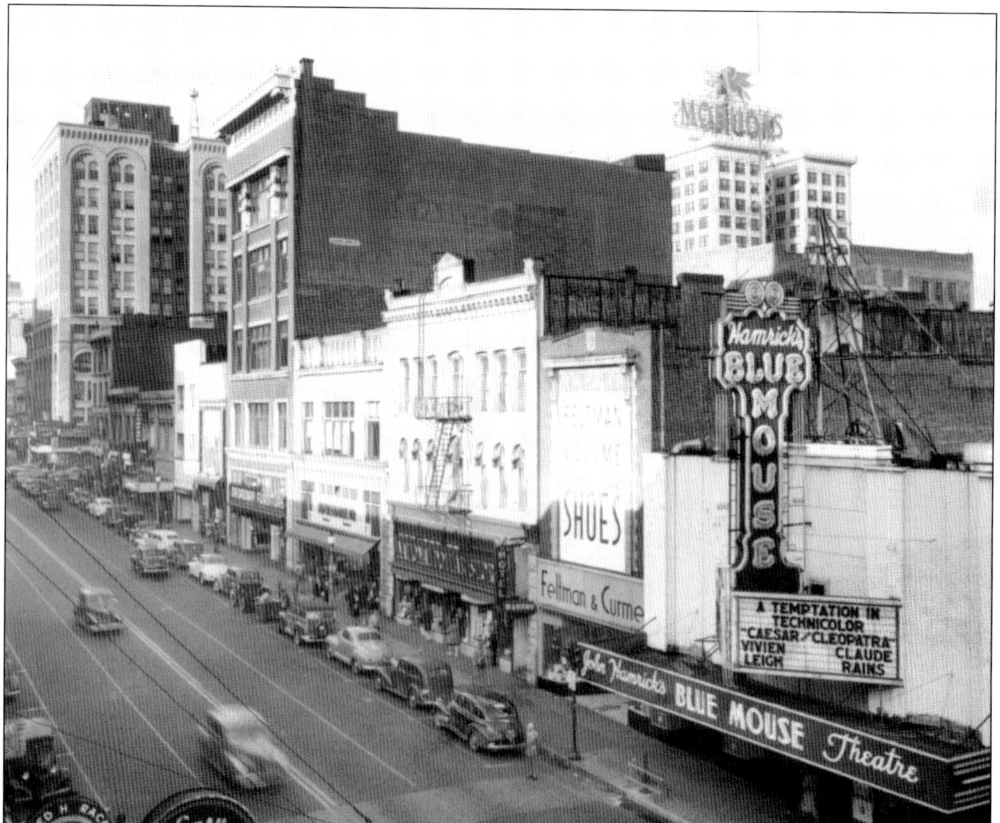

In October 1946, the 1100 block of Broadway was bustling with both car and foot traffic. The large marquee for Hamrick's Blue Mouse Theater is at right, and other businesses on the block include Feltman & Curme (shoes), National Dollar Store, Ted Brown Music Co., and Broadway Furniture. (Courtesy of the Tacoma Public Library.)

Four members of the Tacoma Boys Club were photographed on December 14, 1948, as they rehearsed Christmas songs for their upcoming performance as part of the *Tacoma Times*–sponsored Week of Music festival at Ninth Street and Broadway. More than 200 boys participated in the festive holiday event. (Courtesy of the Tacoma Public Library.)

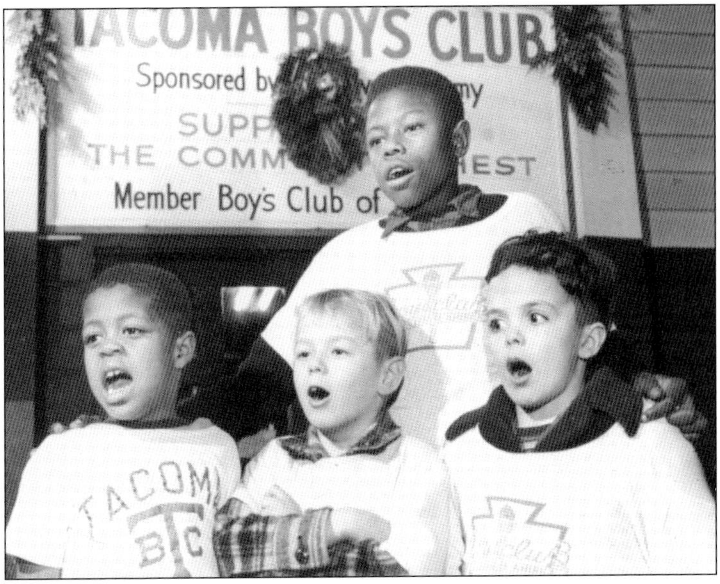

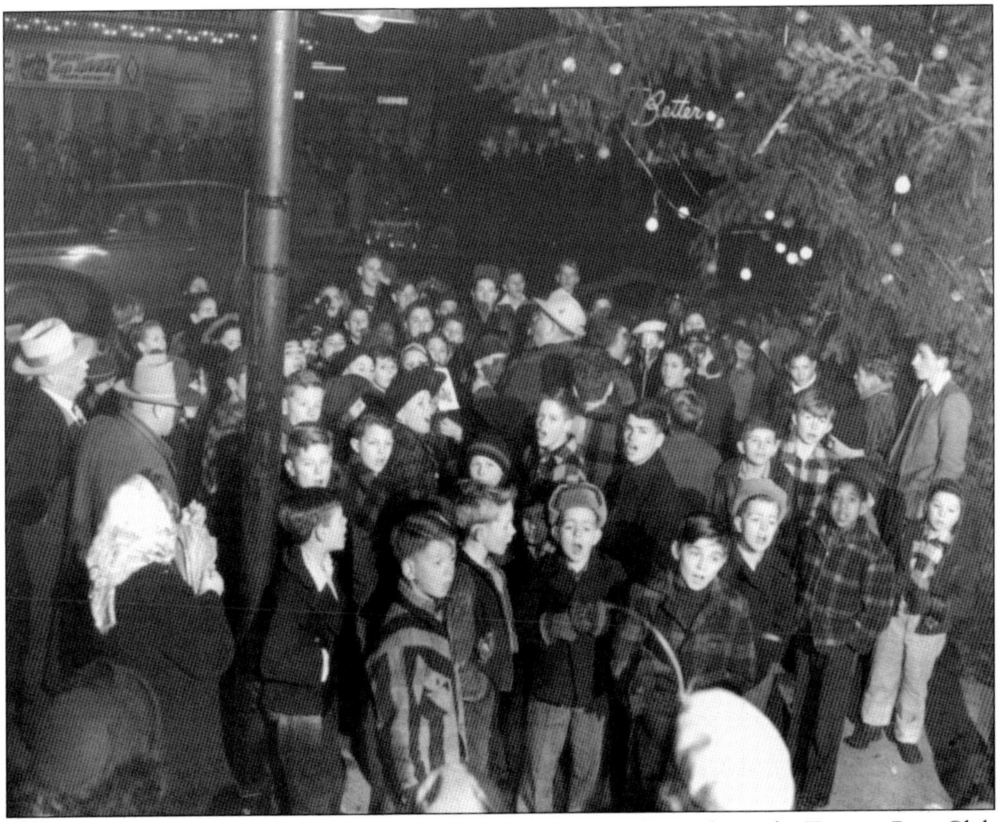

Under the City of Tacoma Christmas tree at Ninth Street and Broadway, the Tacoma Boys Club sang Christmas songs on December 23, 1948, the final evening of the *Tacoma Times*–sponsored Week of Music. The audience that gathered in front of the Roxy Theater (at left) was asked to join the boys in such songs as "Joy to the World" and "Jingle Bells." (Courtesy of the Tacoma Public Library.)

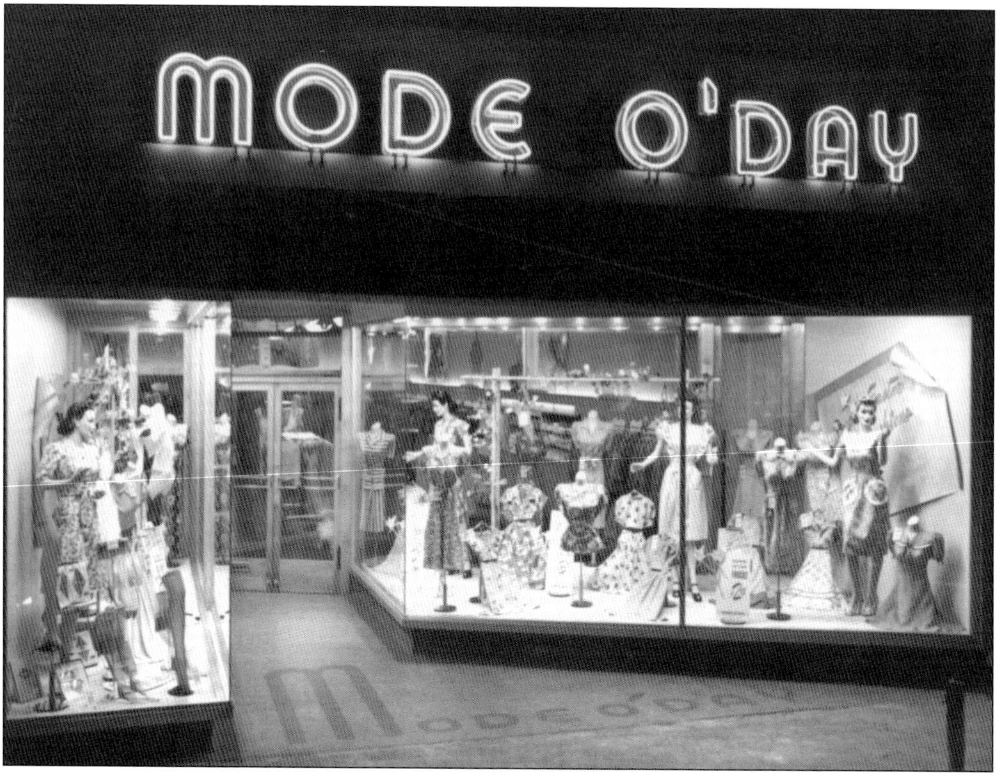

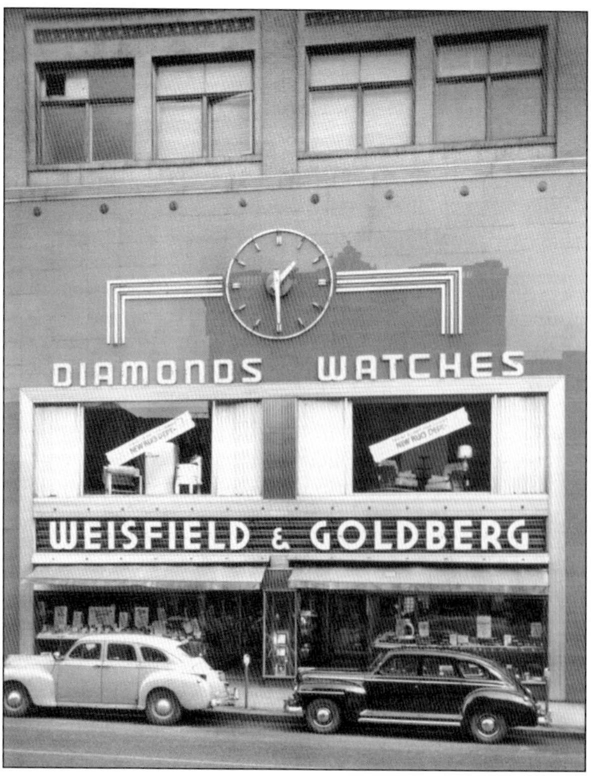

The neon sign for Mode O'Day, a ladies clothing store at 1109 Broadway, glows in this photograph taken after dark during March 1947. Mode O'Day featured a wide selection of fashion clothing and accessories for women of all ages. This Tacoma store was one of the largest in the nationwide chain. (Courtesy of the Tacoma Public Library.)

The roofline of the Pythian temple is reflected in the modern facade of the Weisfield & Goldberg storefront at 925 Broadway in February 1948. The storefront windows display jewelry, and the upper windows feature appliances and furniture and advertise a new rug department. (Courtesy of the Tacoma Public Library.)

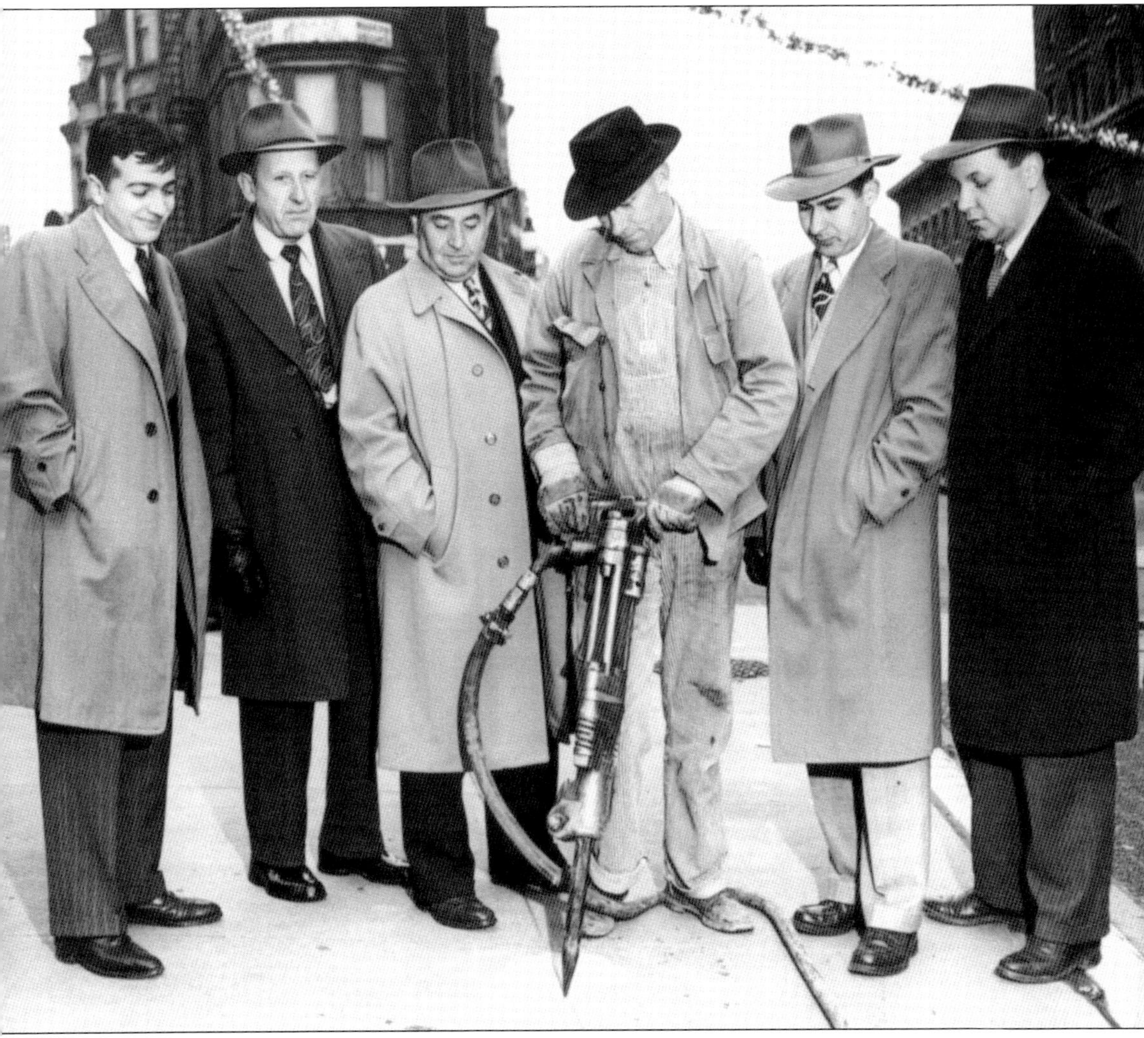

On December 7, 1948, City of Tacoma officials and community representatives watch as Al Gasch of the city's public-works department (holding jackhammer) prepares to drill a hole in the pavement at Ninth Street and Broadway for the city's Christmas tree. The Bostwick Building (left) and Winthrop Hotel (right) can be seen in the background. The 75-foot fir tree was a gift to the city from the US Army through Gen. Harry J. Collins, the commanding officer at Fort Lewis. Although the exact nature of the festivities has changed through the generations, Tacoma's practice of hosting a Christmas tree and some sort of public holiday celebration in December at the intersection of Ninth Street and Broadway has been a tradition for many decades. (Courtesy of the Tacoma Public Library.)

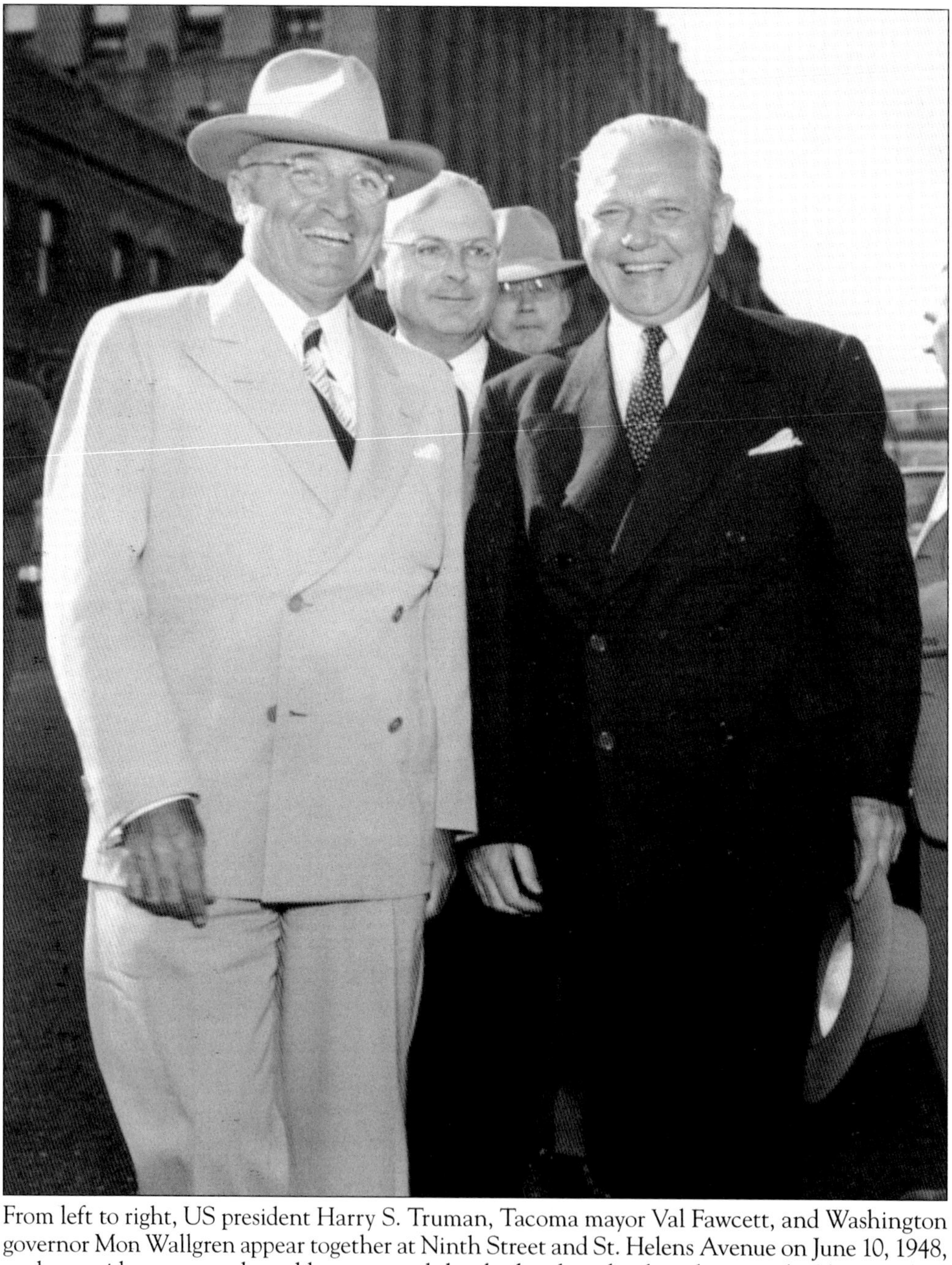

From left to right, US president Harry S. Truman, Tacoma mayor Val Fawcett, and Washington governor Mon Wallgren appear together at Ninth Street and St. Helens Avenue on June 10, 1948, as the president prepared to address a crowd that had gathered to hear him speak. The president and the governor were already acquainted, as Truman had stumped in the state with Wallgren in 1944. The president was in Washington for two days, visiting Olympia, Bremerton, Seattle, and Tacoma. While in the region, he also viewed from the air the damage done by a disastrous flood of the Columbia River. In this, Truman's first visit to Tacoma as president, he spoke about what he called a "special interest Congress," criticizing from afar the Republican-controlled body that was unwilling to go along with his pricing, housing, and farm recommendations. (Courtesy of the Tacoma Public Library.)

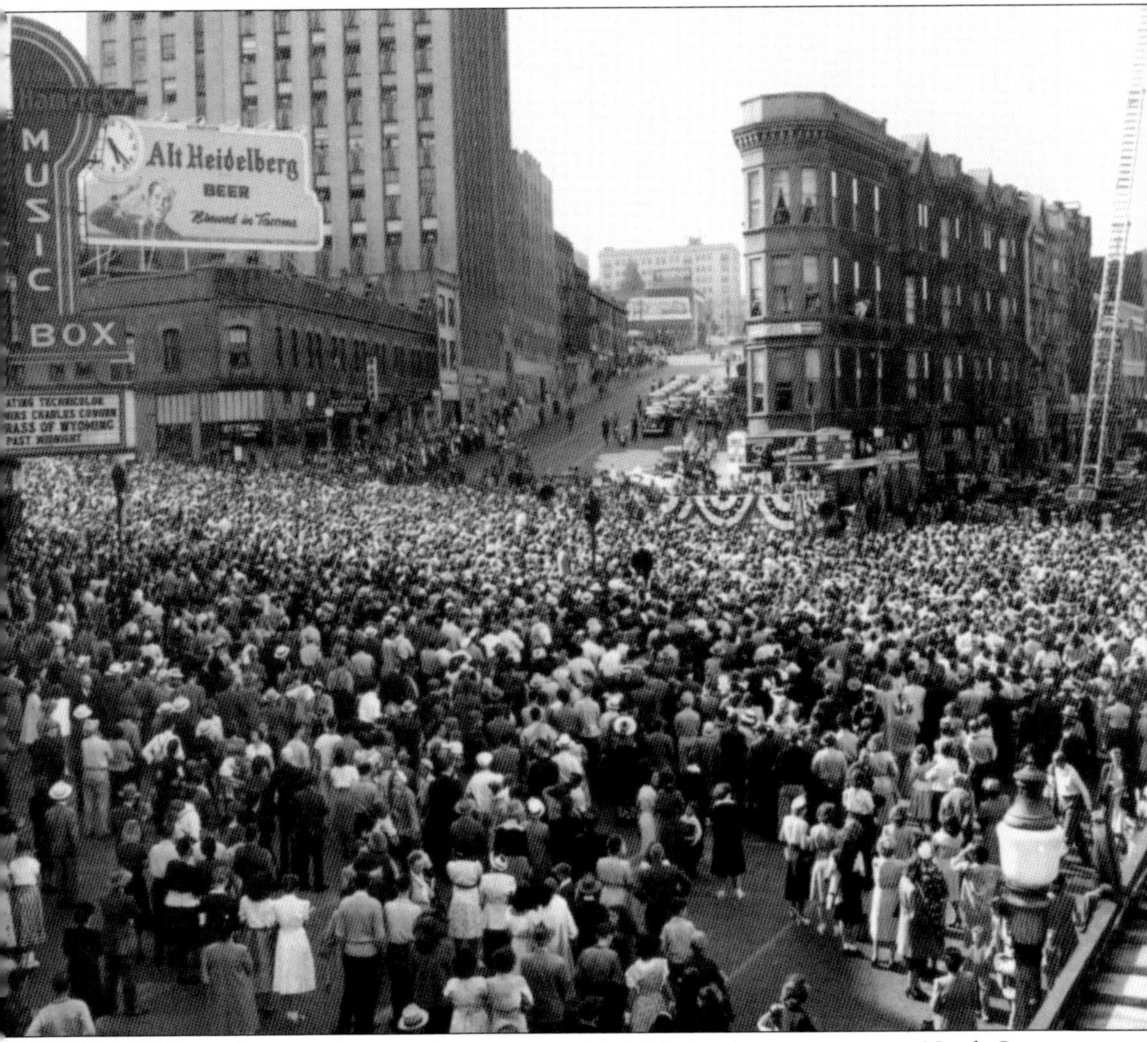

An estimated 9,000 people turned out on June 10, 1948, for the appearance at Ninth Street and Broadway of Pres. Harry S. Truman. The large crowd, which appears to include children as well as men and women of all ages, fills the entire intersection; in addition, several people can be seen leaning out of windows of nearby buildings, especially the tall Medical Arts Building (left rear) and the Bostwick Building, directly above the bunting-wrapped stand from which the president was speaking. A motorcade can be seen halfway up the block on St. Helens Avenue, presumably waiting to take the president to his next location. In spite of the significance of the event, it is otherwise business as usual in the theater district: the Music Box Theater marquee is promoting *Green Grass of Wyoming*, starring Peggy Cummins and Charles Coburn, in "fascinating Technicolor," while a large billboard advertises Tacoma's own Alt Heidelberg beer. (Courtesy of the Tacoma Public Library.)

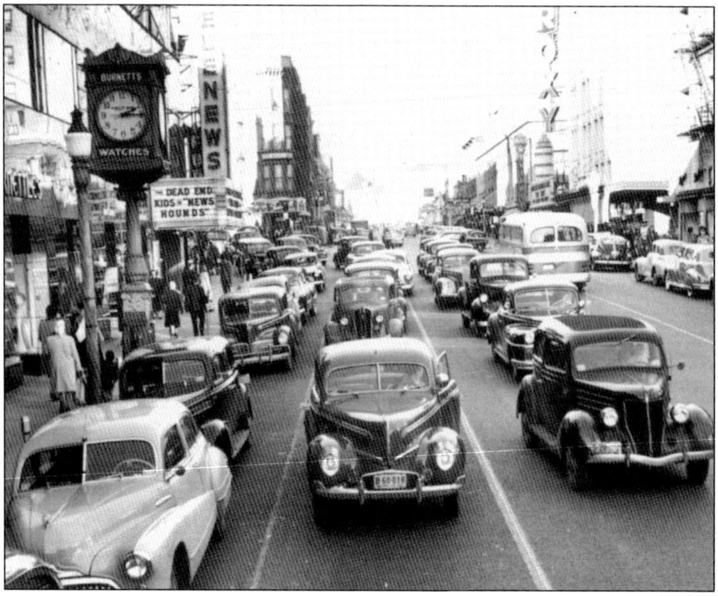

This photograph, featuring congested traffic on Broadway in 1948, was taken for a feature in the *Tacoma Times* inviting reader opinions on the best way to provide more parking for downtown shoppers. Looking north toward the intersection of Ninth Street and Broadway, the Telenews Theater is seen at left, and the Roxy is at the end of the block at right. (Courtesy of the Tacoma Public Library.)

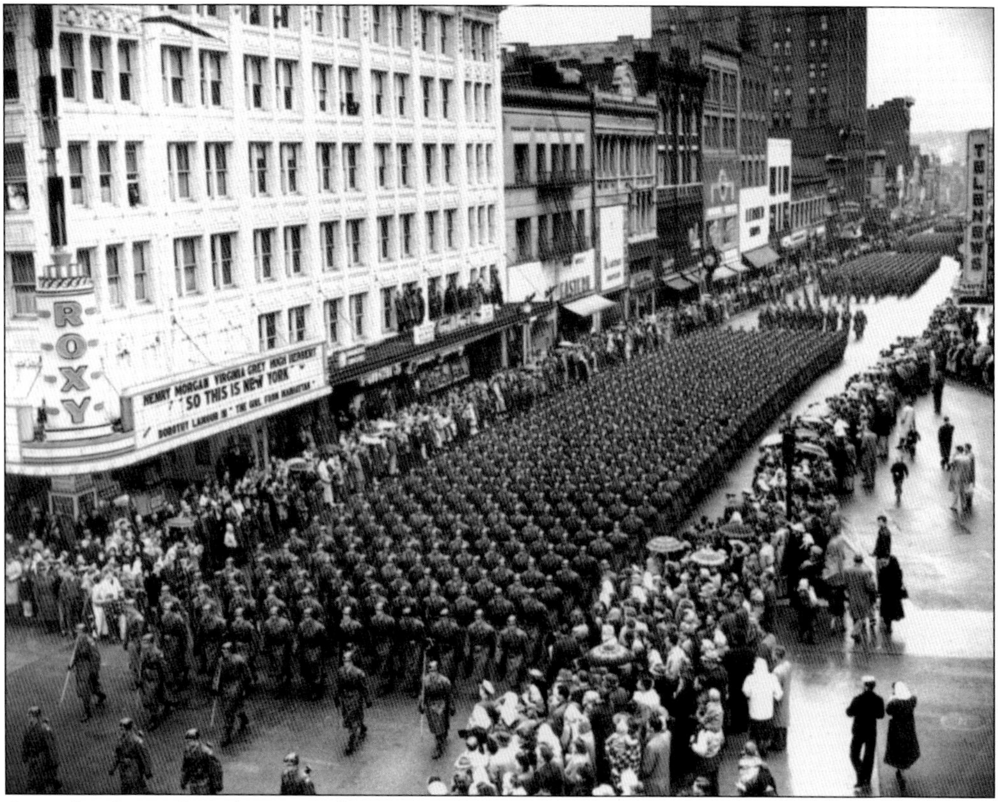

Several infantry battalions, totaling 2,400 men, marched in the Washington birthday military parade on February 22, 1949. This view shows the soldiers at front just about to turn from Broadway onto Ninth Street, in front of the Roxy Theater. Hundreds of spectators line the streets, and several people stand atop the Roxy's awning for a better view. (Courtesy of the Tacoma Public Library.)

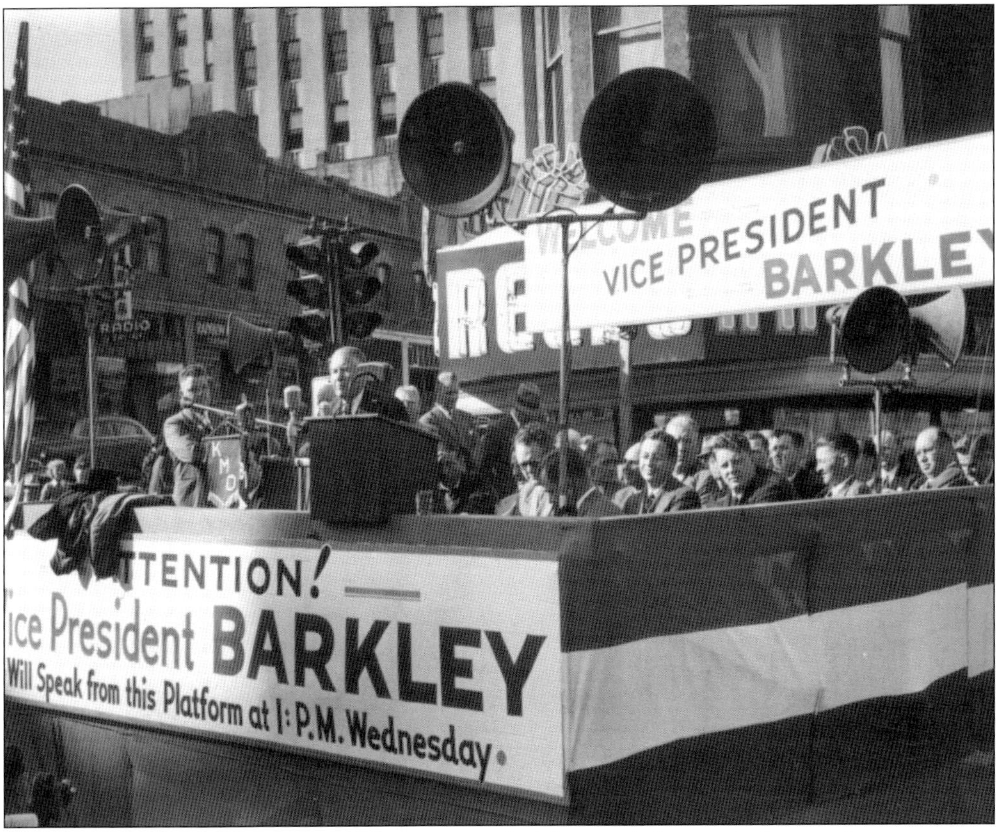

US vice president Alben Barkley addresses a crowd of thousands from a platform at the intersection of Ninth Street and Broadway on October 11, 1950. This platform was in the same location as the one from which President Truman spoke on his visit to Tacoma two years earlier. Joining Barkley on the platform are, among others, Tacoma mayor John Anderson, Rep. Hugh Mitchell, and Sen. Warren G. Magnuson. The mayor presented the vice president with a key to the city during the event. Multiple microphones capture the vice president's words, both to carry his voice over loudspeakers to the large crowd and broadcast his speech over local radio stations KMO and KTBI. (Both, courtesy of the Tacoma Public Library.)

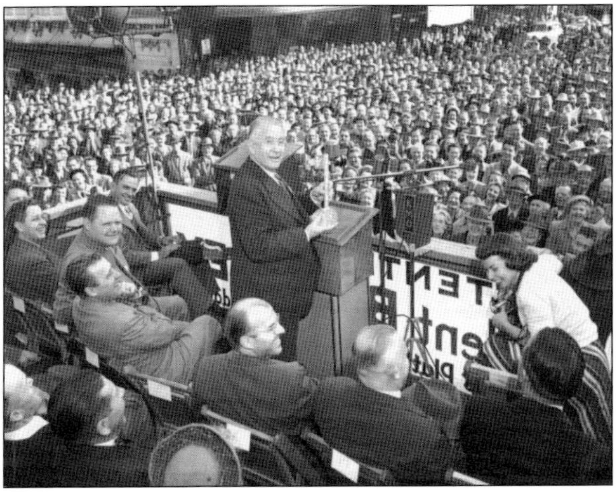

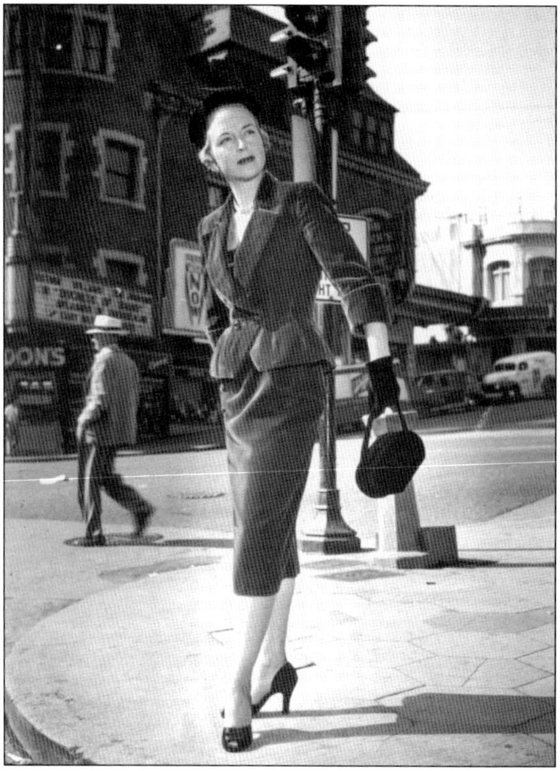

In September 1950, Maurita Runions poses at the corner of Ninth Street and Broadway, clad entirely in attire and accessories from Lou Johnson Specialty Shop for Women and Misses at 755 Broadway. The Music Box (left) and Rialto (right) theaters are in the background, as Runions's gaze is directed north along Broadway. (Courtesy of the Tacoma Public Library.)

In February 1950, Reeds Hats occupied the prime corner storefront of the Bostwick Building, with frontage on both Broadway and St. Helens Avenue as they intersect with Ninth Street. A tiered display features mannequin heads showing off a variety of hat styles. Reeds had previously done business in the 900 block of Broadway. (Courtesy of the Tacoma Public Library.)

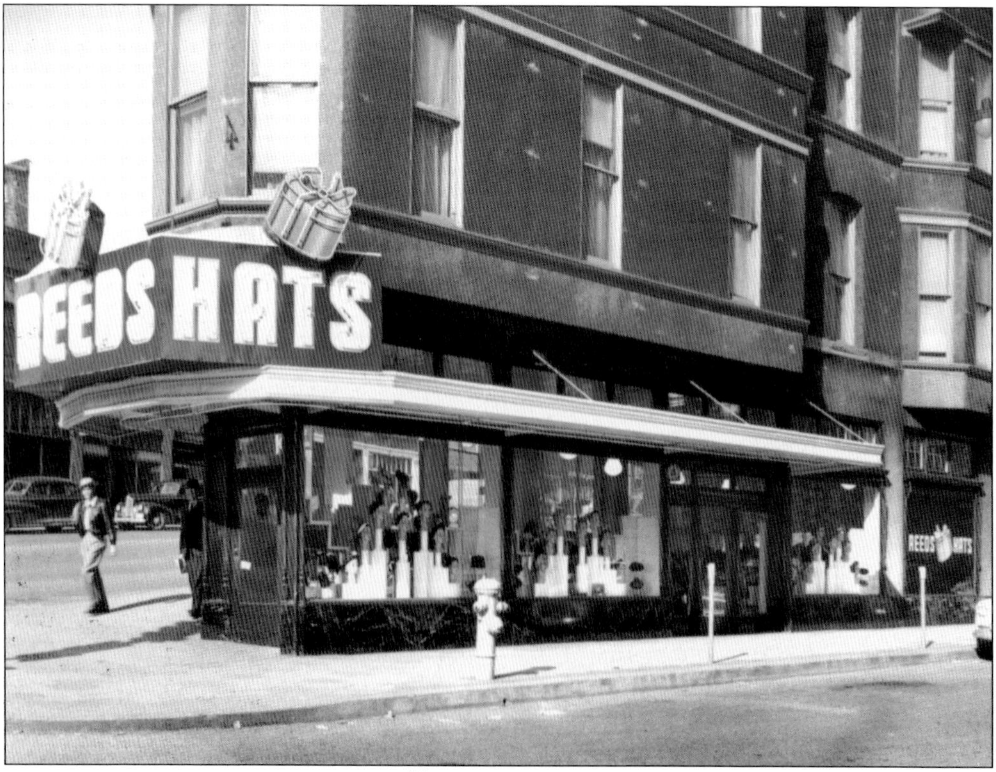

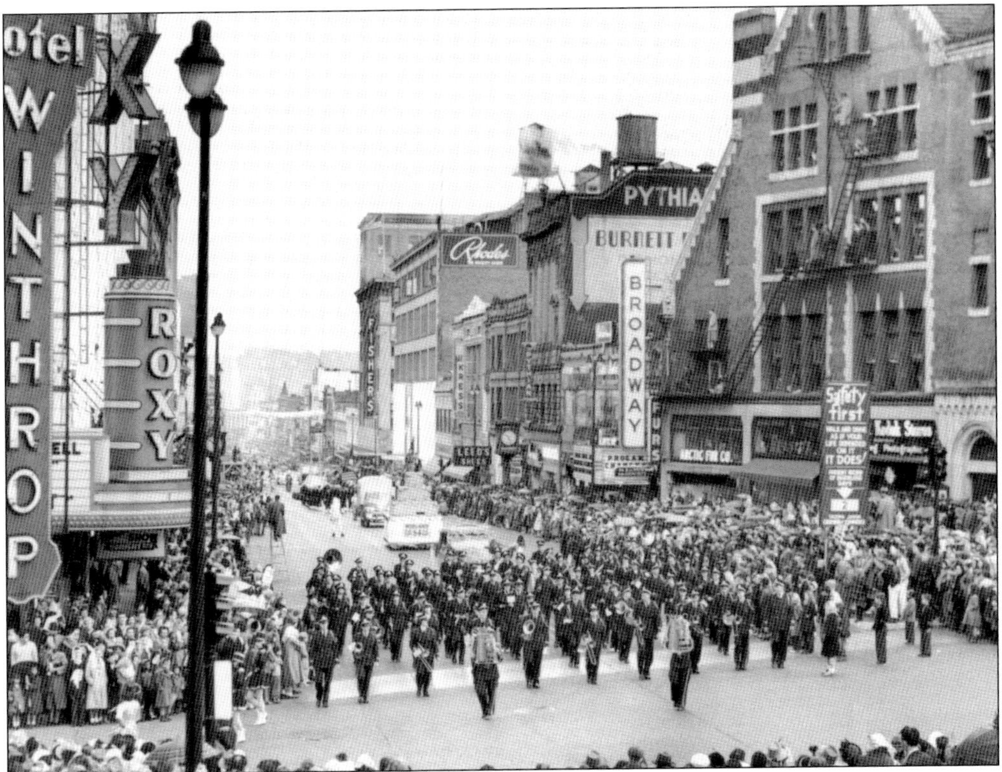

These two images capture the excitement of the 1950 Daffodil Parade, on Saturday, April 1, from the vantage point of the northeast corner of Ninth Street and Broadway. Thousands line the parade route along several blocks of Broadway, watching from street level and from windows and rooftops as a variety of floats, dance troupes, and marching bands pass by. At left are signs identifying the Hotel Winthrop and the Roxy Theater. On the right side of the street are the Music Box Theater (foreground), the Pythian temple, and several department stores: Kress, Rhodes Brothers, Fisher's, and in the far distance, Sears. (Both, courtesy of the Tacoma Public Library.)

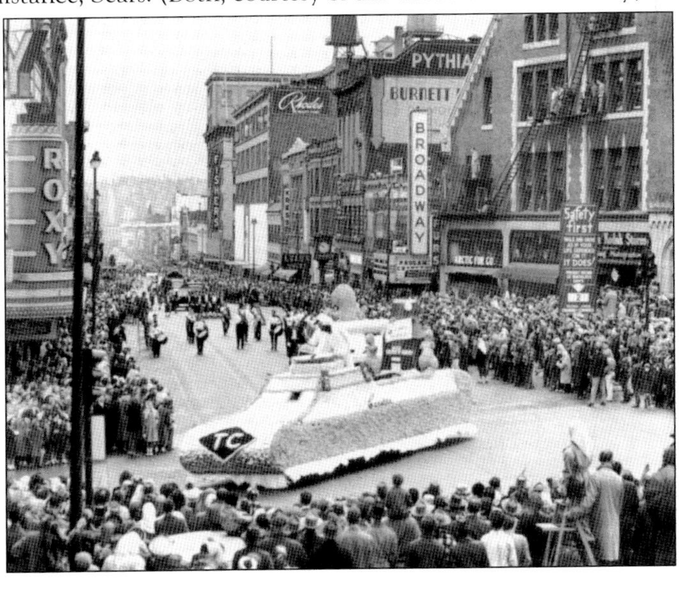

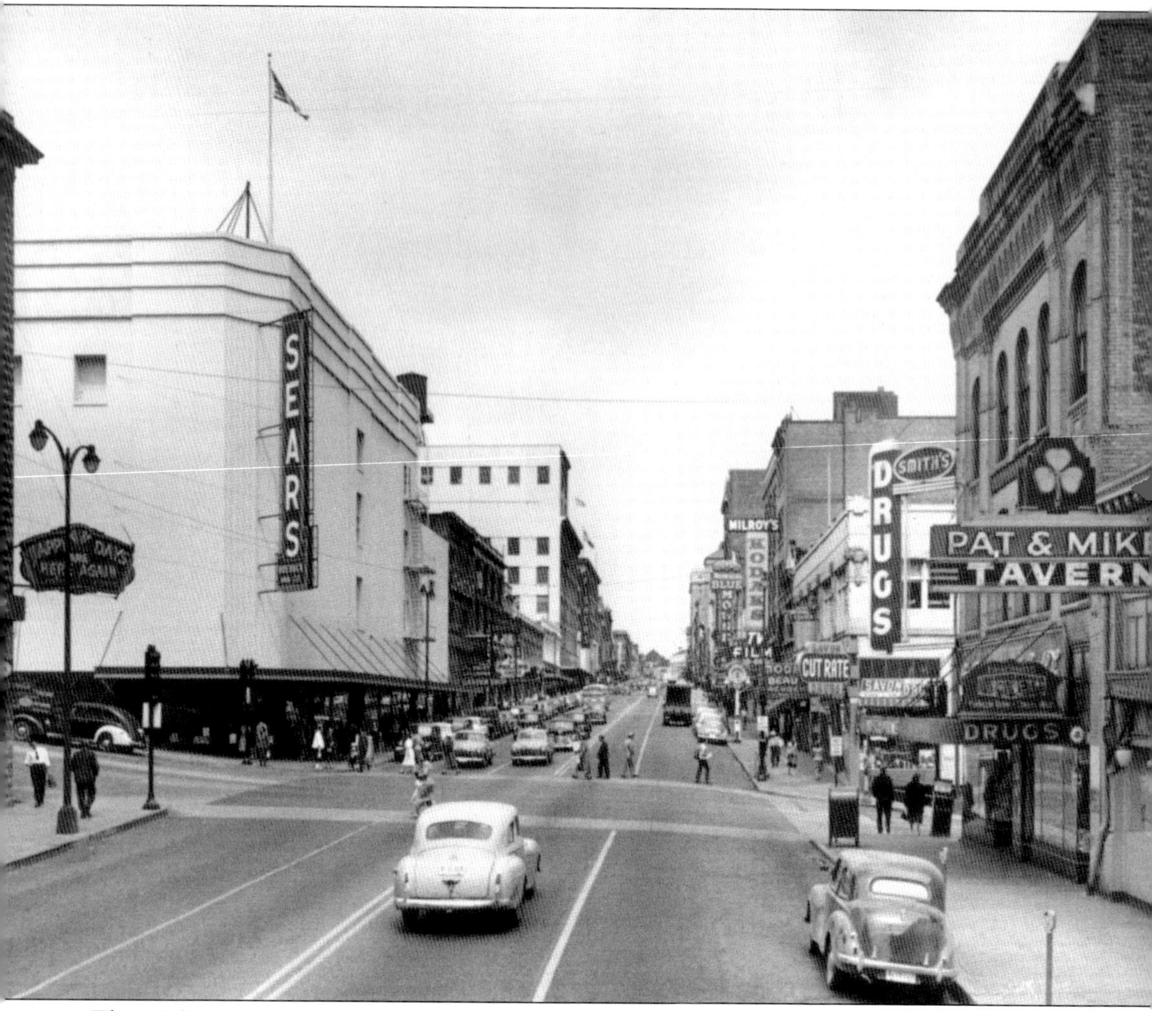

This 1951 image of Broadway, taken looking north from just south of the intersection with Thirteenth Street, captures a busy shopping district with a wide range of establishments. In the foreground are two taverns: Happy Days at left, and Pat & Mike's at right. On the left side of the street, the 1100 block of Broadway is anchored on the north by Fisher's department store and on the south by Sears, Roebuck and Co., which had recently opened a free parking lot for customers. On the right, Hamrick's Blue Mouse Theater occupies the center of the block at 1131 Broadway. Signs can be seen advertising the many smaller shops, including Johnson's Paint & Wallpaper, Savon Drugs, and Modern Beauty Academy. The distinctive shape of the Bostwick Building and the Winthrop Hotel's upper floors can be seen in the far distance. (Courtesy of the Tacoma Public Library.)

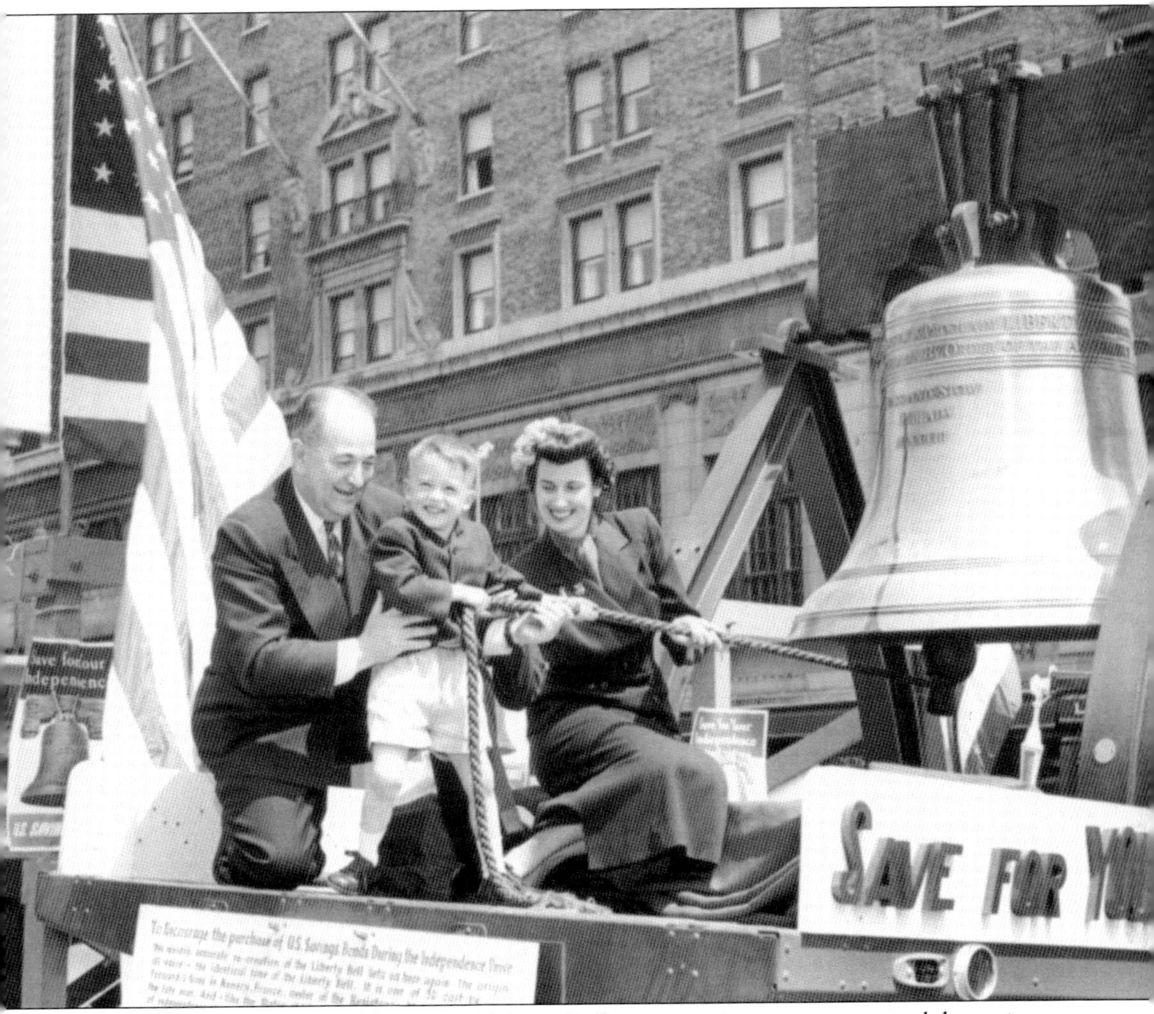

On May 15, 1950, replicas of the original Liberty Bell were rung in every state around the nation to officially open the 1950 independent savings bond drive. The bells were made in Annecy, France, of materials donated by six American copper companies and were then returned to the United States as a gift of the people of Annecy. In Tacoma, a bell was rung at the corner of Ninth Street and Broadway, with the Winthrop Hotel as a backdrop. Reno Odlin, state chairman of the Savings Bond Division, holds on to Sandy Custis, son of Neal and Nancy Hestin, as he and Margaret Marshall of Seattle ring the bell. Marshall was a descendant of chief justice John J. Marshall, at whose funeral procession the original Liberty Bell cracked in 1835. In radio remarks broadcast across the nation that day, President Truman encouraged Americans to "save for our independence" through the purchase of US savings bonds. (Courtesy of the Tacoma Public Library.)

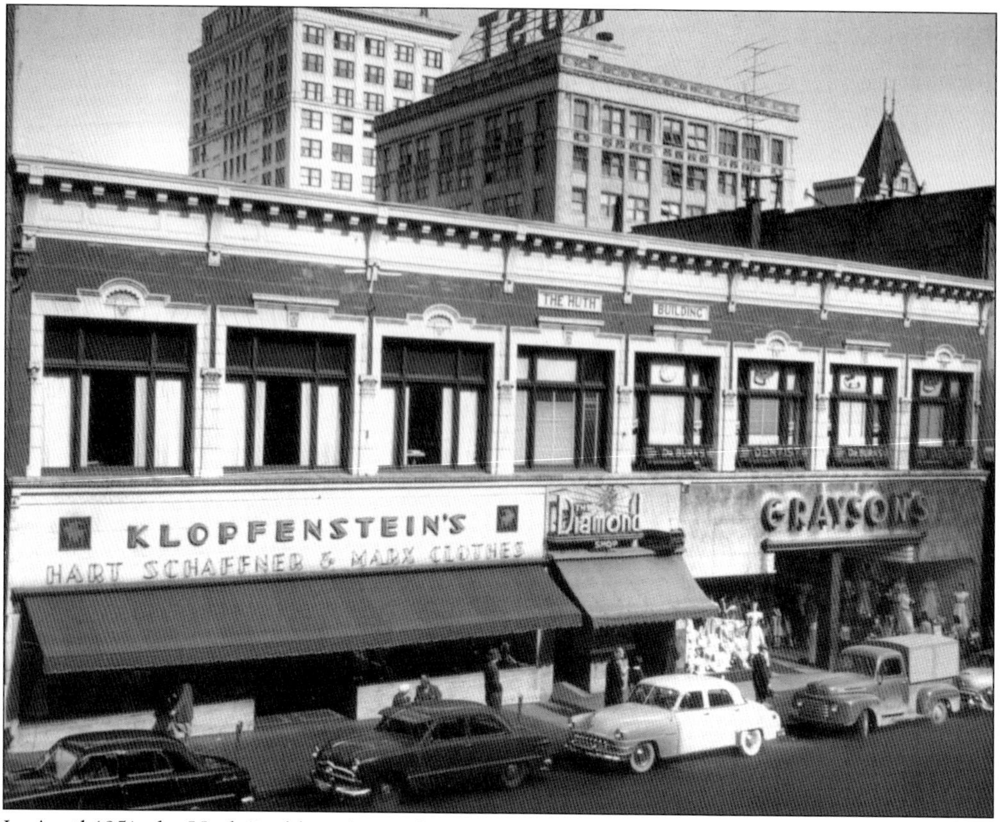

In April 1951, the Huth Building, located at 935–941 Broadway, was home to the Diamond Shop, the dental practice of a Dr. Burns, and two clothing stores: Klopfenstein's, specializing in Hart Schaffner & Marx men's suits, and Grayson's, offering women's apparel. (Courtesy of the Tacoma Public Library.)

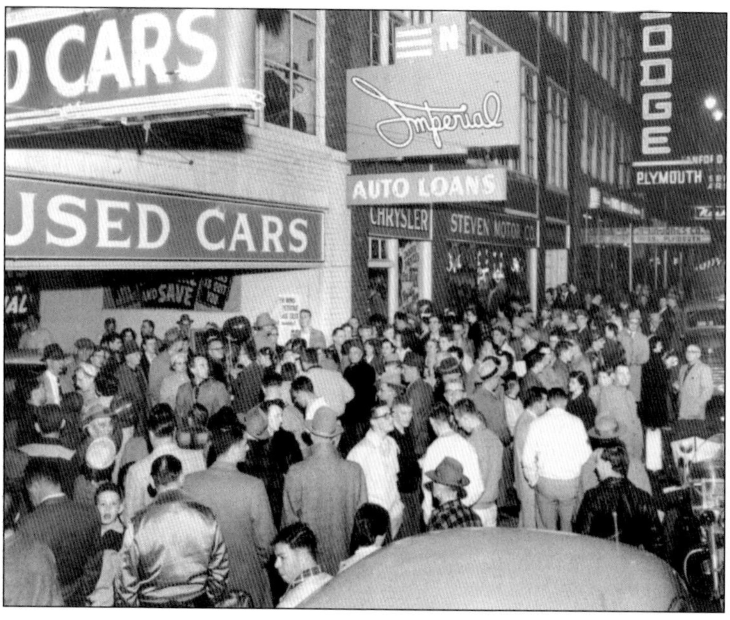

Steven Motor Co., a Chrysler and Plymouth dealer at 738 Broadway, welcomed a crowd of potential car buyers to an open house on the evening of March 1, 1957. Local residents were invited to look around at the many cars and competitive prices. The dealership sold both used and new cars. (Courtesy of the Tacoma Public Library.)

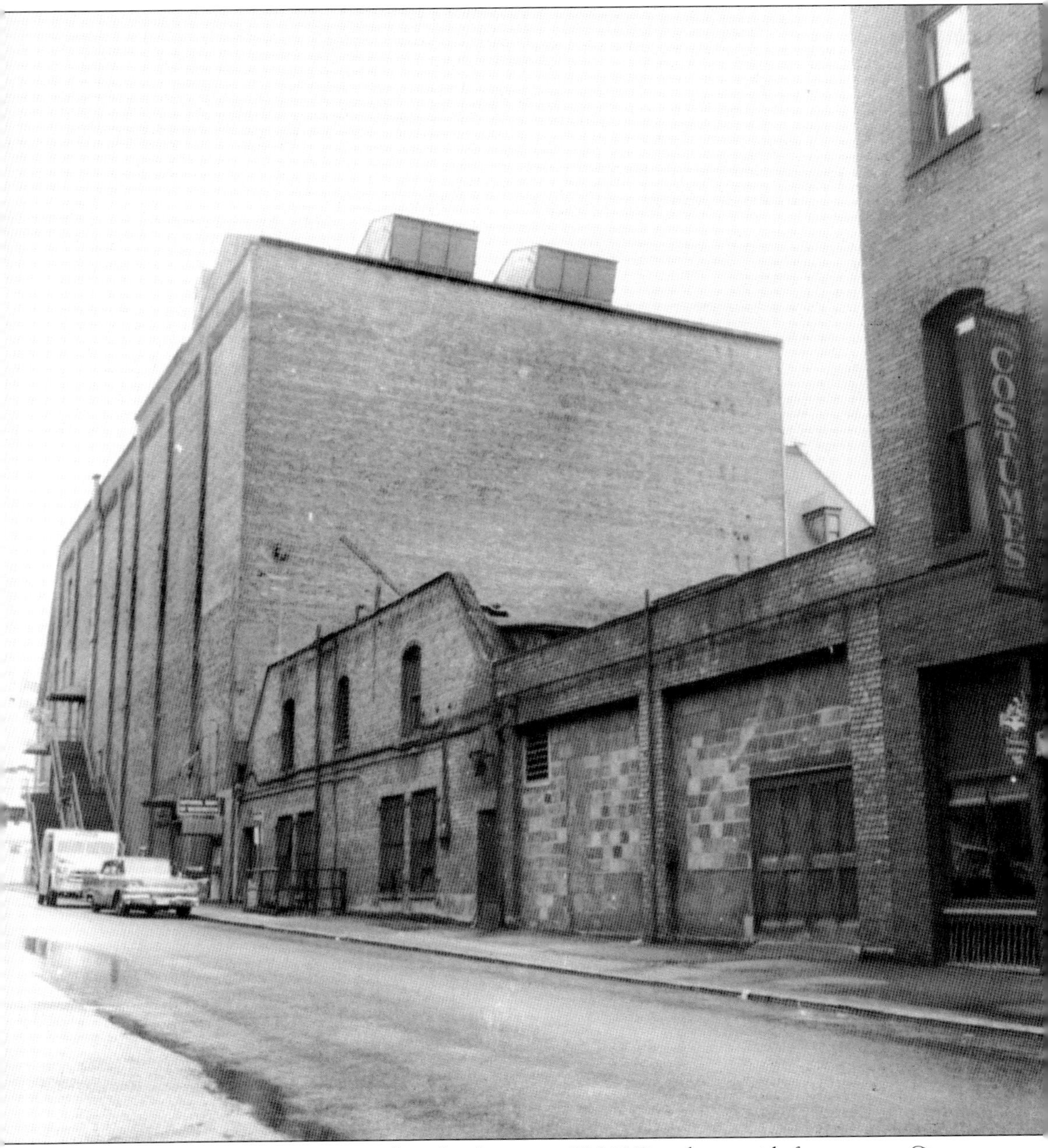

Thorsen's Costume Shop operated in this location, 926 ½ Broadway, with frontage on Court C, from 1926 until 1971. The business serviced the needs of the neighboring theaters as well as the community at large. Their inventory included a wide range of costumes, tuxedos, wigs and toupees, hair dyes, and masks as well as supplies for tricks, jokes, and magic. Neal E. Thorsen managed the business until his death in 1955, at which point his widow, Edythe, took over. This photograph is from the early 1960s and provides a unique view of the windowless backside of the Music Box Theater. Also visible is a rear entrance to the National Bank of Washington branch, which opened at 912 Broadway in 1960. (Courtesy of the Tacoma Public Library.)

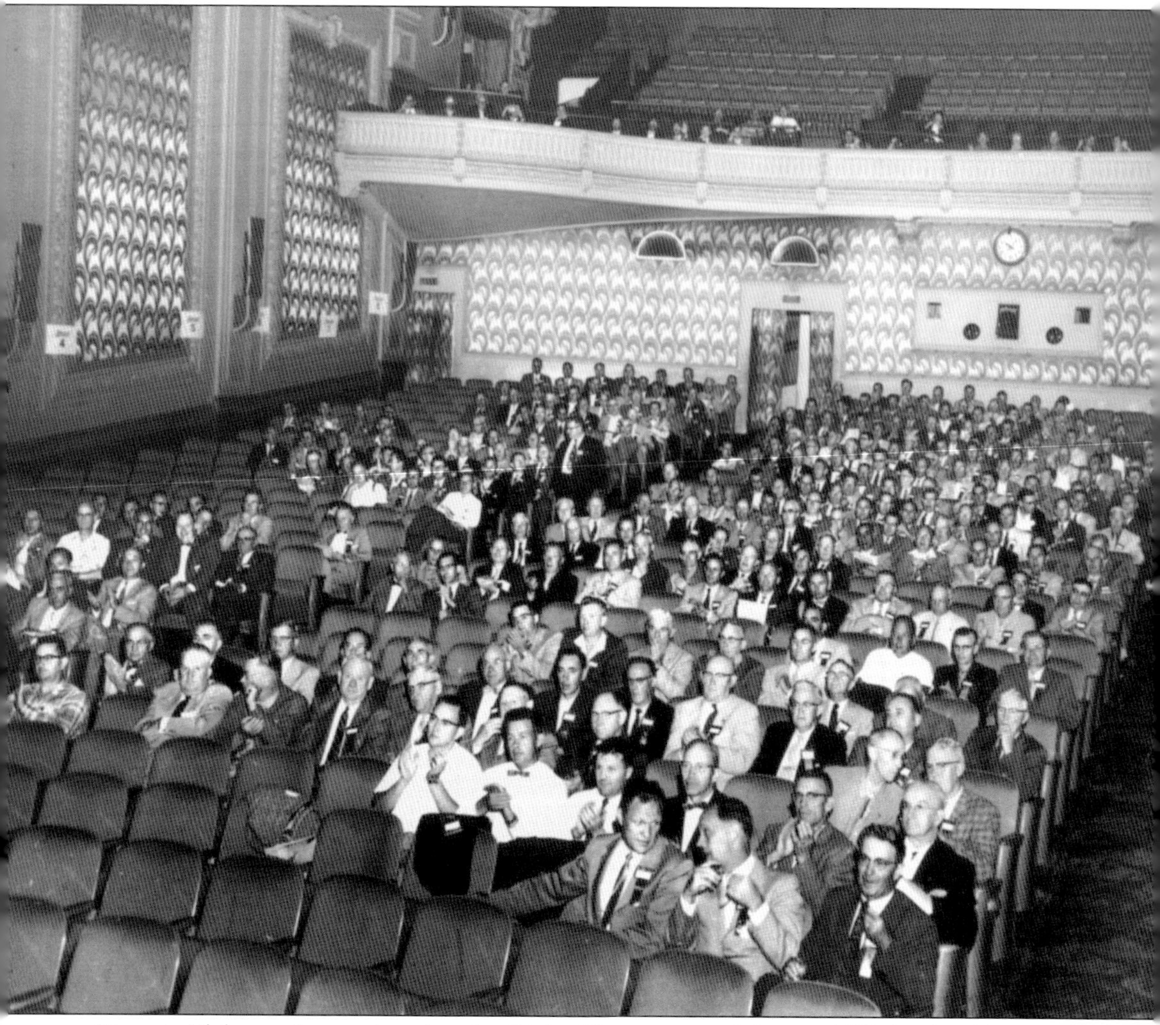

Kiwanis Club members gathered at the Rialto Theater in mid-August 1958 for the 41st annual convention of the Pacific Northwest District of Kiwanis International. It was the first time in 20 years that the regional gathering had been held in Tacoma. Nine Tacoma-area Kiwanis clubs joined to host the convention, which drew 1,200 to 1,500 delegates and their families to Tacoma for three days, August 17–19. In this image, club members wearing name tags with ribbons are likely gathered to elect officials for 1959. In addition to meetings such as this, the convention also included a giant salmon bake on Owen Beach in Point Defiance Park for Kiwanis Club members and their families. Aside from capturing the gathering itself, this photograph provides a rare view of the interior of the Rialto as it looked during this era. (Courtesy of the Tacoma Public Library.)

Five

Fire, Change, Renovation, and Rebirth

On April 29, 1963, the Tacoma City Council met to discuss their plans for what is now called Tacoma's theater district. The city had hired a prominent San Francisco architect to design a pedestrian plaza, and the Music Box was identified as a focal point for the project. The theater was virtually unchanged since its 1927 remodel and remained a dramatic structure around which to renew the district.

The following evening, during a showing of Alfred Hitchcock's *The Birds*, a burned-out bearing in a ventilating fan sparked a fire. By the time firefighters arrived, flames were out of control, quickly spreading to consume the entire roof. Fortunately, no lives were lost; there were only a few minor injuries as the audience was evacuated and firefighters worked to contain the blaze.

The following morning, local papers bemoaned the tragedy, highlighting the unfortunate irony of the fire's timing:

> A dramatic redevelopment plan for downtown Tacoma, to include a Broadway mall, one new park and lots of new parking, was unveiled for the City Council and civic leaders yesterday by the city's consultants. Ironically, the San Francisco architects retained by the city had singled out the Music Box Theater as one of the architecturally sound buildings which downtown should be rebuilt around. The building was destroyed by fire a few hours later.

In spite of the loss of this important structure, redevelopment plans for the district proceeded. Broadway was transformed into a pedestrian plaza. Several buildings were demolished to create new parking garages. The district suffered through hard times as downtown merchants left, many moving to the new Tacoma Mall.

Even with these many challenges and setbacks, Tacoma's theater district persevered. The city eventually purchased the Roxy Theater, and after a decade-long effort, celebrated the reopening of a fully restored facility—once again called the Pantages—in February 1983. The Rialto soon followed, with its own renovation completed in 1991. A third facility, the newly constructed Theater on the Square, opened in 1993. Today, the theater district is once again a vibrant center for performance, entertainment, and community gathering.

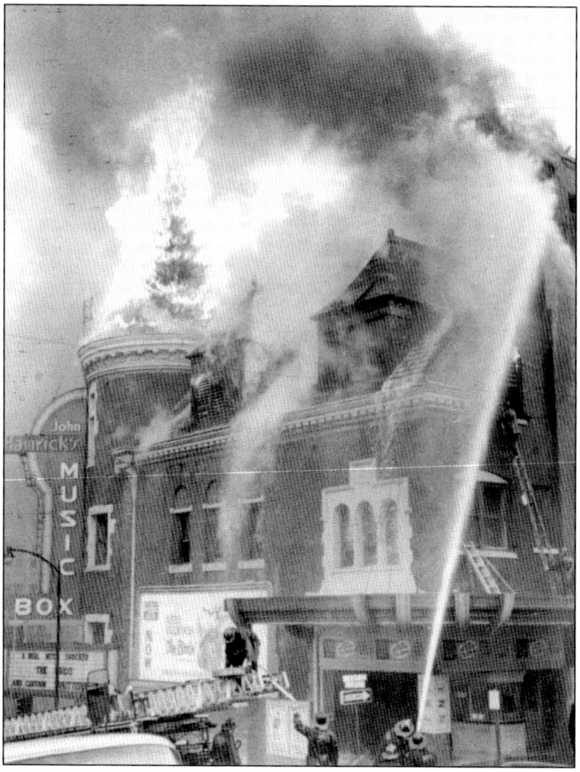

About 300 Tacoma firemen, civil-defense workers, and volunteers fought a raging fire that engulfed the roof of the Music Box Theater on the evening of April 30, 1963, during a 5:45 p.m. showing of Alfred Hitchcock's *The Birds*. The landmark theater's cupola dome collapsed early in the fire. Fortunately, the audience of about 100 was safely evacuated, and there were only a few minor injuries, as a large crowd gathered outside the theater to watch the firefighting efforts. Although the 1890 theater had undergone some modernization over the decades, fire chief James Reiser noted in his comments to the *News Tribune* the following day that the building did not have a sprinkler system. The cause of the fire was a burned-out bearing in a ventilating fan, located in the fan room beneath the projection room. (Both, courtesy of the Tacoma Public Library.)

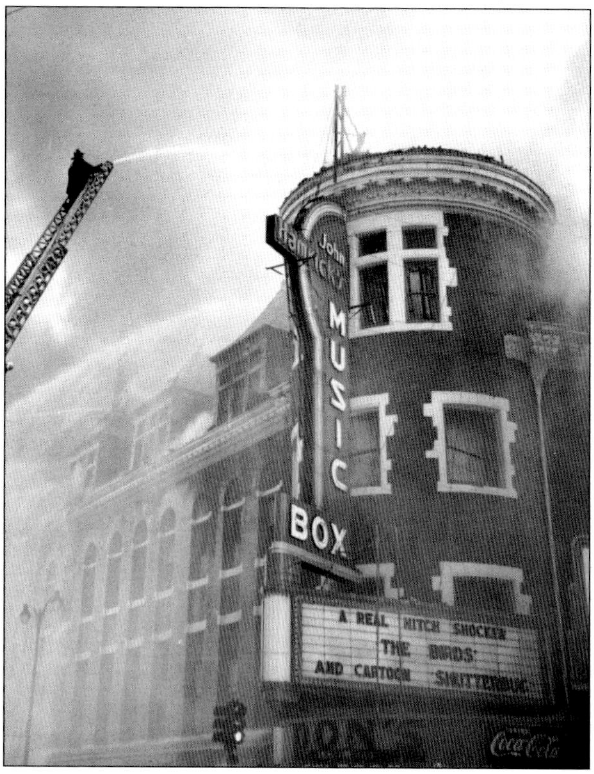

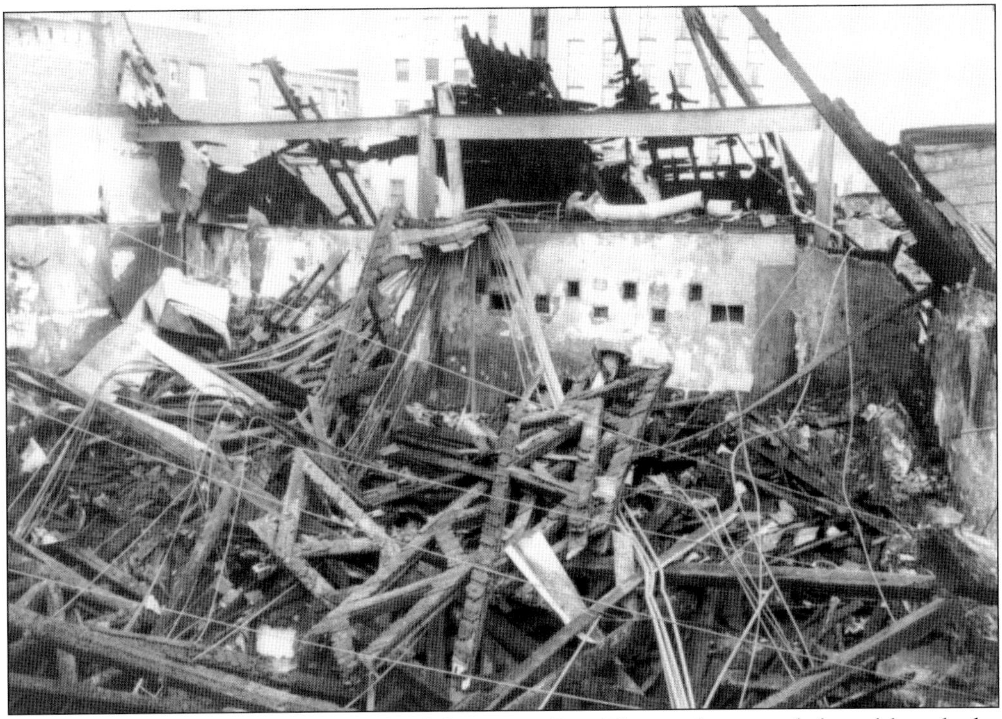

Photographs taken in the aftermath of the Music Box Theater fire reveal that although the exterior walls and stage remained intact, the entire weight of the roof and the auditorium's plaster ceiling had collapsed into the interior of the building. The intricately carved wood trim of the proscenium arch appears relatively undamaged, and a few signs appear to have escaped the flames, including one advertising "Special Laff Seats." Charred beams and roof materials, however, cover the stage, orchestra pit, and entire auditorium seating area. The destroyed theater would be torn down by the summer of 1963. (Both, courtesy of the Tacoma Public Library.)

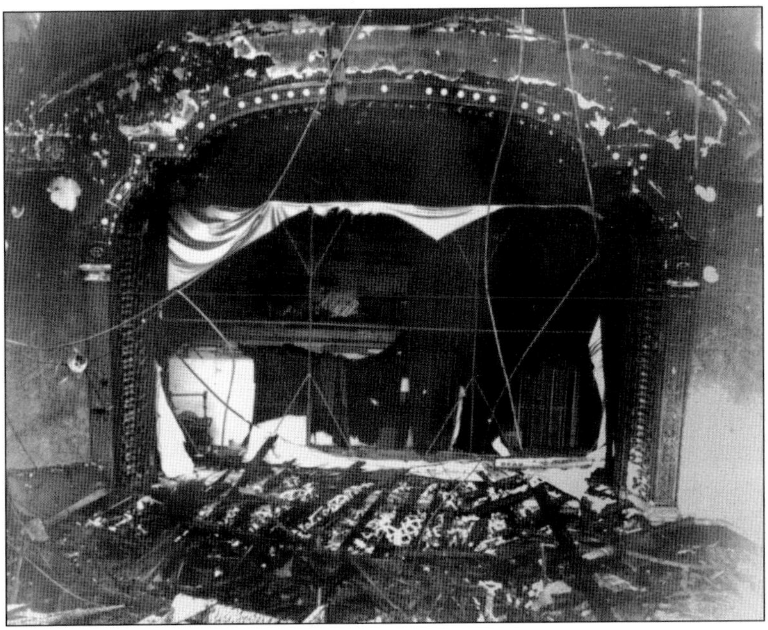

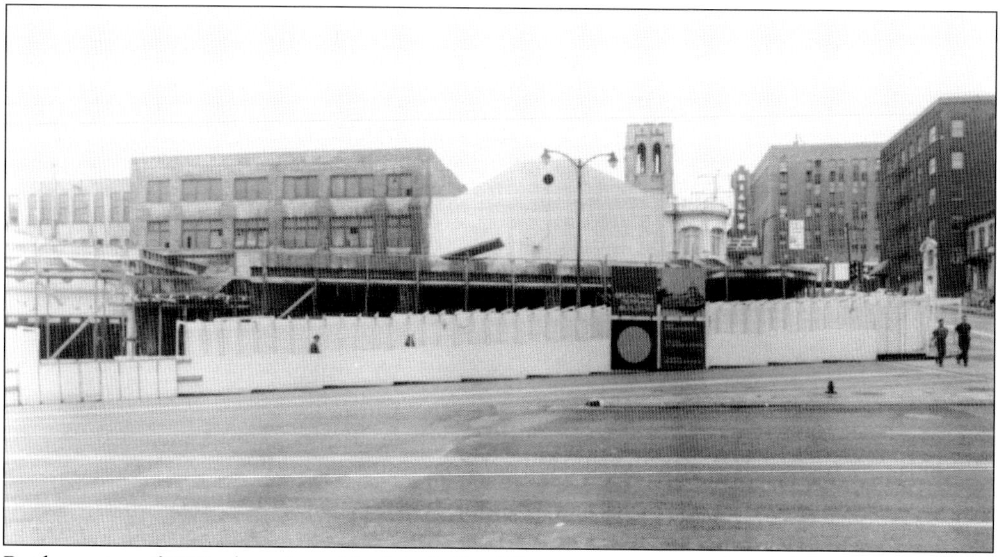

By the spring of 1964, the ruins of the Music Box Theater were removed, and the site was prepared for construction of the new Broadway Terrace Building. The marquee of the Rialto Theater and the bell tower of First Baptist Church are visible in this view from the front of the Pantages. (Courtesy of the Tacoma Public Library.)

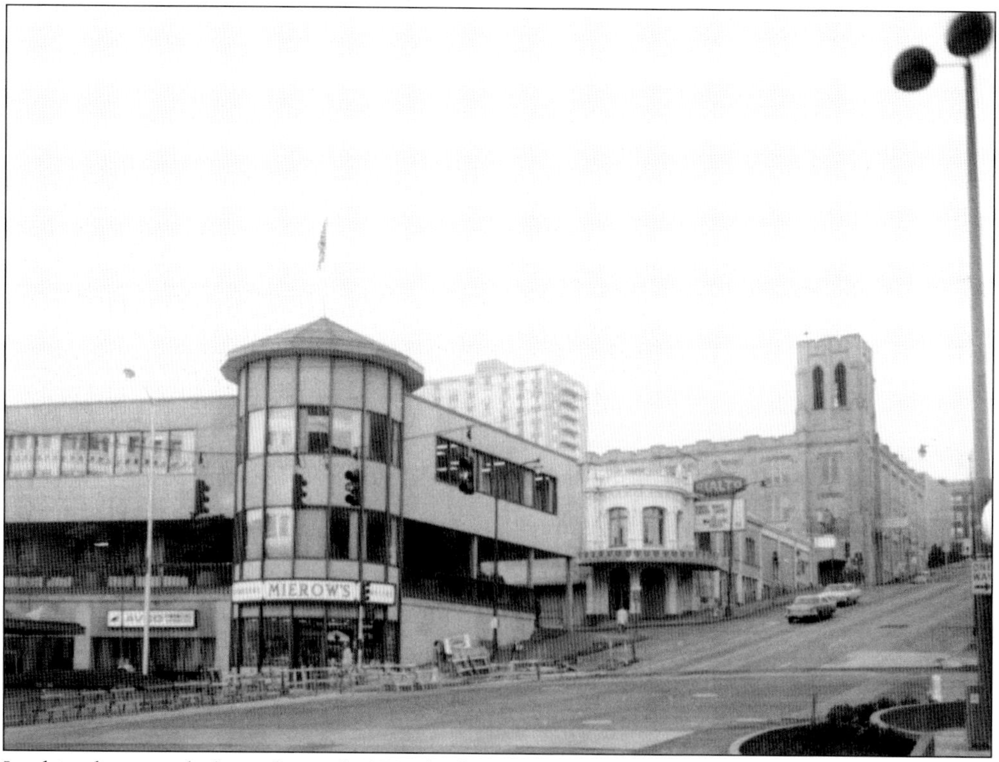

In this photograph from the mid-1970s, looking southwest across Ninth Street, the Broadway Terrace Building now occupies the site of the former Music Box Theater. The marquee of the Rialto advertises two films, *Dirty Mary, Crazy Larry* (1974) and *White Line Fever* (1975). (Courtesy of the Tacoma Public Library.)

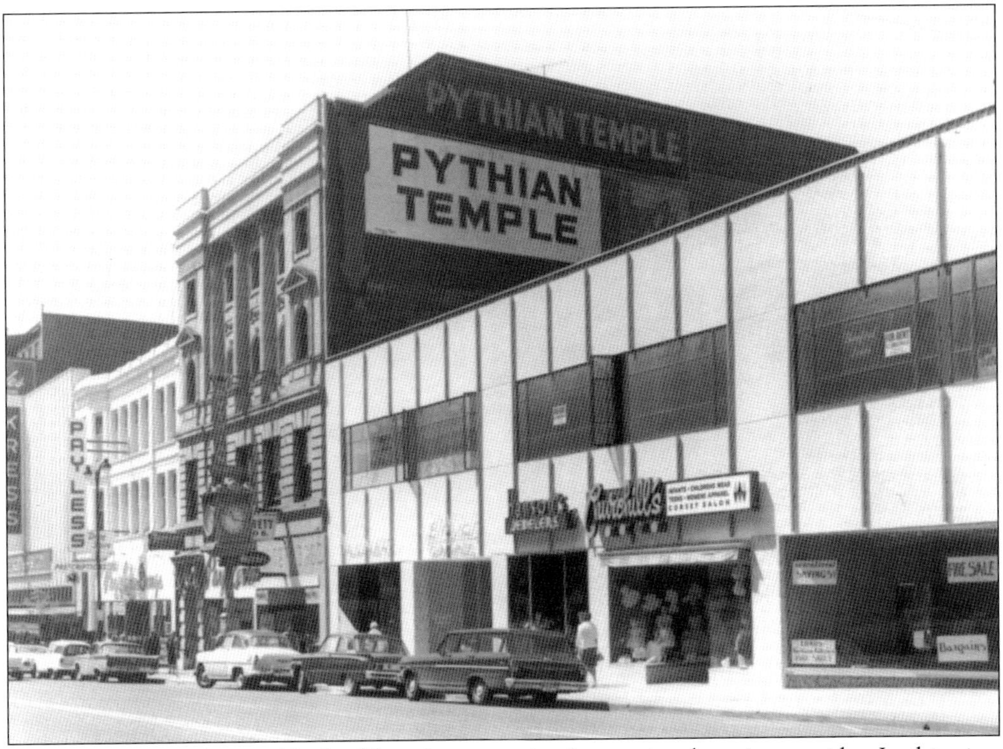

In the mid-1960s, the 900 block of Broadway remained an active shopping corridor. In this view looking south are Churchill's Apparel, Hanson's Jewelers, Burnett Bros., Payless Drugs, Kress department store, and just out of view, Rhodes Brothers department store. Many of these shops would close their doors within the next decade. (Courtesy of the Tacoma Public Library.)

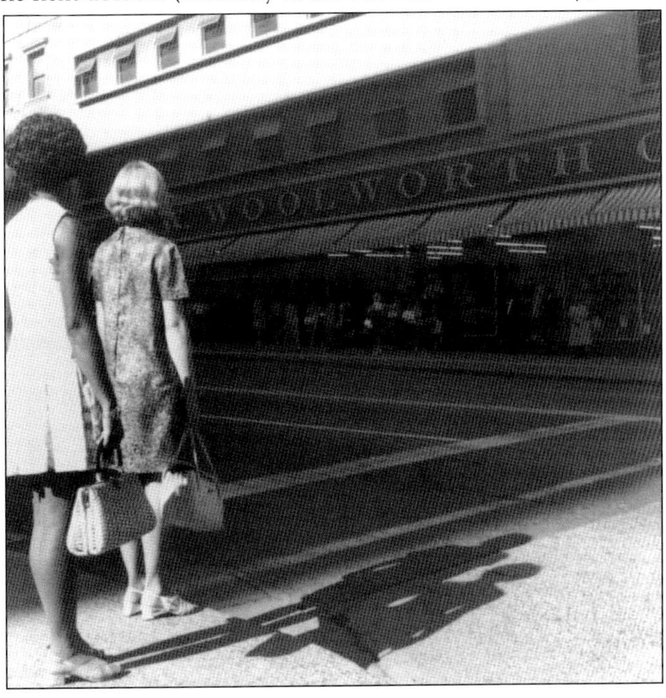

Two women with handbags wait to cross Broadway at Eleventh Street in the mid-1960s. The attention of both women seems to be drawn to the entrance of F.W. Woolworth's, a popular department store and lunch counter that had opened at this corner in 1950. The store closed in 1993 when Woolworth's closed half of its locations nationwide. (Courtesy of the Tacoma Public Library.)

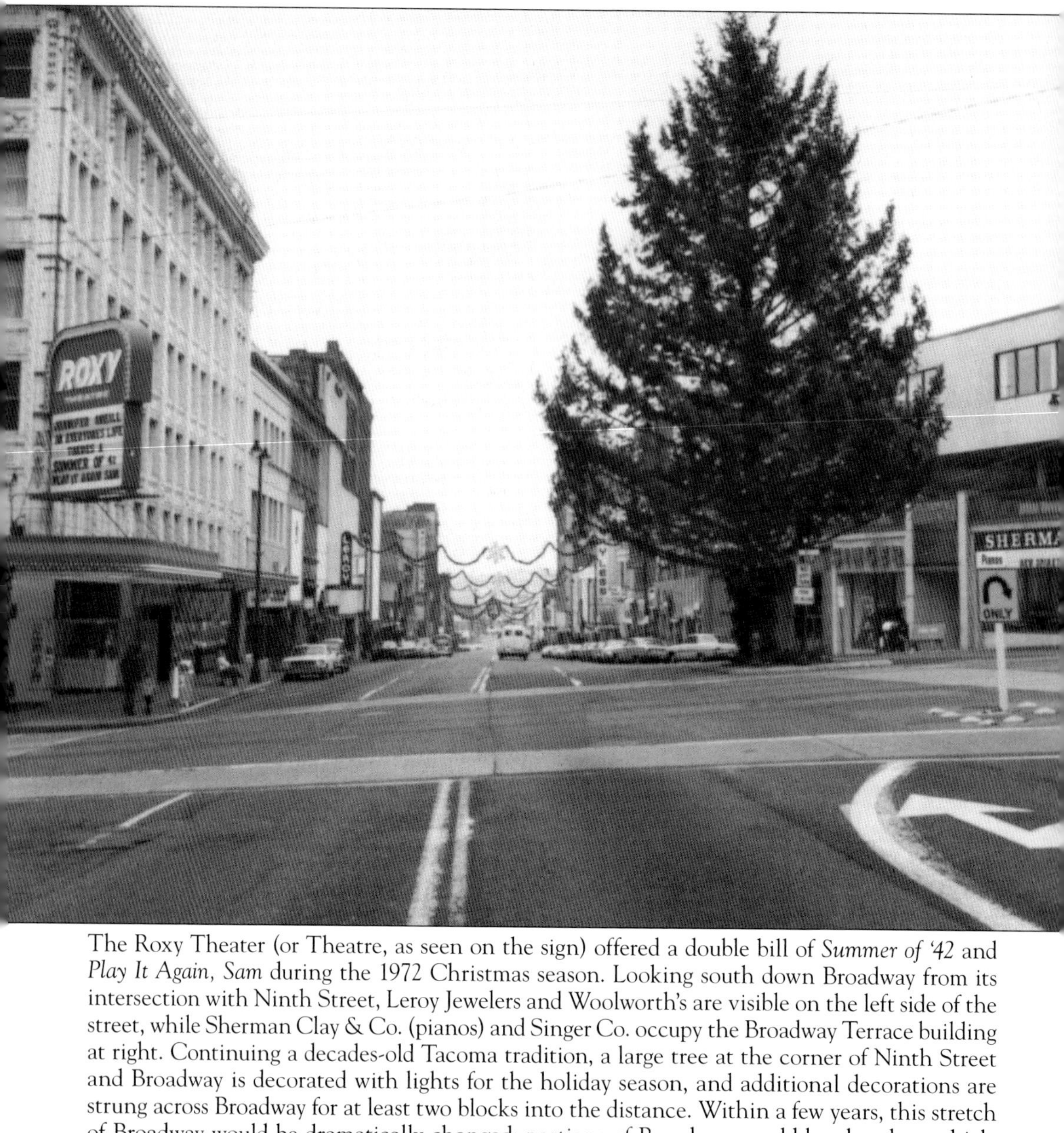

The Roxy Theater (or Theatre, as seen on the sign) offered a double bill of *Summer of '42* and *Play It Again, Sam* during the 1972 Christmas season. Looking south down Broadway from its intersection with Ninth Street, Leroy Jewelers and Woolworth's are visible on the left side of the street, while Sherman Clay & Co. (pianos) and Singer Co. occupy the Broadway Terrace building at right. Continuing a decades-old Tacoma tradition, a large tree at the corner of Ninth Street and Broadway is decorated with lights for the holiday season, and additional decorations are strung across Broadway for at least two blocks into the distance. Within a few years, this stretch of Broadway would be dramatically changed: portions of Broadway would be closed to vehicle traffic and replaced with a pedestrian plaza. Additionally, many downtown shops would close, succumbing to competition from the Tacoma Mall (opened 1963) and Villa Plaza in Lakewood (opened 1957). (Courtesy of the Tacoma Public Library.)

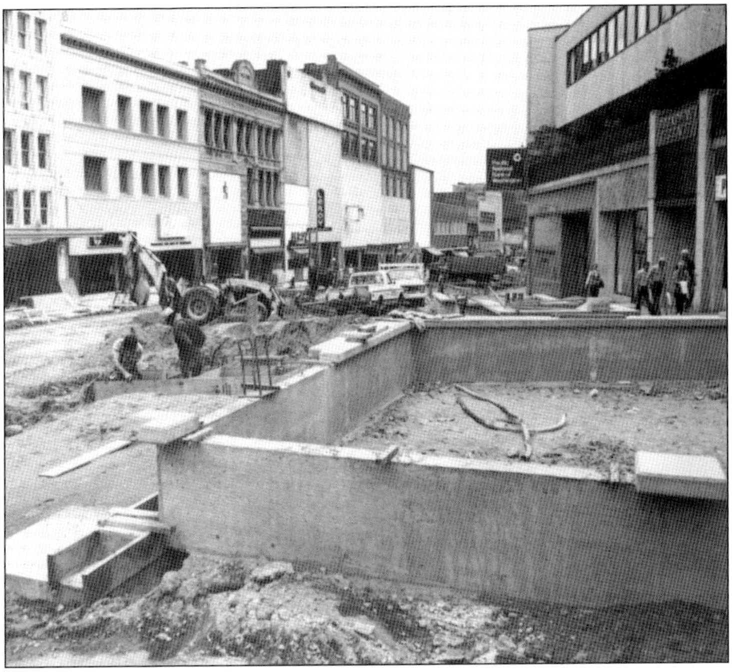

Work began in May 1973 for the new pedestrian plaza on the 900 block of Broadway. Several storefronts display signage, and a few shoppers walk a sidewalk at right, but it appears that many of the businesses on this block were closed during the construction project. (Courtesy of the Tacoma Public Library.)

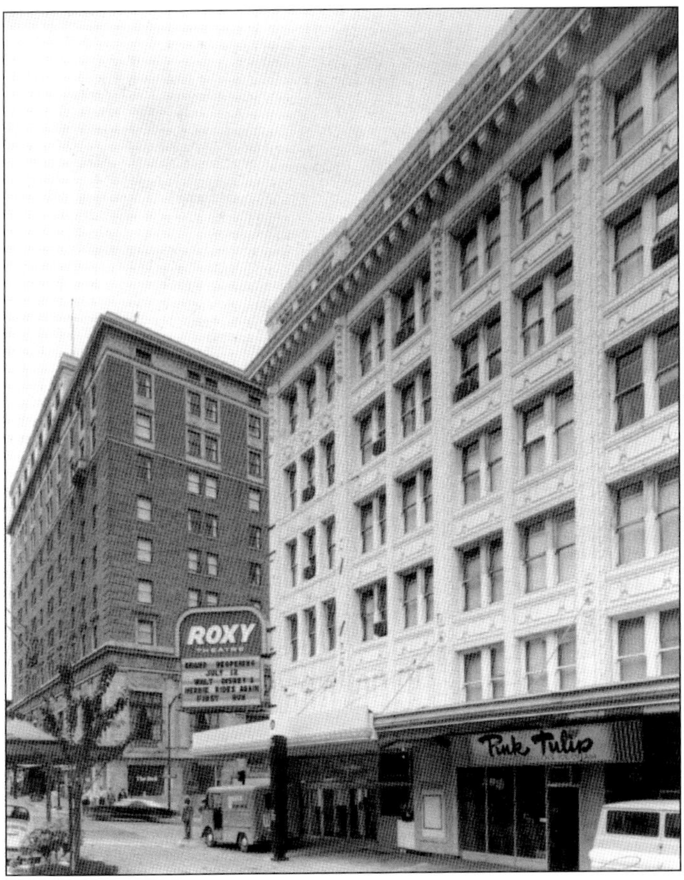

July 12, 1974, was the date of the grand reopening of the Roxy Theater, located at 901 Broadway. A family film, Disney's *Herbie Rides Again*, was the first-run feature in the newly remodeled and refurbished motion-picture theater. The Roxy had been closed since May 1973, coinciding with the construction of Broadway Plaza. The Winthrop Hotel is at left. (Courtesy of the Tacoma Public Library.)

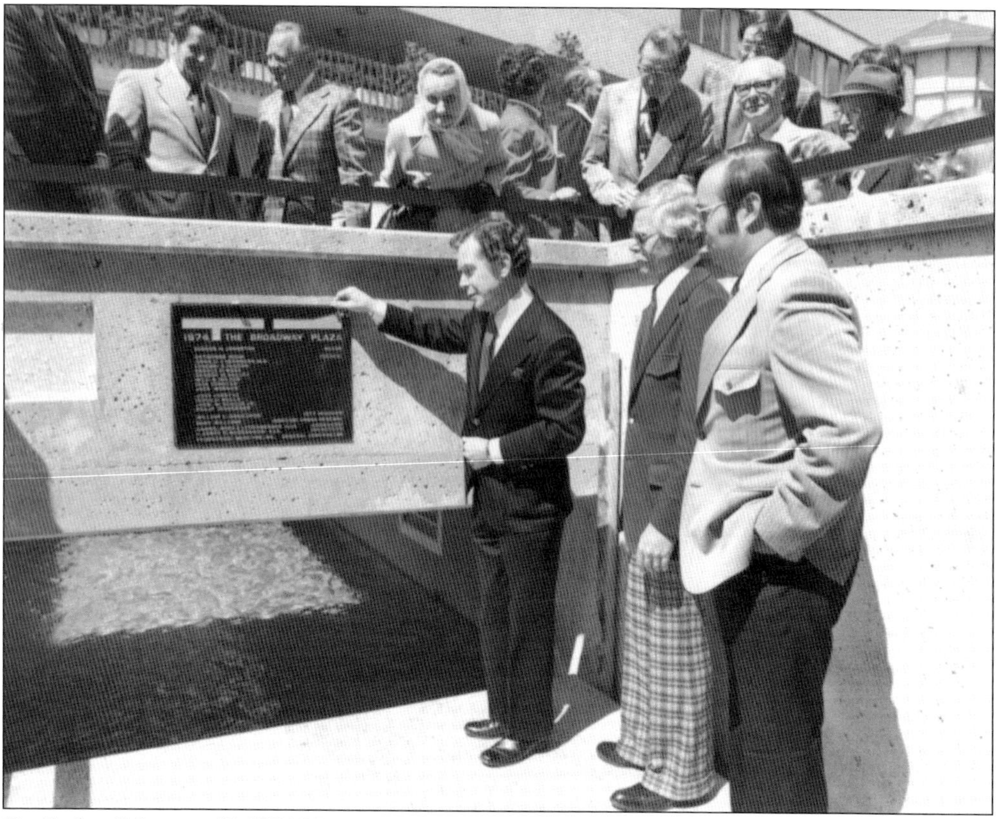

On Friday, February 15, 1974, Tacoma mayor Gordon Johnson led dedication events for Broadway Plaza. The mayor can be seen here speaking to a small crowd gathered for the event, and admiring the plaque affixed to one of the concrete structures on the plaza. Nile B. Paull, deputy area director for the federal Department of Housing and Urban Development, also spoke at the event, commending "the people of Tacoma for being a leader among the nation's cities to construct a downtown pedestrian mall under a Congress-passed program to help eliminate urban decay and blight." Following the dedication ceremony, a "Four Day Circus" commenced, welcoming the public to the new plaza with a range of entertainment events. (Both, courtesy of the Tacoma Public Library.)

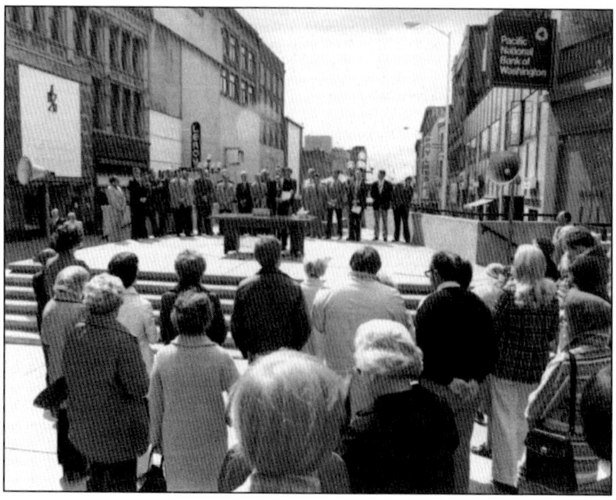

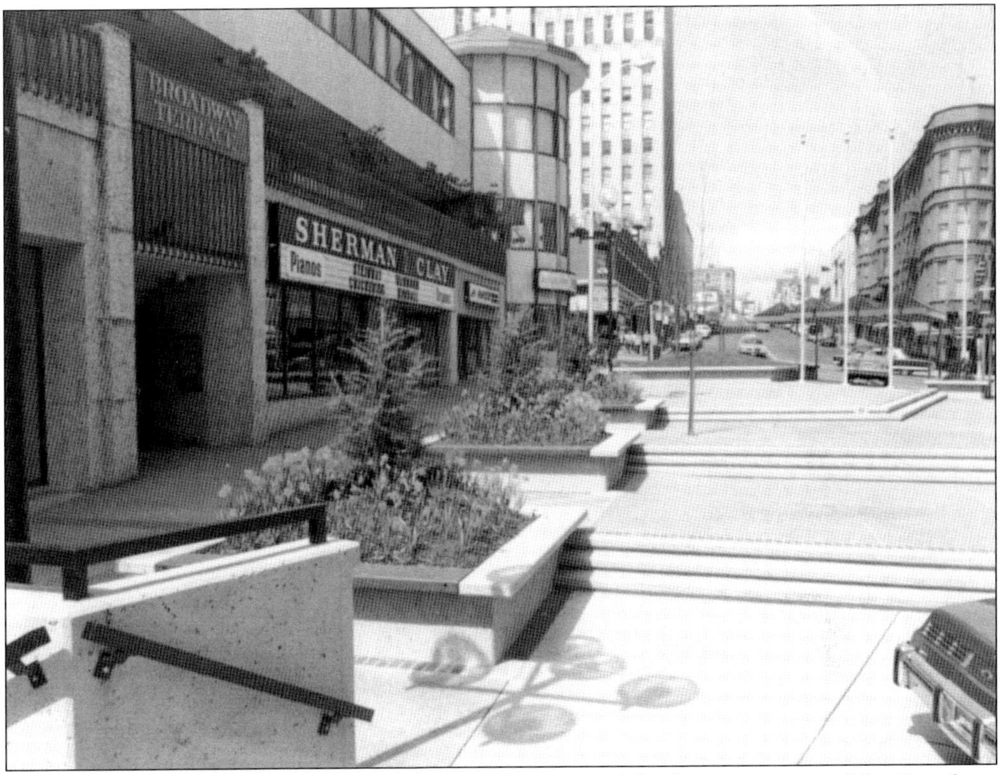

Sherman Clay Co., dealer of pianos and organs, was one of the first occupants of the Broadway Terrace building, at left, when it opened in 1964. The store is seen here in the 1970s, following the completion of the Broadway Plaza project. Past Ninth Street, the 700 block of St. Helens Avenue appears relatively unchanged from earlier decades. (Courtesy of the Tacoma Public Library.)

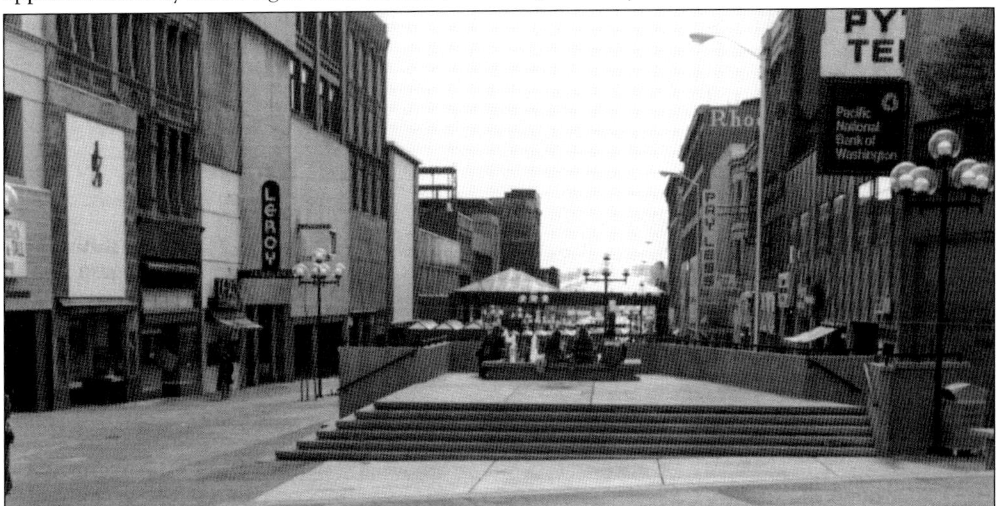

The exact date of this photograph, looking south down the 900 block of Broadway, is not known. A few people gather or walk along the pedestrian plaza, but there also appears to be a large number of empty storefronts, particularly on the left side of the street. (Courtesy of the Tacoma Public Library.)

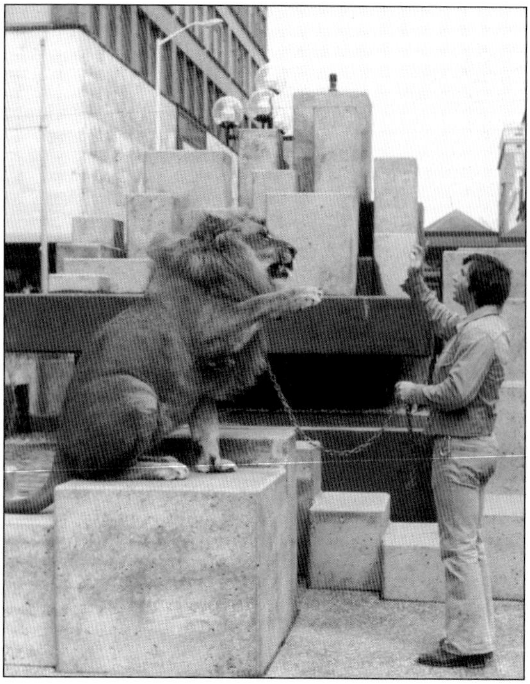

In May 1974, Circus Vargas and its 150 animals made a three-day appearance at Tacoma's recently opened Broadway Plaza pedestrian mall. One of the circus's animals, two-year-old Zamba, is seen here with his trainer, Ron Whitfield, posing on the fountain at the corner of Eleventh Avenue and Broadway. (Courtesy of the Tacoma Public Library.)

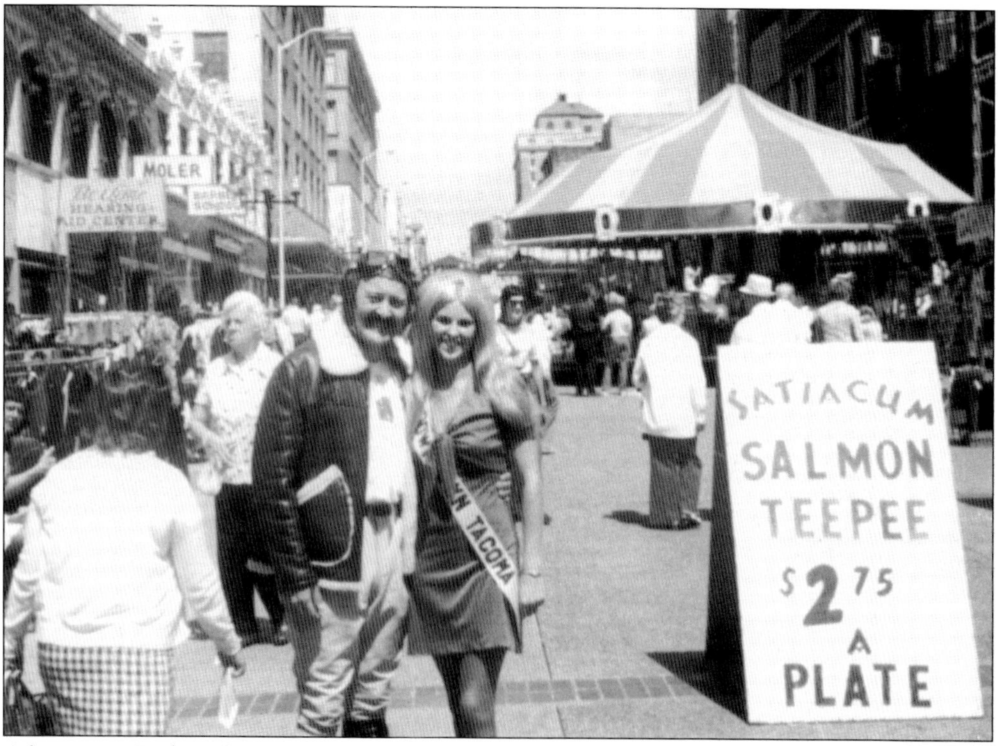

Adman "Ace Busby" of Puget Sound National Bank and Miss Downtown Tacoma Donna McNamara smile for the camera during celebrations taking place in May 1975 to encourage people to visit the new Broadway Plaza. A carousel can be seen in the background, and a sandwich board advertises Satiacum's Salmon Teepee for $2.75 a plate. (Courtesy of the Tacoma Public Library.)

Built in 1929 and operating until 1962 as the Riviera, this theater at 906–908 Pacific Avenue briefly closed and then reopened as the Capri in 1964. Aside from the new name on the marquee, the exterior of the theater appears relatively unchanged over the decades. (Courtesy of the Tacoma Public Library.)

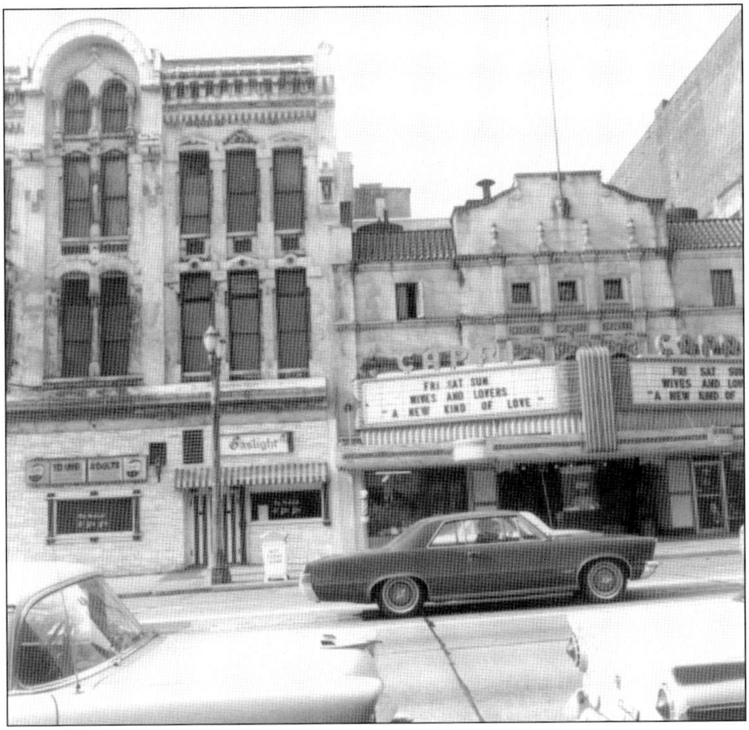

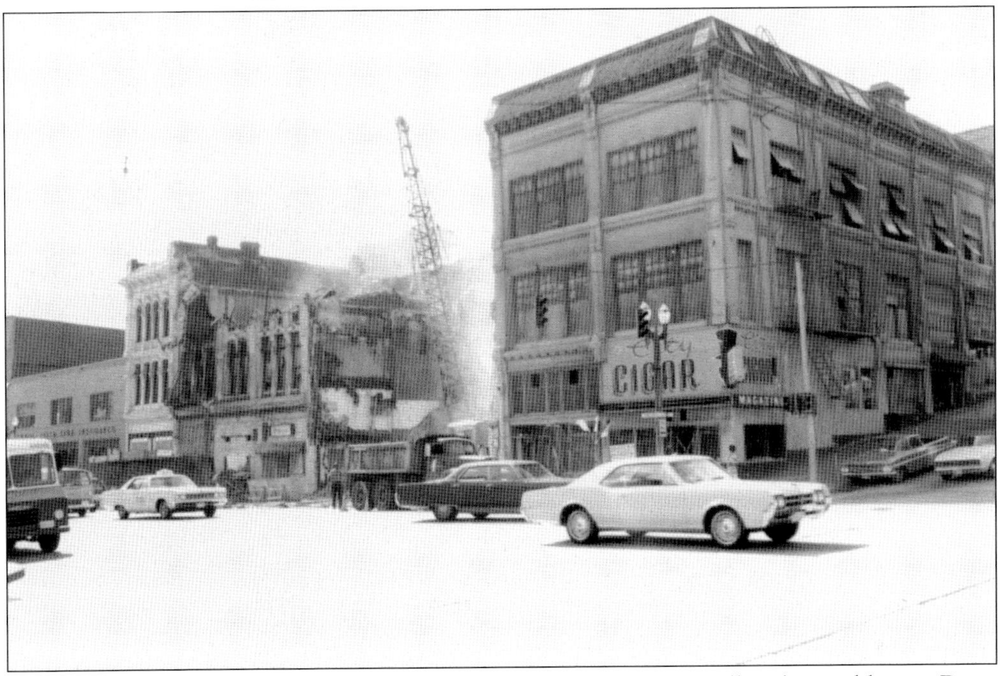

The Capri (formerly Riviera) Theater at 906–908 Pacific Avenue, as well as the neighboring Davis Block (910–912 Pacific Avenue), which had once housed the first Pantages Theater, were being demolished when this photograph was taken in 1969. Much of this west side of the 900 block of Pacific Avenue would eventually be cleared to make way for the Park Plaza North parking garage. (Courtesy of the Tacoma Public Library.)

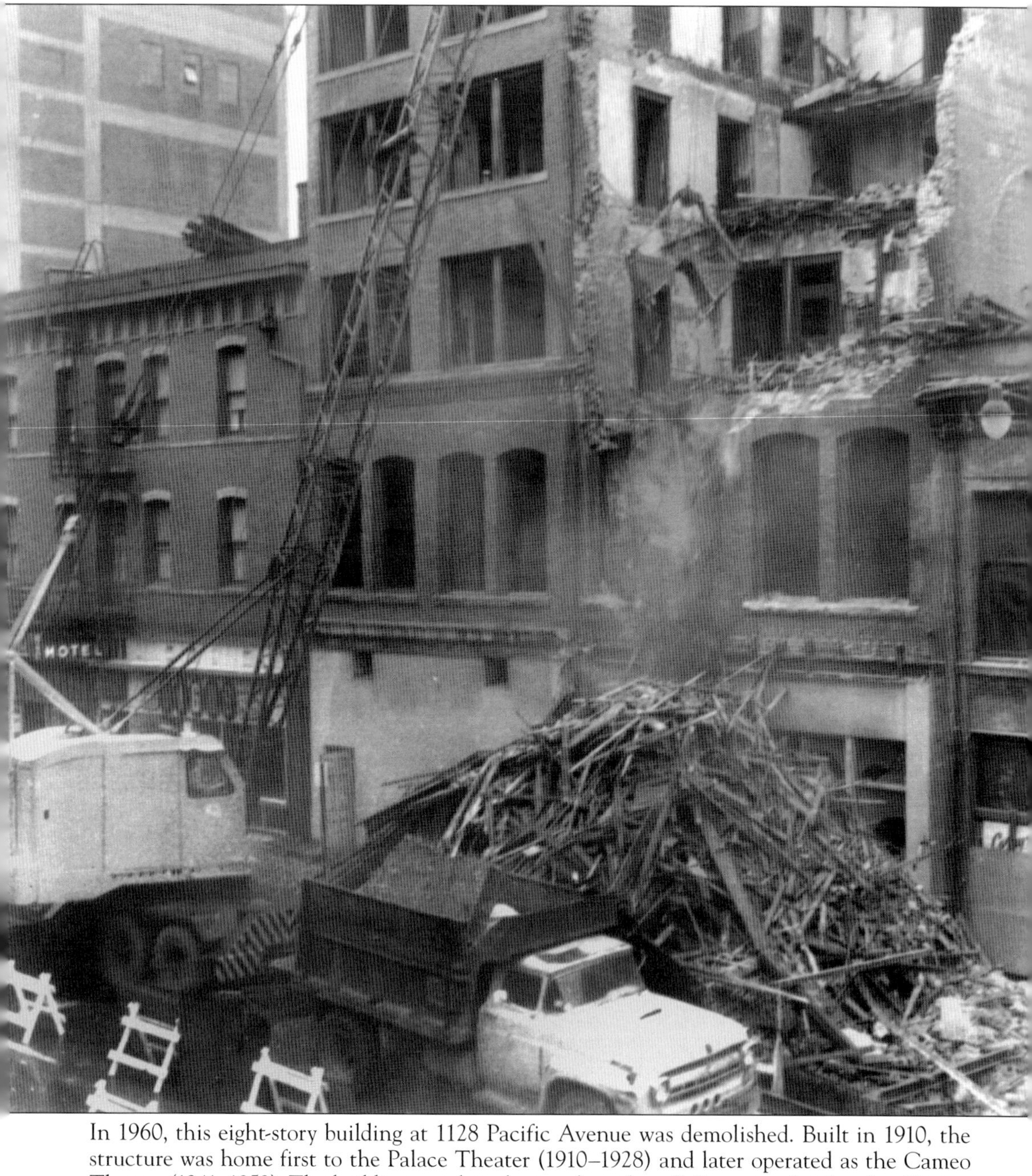

In 1960, this eight-story building at 1128 Pacific Avenue was demolished. Built in 1910, the structure was home first to the Palace Theater (1910–1928) and later operated as the Cameo Theater (1941–1959). The building weathered a number of small fires over the decades. During World War II, space in the building was donated for use by the Red Cross by the Cameo Theater's manager, Vito Cuttone. The building was being demolished to make way for the Tacoma Escalade, a moving sidewalk, which was built at a cost of $205,000 to make climbing the steep hills of downtown Tacoma a bit easier for pedestrians. In addition to the building pictured here, the Blue Mouse Theater in the 1100 block of Broadway was also demolished for the escalade project. A bond issue passed in 1958 had set aside $875,000 to build the moving sidewalks downtown. (Courtesy of the Tacoma Public Library.)

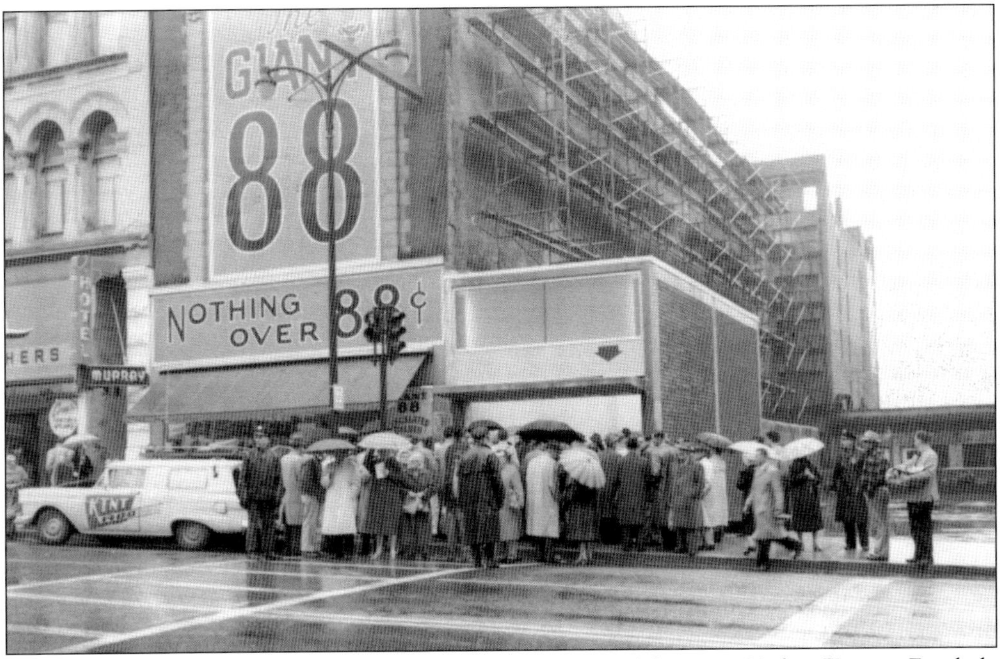

On February 27, 1961, hundreds gathered for the dedication of the new 100-foot Tacoma Escalade at 1129 Broadway, the former site of the Blue Mouse Theater. Unlike a typical escalator, the escalade had no steps, but it did have a moving handrail. It moved at a speed of about 120 feet per minute, or slightly slower than the average walking pace. On another date in February, Tacoma mayor Ben Hanson, deputy mayor James Porter, and several members of the city council were photographed enjoying a trip on the new escalade. Councilwoman Ellen Price and Mayor Hanson lead the group riding uphill from Commerce Street to Broadway. (Both, courtesy of the Tacoma Public Library.)

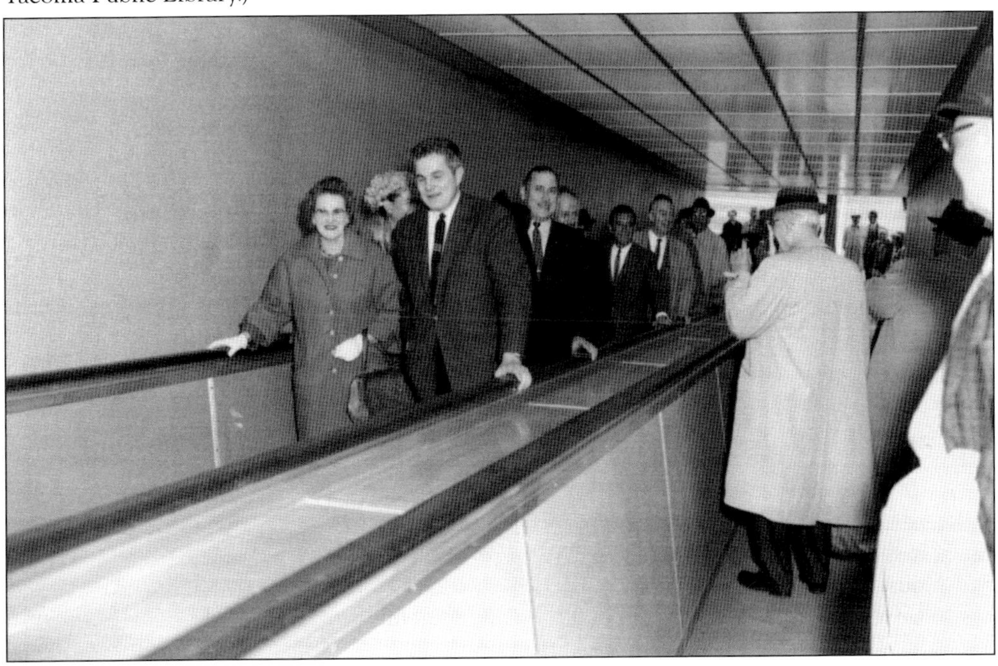

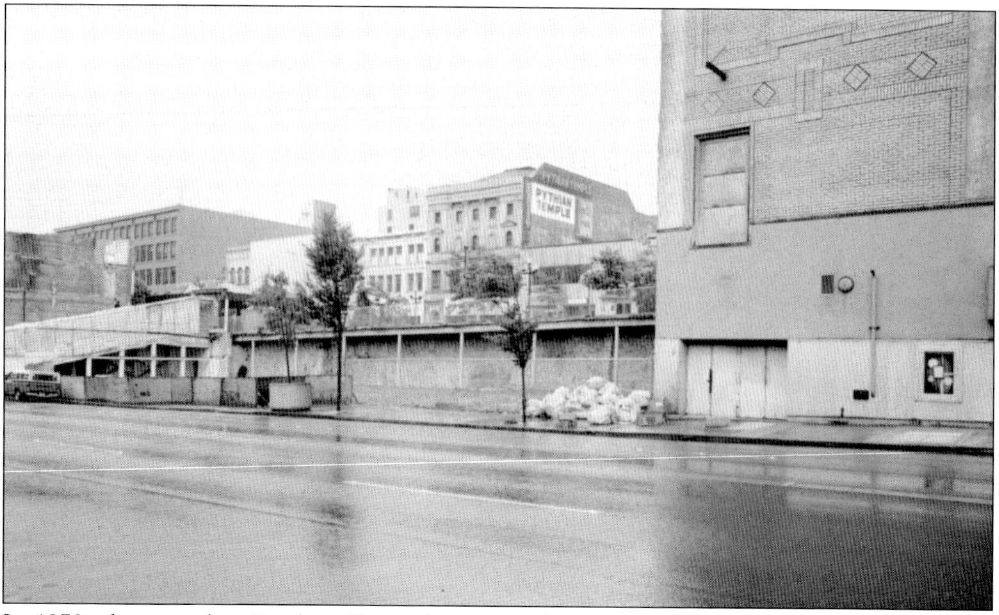

In 1979, photographer Stephen Cysewski captured this view from the corner of Ninth and Commerce Streets, looking southwest toward the 900 block of Broadway. The Tenth Street Escalade, which would close in 1983, can be seen at far left. Many of the buildings that once stood between Broadway and Commerce Street have been demolished. At right is the rear of the Pantages Theater. (Courtesy of the Tacoma Public Library.)

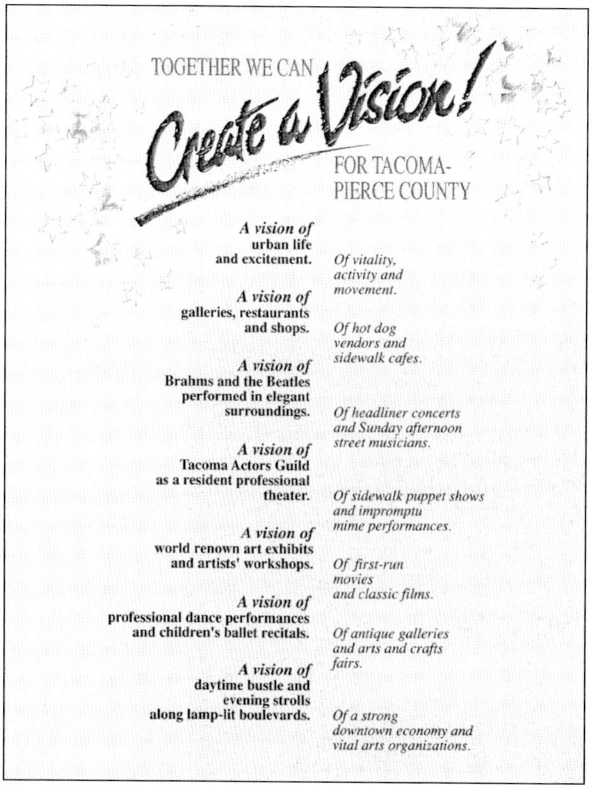

Following the renovation of the Pantages Theater in the early 1980s, the Broadway Theater District Task Force was formed around the vision of reinvigorating the theater district. This image is one page from a brochure titled "A Vision of the Broadway Theater District," which detailed plans to renovate the Rialto Theater and build a new facility to house the Tacoma Actors Guild. (Courtesy of the Tacoma Public Library.)

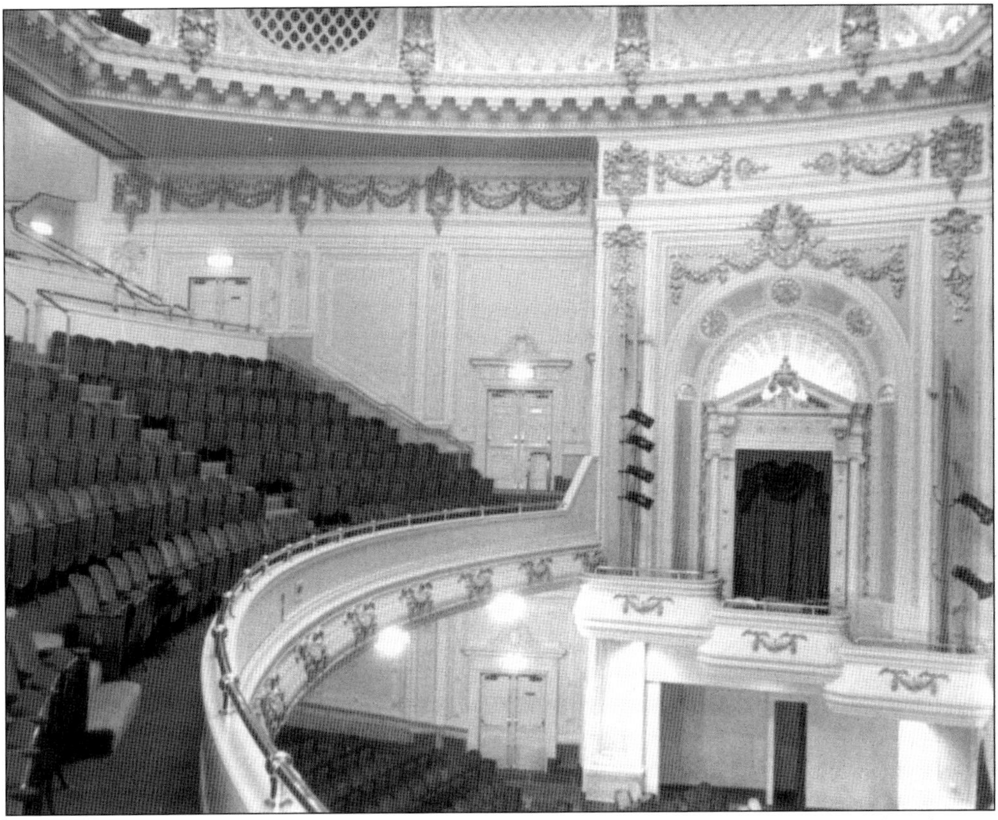

In December 1974, after several ownership changes, the Pantages Theater went into foreclosure, providing the City of Tacoma with the opportunity to buy and restore the theater, an effort that began in 1978. As these photographs taken after the restoration illustrate, the project allowed the theater's stunning interior to shine once again, while also bringing the facility up to modern standards of safety and staging capabilities. The theater reopened on February 12, 1983, and is now the oldest of the Pantages Theaters still in operation. (Both, courtesy of the Tacoma Public Library.)

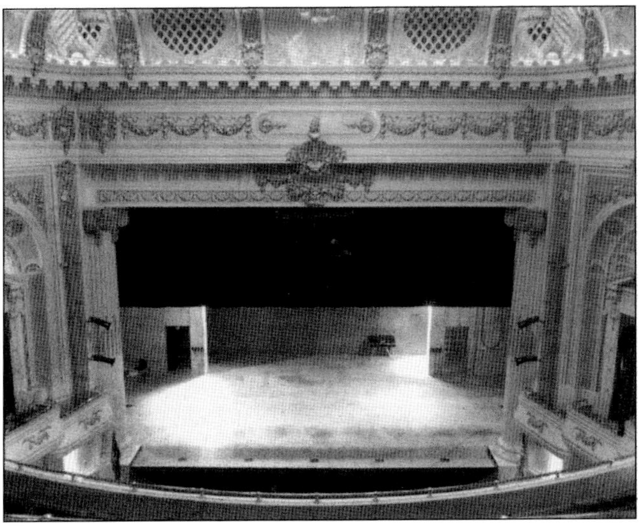

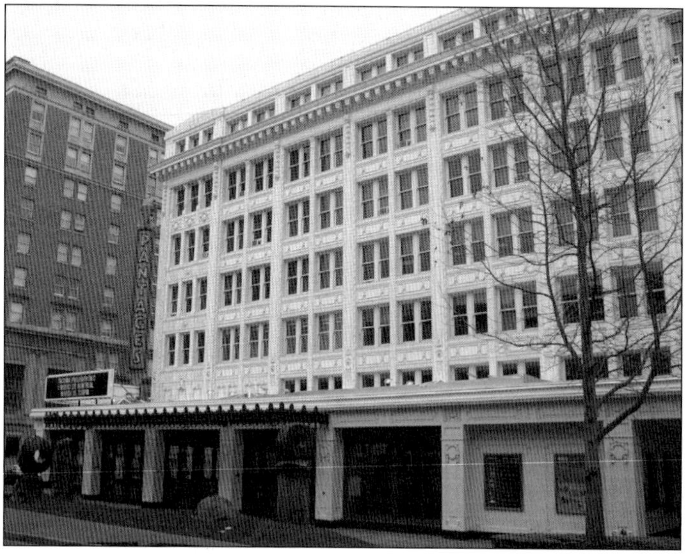

In 1930, all traces of the Pantages name were removed from the theater at 901 Broadway when it became the RKO Orpheum. With the facility's renovation and reopening, prominent Pantages signage once again graced the building. This photograph from 2008 captures the full Broadway-facing view of the grand theater, with the Winthrop Hotel in the background. (Courtesy of the Puget Sound Theater Organ Society.)

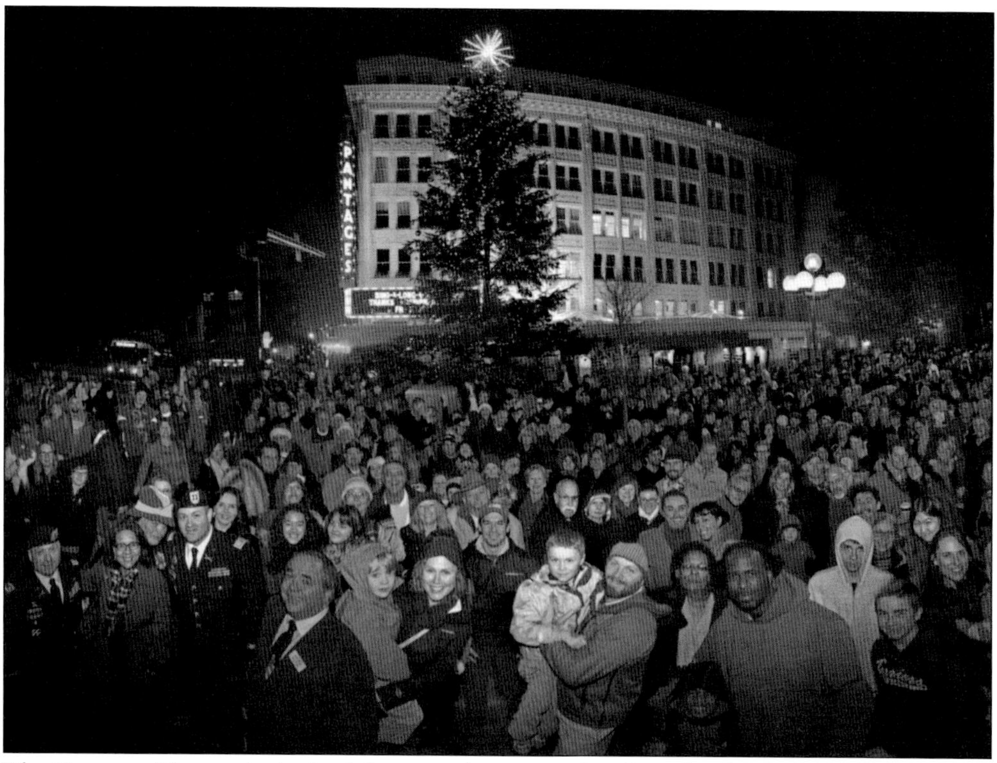

The Pantages Theater is the backdrop as a large crowd gathers for the 68th Annual Tacoma Holiday Tree Lighting on November 30, 2013. Activities included a sing-along and opportunities for children to be photographed with Santa Claus. Tacoma mayor Marilyn Strickland is in the foreground, second from left. (Courtesy of Chip van Gilder.)

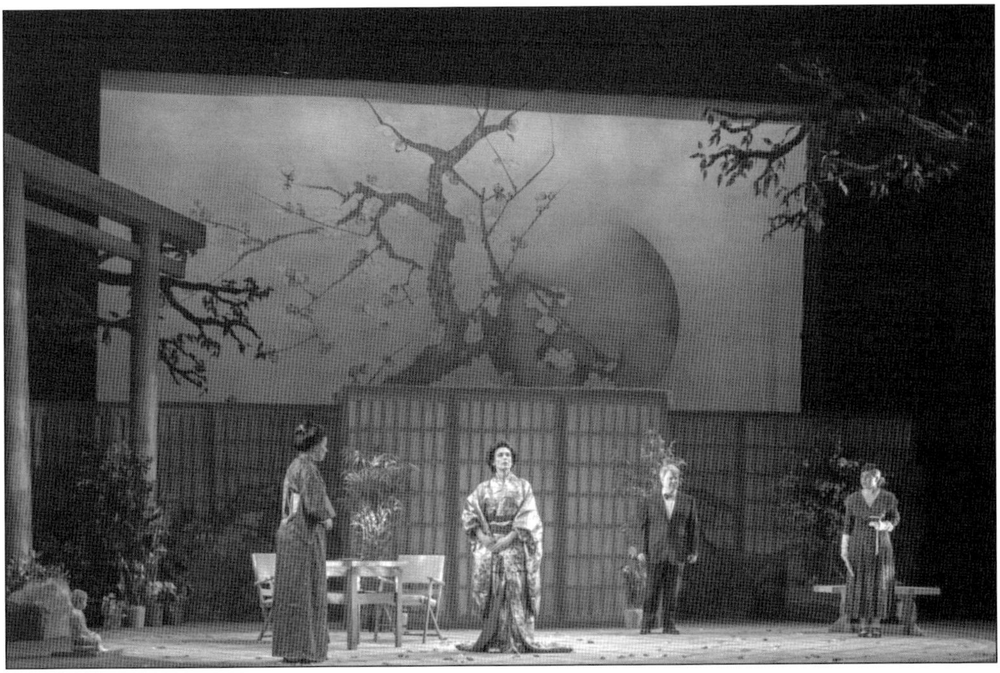

With the renovated historic and new structures that make up Tacoma's Broadway Center, Tacoma's many amateur and professional arts organizations have fine facilities to call home. The Tacoma Opera's production of *Madame Butterfly* in April 2014 delighted audiences with its beautiful staging at the Pantages Theater. (Courtesy of Peter Serko.)

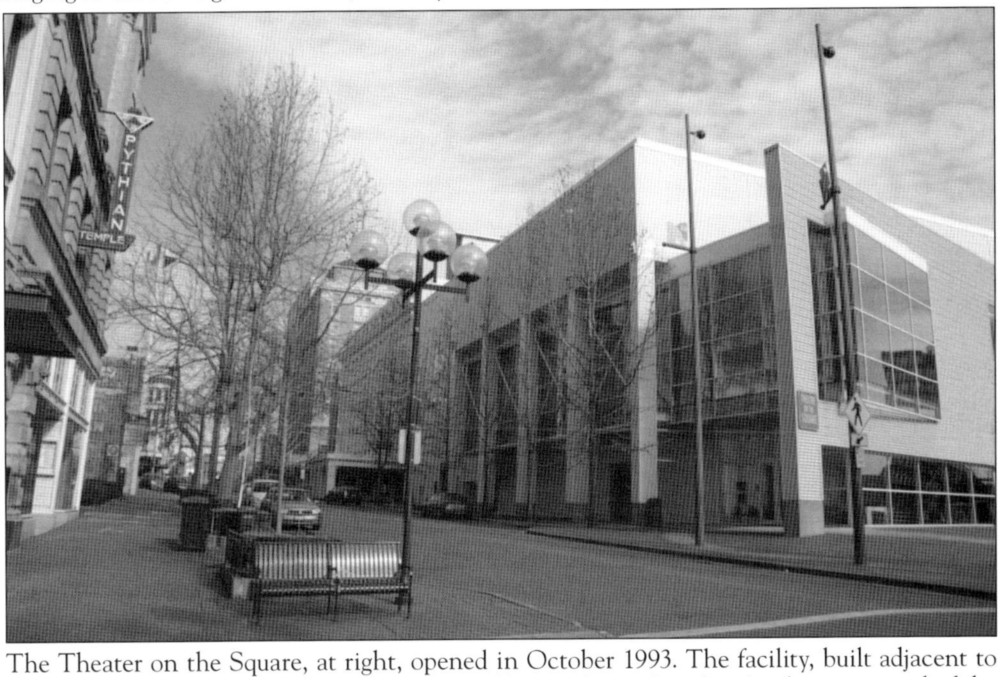

The Theater on the Square, at right, opened in October 1993. The facility, built adjacent to the Pantages, contains a 302-seat theater as well as a rehearsal studio. As the centennial of the opening of the Pantages and Rialto Theaters approaches, new plans for growth and development for Tacoma's Broadway Center are underway. (Author's collection.)

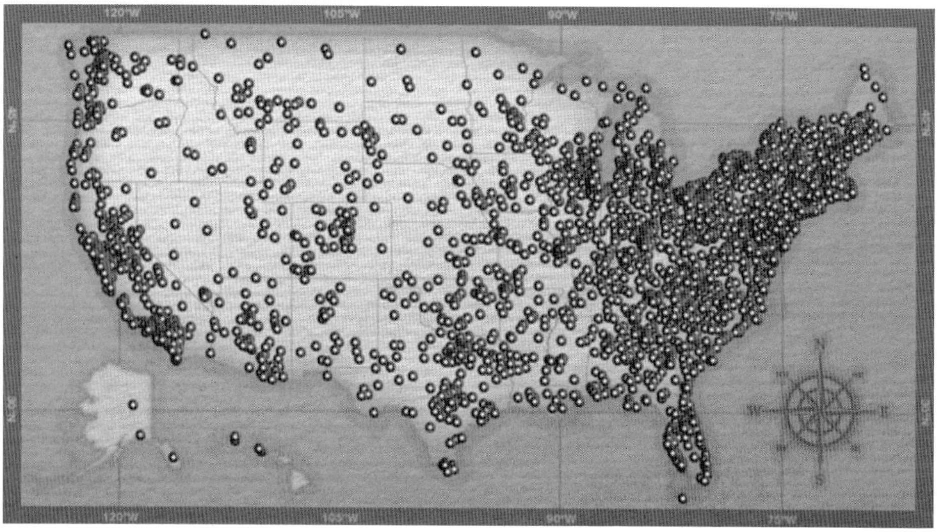